The Special Education
CONSULTANT TEACHER

The Special Education

CONSULTANT TEACHER

Enabling Children with Disabilities to be Educated with Nondisabled Children to the Maximum Extent Appropriate

By

EDWARD BURNS, PH.D.

State University of New York at Binghamton

CHARLES C THOMAS • PUBLISHER, LTD.
Springfield • Illinois • U.S.A.

Published and Distributed Throughout the World by

CHARLES C THOMAS • PUBLISHER, LTD.
2600 South First Street
Springfield, Illinois 62704

©2004 by CHARLES C THOMAS • PUBLISHER, LTD.

ISBN 0-398-07510-7 (hard)
ISBN 0-398-07511-5 (paper)

Library of Congress Catalog Card Number: 2004047879

With THOMAS BOOKS *careful attention is given to all details of man-
ufacturing and design. It is the Publisher's desire to present books that are satisfactory as to their physical qualities and artistic possibilities and appropriate for their particular use.* THOMAS BOOKS *will be true to those laws
of quality that assure a good name and good will.*

Printed in the United States of America
CR-R-3

Library of Congress Cataloging-in-Publication Data
Burns, Edward, 1943-
     The special education consultant teacher : enabling children
with disabilities to be educated with nondisabled children to the
maximum extent appropriate / by Edward Burns.
          p. cm.
     Includes bibliographical references and index.
     ISBN 0-398-07510-7 --ISBN 0-398-07511-5 (pbk.)
     1. Children with disabilities--Education---United States. 2. Inclusive
education--United States. 3. Special education teachers--United States.
I. Title.

LC4031.B697 2004
371.9'046--dc22
                                                                          2004047879

PREFACE

Special education is slowly evolving from a **place where services are provided to services provided in the least restrictive environment** with an emphasis on the regular classroom and the regular classroom curriculum. For every child with a disability under the Individuals with Disabilities Education Act (DEA) amendments of 1997 the presumed placement is the regular classroom, and a child can be removed from the regular classroom only if special education services and accommodations (i.e., supplementary aids and services) are not successful.

In order to achieve successful regular classroom participation for children with disabilities with supplementary aids and services, consultant teacher services are essential. Just as the function of special education from a place to a service is changing, so too is the role of the special education teacher from that of a self-contained classroom teacher to a very versatile professional providing direct teaching in the regular classroom and indirect supportive services to promote regular classroom participation.

The Special Education CONSULTANT TEACHER: Enabling Children with Disabilities to be Educated with Nondisabled Children to the Maximum Extent Appropriate is intended for special education teachers and other professionals providing special education services with information, guidelines, and suggestions relating to the role and responsibilities of the special education consultant teacher. Every state must provide a continuum of alternative placements (e.g., regular classroom, resource room, self-contained setting), but the focus of this guide is participation in the regular classroom and/or regular curriculum "to enable children with disabilities to be educated with nondisabled children to the maximum extent appropriate."

This handbook is comprised of several parts. Part I deals with basic consultant teacher responsibilities and regulatory concerns; Part II focuses on planning, individualized planning and IEP consultant teacher services; Part III outlines the various consultant teacher indirect services, and Part IV describes direct consultant teacher services; Part V concerns the importance of the regular classroom and the regular classroom teacher for the consultant teacher; Part VI identifies the many Least Restrictive Environment, inclusion and mainstreaming issues important to the consultant teacher, and Part VII addresses the varied supervisory and job responsibilities of the consultant teacher.

In many ways this is simply an "idea" book comprised of many suggestions concerning what the special education consultant teacher can and should do to enable children with disabilities to be educated with nondisabled children. But no matter whether the special education teacher is called a consultant teacher, consulting teacher, mainstreaming teacher, inclusion specialist, special education consultant teacher, or simply special education teacher, direct and indirect services provided to enable children with disabilities to be educated with nondisabled children is how special education becomes a service rather than a place, and how children with disabilities are educated with nondisabled children to the maximum extent appropriate.

E. B.

CONTENTS

PART III - INDIRECT SERVICES AND THE CONSULTANT TEACHER

PART IV - DIRECT SERVICES AND THE CONSULTANT TEACHER

PART V - THE REGULAR CLASSROOM AND THE CONSULTANT TEACHER

PART VI - THE LEAST RESTRICTIVE CONSULTANT TEACHER

PART VII - CONSULTANT TEACHER ESSENTIALS

The Special Education
CONSULTANT TEACHER

Part I
Basic Consultant Teacher Services

The special education consultant teacher's goal: to provide services to enable successful participation in the regular classroom to the maximum extent appropriate.

CONSULTANT TEACHER SERVICES

We note that these experts challenged the School District's view that readiness for mainstreaming or inclusion could successfully be developed within a desegregated setting and argued that it is illusory and perhaps even pretextual, to contend that segregation can breed readiness for inclusion.[1]

To some degree every special education teacher will provide consultant teacher services for children with disabilities to maximize each child's participation in the regular classroom and regular curriculum. For every child with a disability who needs special education under the Individuals with Disabilities Education Act (IDEA) amendments of 1997, the presumed setting for services and accommodations is the regular classroom. When a child with a disability cannot be educated successfully in the regular classroom, an alternative placement might be necessary. Nonetheless, for children who do require an alternative placement, education with nondisabled children is required to the maximum extent appropriate. The primary role of the consultant teacher is to enable children with disabilities to successfully participate in regular education classes and the regular curriculum.

The Mainstreaming Requirement

The courts have interpreted the least restrictive environment clause as Congress' "strong preference in favor of mainstreaming" (Daniel v. State Board of Education, P. 1044).

The Senate Report (SR 105-17) for IDEA refers to "a presumption that children with disabilities are to be educated in regular classes" (SR 105-17).

The IDEA mandates that children with disabilities are educated with children who are not disabled, and that the removal of children with disabilities from the regular education classes occurs only when the nature or severity of the disability of a child is such that education in regular classes with the us of the supplementary aids and services cannot be achieved satisfactorily (20 U.S.C. 1412[a][5][A]).

The work of the consultant teacher centers about the education of children with disabilities with nondisabled children to the maximum extent appropriate. This is accomplished by providing direct (viz., teaching in the regular classroom) and indirect services (e.g., support for the regular classroom teacher) to enable participation in the regular classroom and/or regular curriculum.

Although the task is to provide direct and indirect services, the consultant teacher is also involved in developing pre-referral interventions "to reduce the need to label children as disabled in order to address their learning needs,"[2] assisting children with disabilities who have disabilities but do not need special education (and therefore are not served under IDEA), and for children who have been declassified.

The consultant teacher must meet the many diverse activities required to implement the least restrictive environment or mainstreaming provision of IDEA. Whether the task is to enable a student to participate in a regular third grade classroom, high school biology class, or to enable a student in a self-contained classroom to participate in regular seventh grade social studies curriculum, the consultant teacher is responsible for providing "the full range" of direct and indirect services to maximize classroom and curriculum participation.

Every special education teacher should be involved in enabling children with disabilities to be involved in the regular classroom to the maximum extent appropriate. What distinguishes the consultant teacher from a special education teacher in a resource room setting, a self-contained classroom, or a residential setting is the emphasis on the regular classroom and the regular curriculum. The consultant teacher's focus is entirely on maximizing participation in the regular classroom and the general curriculum. To this end the consultant teacher might work in the regular classroom on a one-to-one basis, or with all children in the regular classroom to achieve this goal. In other situations the consultant teacher might observe a child's regular classroom behavior, plan and collaborate with the regular classroom teacher, design a plan with the classroom teacher to manage classroom behavior, or to provide and supervise general classroom and curriculum accommodations. When appropriate, the consultant teacher might provide services to children with disabilities in more restrictive settings that will result in regular classroom and general curriculum participation.

Keep an eye on the ball. Consultant teaching is not about the consultant teacher; consultant teaching is about enabling children with disabilities to function as independently as possible in the regular classroom. If the consultant teacher always provides the same service, always provides a set amount of instructional support in the classroom, and never seeks to increase independent classroom performance, the services provided might be excellent when considered in isolation, but certainly not effective if the goal of successful classroom performance is not advanced.

A SERVICE AND NOT A PLACE

*We conclude that in the field of public education the doctrine of
separate but equal has no place. Separate educational facilities
are inherently unequal.*
                                        Brown v. Board of Education

Special education is not a place and not an alternative to the regular class-room. True, a child might require an alternative setting but this is neither the purpose or the intent of special education. Special education has a very unique responsibility which, sadly enough, has often been misunderstood or simply ignored. In *Brown v. the Board of Education* the Warren court declared that "in the field of public education the doctrine of 'separate but equal' has no place. Separate educational facilities are inherently unequal. Therefore, we hold that the plaintiffs and others similarly situated for whom the actions have been brought are, by reason of the segregation complained of, deprived of the equal protection of the laws guaranteed by the Fourteenth Amendment." Special education is founded in this seminal civil rights land-mark case. No child, regardless of race or disability, should be segregated.

But special education presents a bit of dilemma when the appropriateness of a segregative environment is considered. For some children with disabili-ties a separate environment or facility might be appropriate and might actu-ally prevent discrimination by providing *appropriate* services and an appro-priate educational program. Special education provides a legal by-pass to the *Brown* decision by permitting a segregative placement because such a place-ment is thought to best meet a child's needs.

How does special education reconcile the possible need for a segregative setting with mandate by the Warren court in *Brown* that "separate educa-tional facilities are inherently unequal?" The only way to overcome this Supreme Court hurdle is by mandating that removal from regular classes is as least restrictive as possible and that children are educated in regular class-es to the maximum extent appropriate. This is no trivial matter and ignoring this basic tenet of IDEA can result in blatant discrimination. Every teacher who provides consultant teacher services is entrusted with the fundamental obligation to enable children with disabilities to be educated with nondis-abled children to the maximum extent appropriate. If a student with a dis-ability is capable of participating in high school math but the student's place-ment does not provide high school math, the placement is discriminatory. If a child is able to participate in the regular classroom fifty percent each day,

7

but the child is placed in a self-contained classroom where mainstreaming is not practiced, the placement is discriminatory. Whether working with regular classroom teachers, other special education teachers or school specialists (e.g., reading teachers, physical therapists, speech and language specialists), the consultant teacher is concerned with meeting this elemental special education requirement that children with disabilities are required to be educated with nondisabled children.

The special education consultant teacher's focus is to maximize the extent a child with a disability can be educated with nondisabled children. This task is accomplished by ensuring each child is placed in the **least restrictive environment** or **LRE** to the maximum extent appropriate. The often repeated phrase "maximum extent appropriate" is essential for providing each child with the LRE. The regulations identify a series of alternate placements as part of the **continuum of placements** to achieve the LRE.

Instruction in Regular Classes
Special Classes
Special Schools
Home Instruction
Instruction in Hospitals and Institutions

The continuum of alternative placements is arranged in terms of the **relative degree of restrictiveness**; that is, instruction in regular classes is less restrictive than special classes, and instruction in special classes is less restrictive than special schools, etc. The continuum of alternative placements listed in the regulations is illustrative in that alternate placements can vary in terms of the degree to which the placement restricts involvement in the regular classroom or regular curriculum. Placement in a regular classroom where all services are provided by an untrained and unsupervised aide might be more restrictive than services provided in a resource room or even a self-contained classroom where more actual participation in classroom activities and the general curriculum provided. Restrictiveness is partly defined by the placement setting, but the actual degree of restrictiveness is defined by the interaction of accommodations, interventions and placements which allow a child to participate as independently and successfully as possible.

The Regulations

The regulations refer to the final regulations for IDEA provided by the Office of Special Education and Rehabilitative Services (OSERS), Department of Education. The "regulation" for the continuum of services is cited in Title 34, Part 300, Section 26 and in Title 34, Part 300, Section 551 of the Code of Federal Regulations (CFR) or 34 CFR 300.26 and 34 CFR 300.551.

The placement choice is not between the regular classroom and a special class or other restrictive setting, but to provide maximum participation in the least restrictive setting. The placement decision is not to select one of a series of placements, but to select the appropriate mix of placements that maximizes independent and successful classroom behavior. For example, a child might be able to participate in the regular classroom for one hour a day, in a resource room for one hour, and in special classes for three hours.

The following guidelines concern the IEP teams determination of the least restrictive placement (Part VI provides specific placement guidelines for the consultant teacher).

Determining the Least Restrictive Placement

1. **Begin with an IEP which specifies needed special education, related services, supplementary aids and services, and measurable annual goals.**

2. **Determine the maximum extent of regular classroom participation.**

3. **Determine the degree of regular *classroom and curriculum* participation if supplementary aids and services are not successful.**

4. **The criterion for the maximum extent is "satisfactory" performance.**

5. **The least restrictive placement is the maximum amount of time in each placement on the continuum, beginning with the regular classroom or "the" least restrictive placement.**

6. **This process is repeated for each setting on the continuum.**

7. **When the maximum amount of time in each placement on the continuum is determined, this is the least restrictive placement.**

8. **The least restrictive placement can involve multiple placements.**

9. **Every child must be able to participate in the regular classroom, regardless of the placement, to the maximum extent appropriate. In other words, a placement cannot "prevent" regular classroom or curriculum participation.**

**10. Ensure that the child is able to participate in the regular cur-
riculum, regardless of the placement, to the maximum extent
appropriate.**

If a child cannot be educated in the regular classroom successfully, a special class might be necessary; if a child cannot be educated in a special class,
a special school might be necessary. The continuum of alternative placements listed in the regulations does not eliminate the need to provide each
child with the least restrictive environment. That is, a single placement,
wherever that placement is, will probably not be the least restrictive if participation in environments that are less restrictive have not been considered
(viz., the regular classroom). One child in a special class might be able to
fully participate in the regular curriculum, while another child might be able
to spend fifty percent of the day in the regular classroom. An alternative
placement, although a required part of the continuum of placements, cannot
be used to meet a child's least restrictive environment needs if the placement
does not permit participation with nondisabled children to the maximum
extent appropriate. A school could not place a child in a restrictive setting
and then use the fact that the child had been placed in a restrictive setting as
a reason to exclude regular classroom participation.

If possible, every child with a disability should be educated in the regular
classroom with direct and indirect special education support; if a child cannot be educated in the regular classroom with support, an effort must be
made to educate the child in the regular classroom. This is what the courts
refer to as the "mainstreaming provision of the Act" which is "that handicapped children be educated alongside nonhandicapped children to the
maximum extent appropriate,"[3] or IDEA's "very strong congressional preference" for mainstreaming."[4] This "preference for mainstreaming" is actually a mandate that children with disabilities be educated with nondisabled
children to the maximum extent appropriate. This is what is meant by the
telling phrase that **special education is a service and not a place**. The
services provided by special education allow for participation in the least
restrictive environment, participation in the regular classroom, and participation in the general curriculum.

The least restrictive environment applies to a child's actual placement but
also to all accommodations, services, and interventions. The consultant
teacher is responsible for ensuring that the extent of services do not exceed
the level of services that are actually required. If a child requires only indirect services and not direct instruction, providing direct instruction by a special education teacher would be excessive; if a child is able to participate in
the general curriculum with limited accommodations but extra accommodations are provided to ensure that the child receives sufficient help, the accom-

modations would be restrictive. The best example of an accommodation that can be excessively restrictive is a complete test exemption. A test exemption might be easier for school personnel, and certainly require less effort and stress on the part of the student, but exempting a child from district-wide and state testing programs can have great programming impact by eliminating access to certain courses, programs, and even graduation with a high school diploma.

This preference for mainstreaming, this presumption that children with disabilities are to be educated in the regular classroom, can only be realized by *providing* direct and indirect services in the regular classroom and other educational settings to enable children with disabilities to participate in the regular classroom and the regular curriculum.

Whether called a special education teacher, inclusion teacher, itinerant special education teacher, resource teacher, etc., the school must assign a qualified teacher to meet the fundamental special education requirement to enable children with disabilities to be educated with nondisabled children to the maximum extent appropriate. The special education teacher who enables a child to participate in the regular classroom could be called an inclusion teacher, a consultant teacher or learning specialist, or simply a special education teacher. Regardless of the title used by the school or district, if the teacher is a qualified special education teacher, and the primary responsibility is to enable regular classroom participation by providing direct and indirect services, the teacher is a consultant teacher.

Special Education Services
34 CFR 300.347(a)(3)

A statement of the special education and related services and supplementary aids and services to be provided to the child, or on behalf of the child, and a statement of the program modifications or supports for school personnel that will be provided for the child--

(i) To advance appropriately toward attaining the annual goals;
(ii) To be involved and progress in the general curriculum in accordance with paragraph (a)(1) of this section and to participate in extracurricular and other nonacademic activities; and
(iii) To be educated and participate with other children with disabilities and nondisabled children in the activities described in this section.

After a child has been determined to have a disability under IDEA and needs special education, an **individualized education program (IEP)** is developed to provide all necessary services and accommodations. At one time, and for some even now, the IEP is a passport to a special education class and restricted access to the regular classroom and curriculum. For the consultant teacher, the IEP is the basis for providing access to the regular classroom and regular curriculum. In keeping with the emphasis on special education as a service and not a place, and the importance of the regular classroom, an IEP is designed "to enable the child to be involved in and progress in the general curriculum" and to meet "each of the child's other educational needs."[5] Essential elements of each child's IEP, elements required for every child with a disability in every IEP, include:

- **Identifying levels of performance that affect academic performance.**

- **Measurable annual goals that address specific areas of performance.**

- **Specially designed instruction necessary to achieve goals.**

- **Classroom modifications.**

- **Teacher supports.**

The IEP and special education is not about placements, and certainly not about special classes, but about identifying needs, developing goals, and then providing services and modifications to achieve these goals. To this end the consultant teacher is a service provider in whatever setting enables a child to participate with nondisabled children.

Historically, special education has been (and often is) regarded as a place where children are assigned. The purpose of such placements, albeit unintentional (and sometimes not), is not necessarily to provide a **Free Appropriate Public Education (or FAPE)**, but to segregate these children into classrooms and other alternative placements which do not enable the children to participate in either the regular classroom or the regular curriculum to the maximum extent appropriate. By having a commitment for FAPE and strong belief that IDEA is about "high expectations" and being educated with nondisabled children to the maximum extent appropriate, the consultant teacher can do much to offset many of the segregative practices, some intentional and some not, long associated with special education.

Why do we have special education? Not to classify, not to label, and not to place, but to provide each child with FAPE. If a placement is not appropriate, or if services are not appropriate, special education is not appropriate. The only rationale for special education is FAPE; the only reason for a special education placement is FAPE. When special education is not predicated on FAPE, special education is harmful, segregative, and statutorily and ethically inappropriate.

"THE CONTINUUM"

Success for the consultant teacher is for a child to participate satisfactorily in the regular classroom and the general curriculum with the least restrictive placement and the least restrictive services.

The regulations for IDEA (34 CFR 300.551) describe the continuum of alternative placements as those "listed in the definition of special education under § 300.26 (instruction in regular classes, special classes, special schools, home instruction, , and instruction in hospitals and institutions." The continuum listed in the definition of special education (§ 300.26) cites "instruction conducted in the classroom, in the home, in hospitals and institutions, and in other settings."

Every state has a continuum of alternative placements, and often the description of these placements simply repeats what is contained in the regulations. No matter what discrete categories are listed, the "continuum" is infinite. In other words, the task is not to select the single most appropriate placement but to select (as described in *Daniel v. the State Board of Education*) the "the appropriate mix" of placements. The following is a somewhat expanded version of the continuum provide in the regulations:

Regular Classroom: No Services

Regular Classroom: Accommodations

Regular Classroom: Indirect Services

Regular Classroom: Direct Services

Resource Rooms

Special Classrooms

Special Schools

Home Instruction

Residential Settings

TEN ESSENTIAL CONSULTANT TEACHER SKILLS

What does the special education consultant teacher need in order to maximize the time children with disabilities can satisfactorily participate in the classroom? The ability to:

1. Identify regular classroom needs,

2. Prioritize needs,

3. Plan individualized programs that result in regular classroom participation,

4. Develop meaningful measurable annual goals,

5. Use a variety of different teaching strategies and interventions in the regular classroom,

6. Work with disabled and nondisabled children in the classroom,

7. Collaborate with the regular classroom teacher, other service providers, and parents,

8. Nurture independent classroom performance,

9. Provide the least restrictive curriculum modifications,

10. Coordinate, supervise and implement regular classroom supports.

The consultant teacher requires a variety of skills and abilities, but maybe the most important is what Congress referred to in IDEA as "high expectations" for children with disabilities. Only when we aim for what children can achieve will be find that elusive "appropriate education" which is the rationale for all special education services.

HUDSON v. ROWLEY
458 U.S. 176 (1982)[6]

Hudson v. Rowley stands next to *Brown v. Board of Education* as having the greatest impact on special education. The case involved a deaf student, Amy, in the Hendrick Hudson Central School District in Peekskill, New York. The Rowleys agreed with the IEP developed by the school but insisted on having a qualified sign-language interpreter for Amy. The District decided that Amy did not need an interpreter, based in part on a report from an interpreter who had been in Amy's kindergarten class on an experimental basis.

First, the Rowley's requested an impartial hearing at which the hearing officer agreed with the District that Amy did not need an interpreter.
Next, the parents appealed to the State which agreed with the hearing officer.
Then, the parents brought suit in district court (483 F.Supp. 528, 531 [1980]) which agreed with the parents that Amy was not receiving a free appropriate public education because she was not achieving her full potential.
In response, the District to the United States Court of Appeals for the Second District agreed with the District court that Amy was not receiving an appropriate education.
So, the District went to the Supreme Court to make the final decision. And they did.

The rationale for the decision was that a reviewing court must base its decision on the "preponderance of the evidence" which does not mean that courts substitute their own notions of educational policy for those of the school. And "a court's inquiry in suits . . . is twofold. First, has the State complied with the procedures set forth in the Act? And second, is the individualized educational program developed through the Act's procedures reasonably calculated to enable the child to receive educational benefits? If these requirements are met, the State has complied with the obligations imposed by Congress and the courts can require no more."

The Supreme Court concluded "that the Court of Appeals erred in affirming the decision of the District Court. Neither the District Court nor the Court of Appeals found that petitioners had failed to comply with the procedures of the Act, and the findings of neither court would support a conclusion that Amy's educational program failed to comply with the substantive requirements of the Act. On the contrary, the District Court found that the 'evidence firmly establishes that Amy is receiving an 'adequate' education, since she performs better than the average child in her class and is advancing easily from grade to grade.' In light of this finding, and of the fact that Amy was receiving personalized instruction and related services calculated . . . to meet her educational needs, the lower courts should not have concluded that the Act requires the provision of a sign-language interpreter. Accordingly, the decision of the Court of Appeals is reversed, and the case is remanded for further proceedings consistent with this opinion."

DIRECT AND INDIRECT
CONSULTANT TEACHER SERVICES

*The consultant teacher can provide indirect and direct services
in any setting as long as the goal is to enable participation in the
regular classroom and regular curriculum.*

The two essential services provided by the consultant teacher are **direct** and **indirect** services which enable participation in the regular classroom and in the regular curriculum. The first array of services considered by the IEP team are those indirect services and supports necessary for a child to be included in the classroom. This might include planning time, curriculum or text format accommodations, accommodations to the classroom environment, classroom supports such as an aide or interpreter. The consultant teacher might be responsible for coordinating these supports, orchestrating planning, and developing and/or supervising classroom and curriculum accommodations.

For the most part the consultant teacher will provide direct services in the regular classroom to children with and without disabilities. Not only might the consultant teacher work directly with a child with a disability in the regular classroom but also work with nondisabled children to support classroom inclusion. However, the consultant teacher must not lose sight of the primary goal to enable classroom and curriculum participation, rather than a goal to provide a particular service or teaching strategy. The primary responsibility of the consultant teacher is not to spend several hours a day providing direct instruction, or to work one-on-one with students, but to enable successful classroom participation. For the consultant teacher successful classroom participation is a level of satisfactory classroom performance achieved with the least restrictive placements, accommodations, and interventions.

The consultant teacher might also provide direct and indirect services for special education teachers in more restrictive settings to enable participation in the regular classroom. A glaring deficiency associated with many restrictive settings is that participation in regular classroom activities to the maximum extent appropriate is not provided. This violation of the least restrictive environment mandate is especially prominent in highly restrictive classrooms, special schools, and institutional settings where lack of proximity to nondisabled children prevents participation in regular classroom to the maximum extent appropriate.[7] This shortcoming could be alleviated, in part, by providing consultant teacher services to assist regular classroom and regular curriculum participation.

The combination of direct and services, the regular and specialized curriculum, and regular and more restrictive special education settings illustrate the potential role of consultant teacher to enable regular classroom and regular curriculum participation. The following model depicts areas in which the special education consultant teacher might make important contributions. The focal point of the consultant teacher's activities is to provide direct and indirect services in the regular classroom. In the figure shown below quadrant #1 indicates direct services in the regular classroom using the regular curriculum; and quadrant #2 denotes indirect services in the regular classroom using the regular curriculum.

Quadrants #3 (direct services) and #4 (indirect services) focus on specially designed curriculum in the regular classroom. For example, a child with a developmental disability, autism, severe learning disability, etc., might be able to participate in the regular classroom but with extensive modifications to the curriculum.

Quadrants #5 and #6 address an important segment of the disability population overlooked when special education becomes more place than service. These quadrants focus on direct and indirect services for children in restrictive settings (e.g., special education classroom) which enable participation in the regular classroom curriculum. For a child in a restrictive setting the consultant teacher might organize and/or supervise the provision of actual curriculum materials (e.g., textbooks, workbooks, actual classroom activities, and quizzes/tests). For children in restrictive settings, the consultant teacher might also supervise mainstreaming activities, or bringing the regular classroom or regular teacher to the restrictive setting (e.g., reverse mainstreaming).

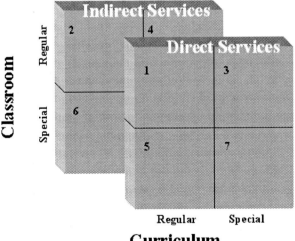

For children in restrictive settings who require not only a special setting but a special curriculum (quadrants #7 and #8) the special education consultant teacher can consult with the special education and provide indirect services (e.g., providing regular classroom and general curriculum materials) to ensure that each child is able to participate in the regular classroom and general curriculum to the maximum extent appropriate. If the consultant teacher does provide direct services in the restrictive setting, the services should focus on skills necessary for regular classroom participation, the direct and indirect services should be within the expertise of the consultant teacher, and depending on the extensiveness of the services appropriate, adjustments should be made to the consultant teacher's caseload.

The consultant teacher must ensure that children in more restrictive settings are participating in the general curriculum by arranging for the use of suitable classroom materials and textbooks, by consulting with the special education teacher concerning the curriculum, measuring progress in the curriculum, and otherwise ensuring that each child is able to participate in the general curriculum to the maximum extent appropriate. If a consultant teacher is not available to provide this service, or the service provider does not have a special education teacher with the designation *consultant teacher*, the special education teacher, or someone qualified as a special education teacher, must assume the role of consultant teacher to ensure that each child in a restrictive setting participates in the regular classroom and the regular curriculum.

The following table illustrates the various combinations of placement, curriculum, and type of service provided by the consultant teacher. To provide these different services not only must a consultant teacher be available to provide basic support and services in the regular classroom, but often special educators in resource room settings or even more restrictive environments will need to assume consultant teacher responsibilities.

#	Placement	Curriculum	Service	Sample Activity
1	Regular Classroom	Regular	Direct	Working with a child and/or class to enable regular classroom participation
2	Regular Classroom	Regular	Indirect	Providing support and accommodations to enable regular classroom participation
3	Regular Classroom	Special	Direct	Direct instruction in the regular classroom but using specialized curriculum
4	Regular Classroom	Special	Indirect	Special accommodations (e.g., Braille), supervising aides, curriculum adaptations

#	Placement	Curriculum	Service	Sample Activity
5	Special Classroom	Regular	Direct	Working in a restricted environment to enable regular curriculum participation
6	Special Classroom	Regular	Indirect	Special education teacher support to enable regular curriculum participation
7	Special Classroom	Special	Direct	Providing direct teaching in ASL, Braille, AT to achieve special curriculum goals
8	Special Classroom	Special	Indirect	Providing support and accommodations to achieve special curriculum goals.

One of the more blatant violations of FAPE is ignoring the general curriculum because a child is in a restrictive setting.[8] This occurs in many self-contained special education classes but is a particular problem for children with disabilities placed in special schools or drawn from a variety of schools and/or districts. In an excellent report on compliance with IDEA by the National Council on Disability, three administrators from California stated that "students identified as seriously emotionally disturbed who are served in a separate school program in the district . . . are not provided adequate opportunities for integration with age-appropriate peers, regardless of individual need." (p. 99).[9] Also, residential facilities are notorious for violating the LRE needs of children with disabilities. This is especially likely to occur when the facility is isolated from regular public schools or when including children in regular education classes becomes difficult because of transportation, scheduling, or staffing reasons.

The consultant teacher must not ignore children in restrictive settings. This is accomplished by ensuring that every child in an alternative placement has an opportunity to participate:

- **In the regular classroom involving the regular curriculum.**

- **In the regular classroom involving specialized curriculum.**

• **In restrictive settings involving the regular curriculum.**

• **In the restrictive setting but with access to the regular classroom to the maximum extent appropriate.**

An important but largely ignored need for children in restrictive settings is participation in the regular curriculum. This can be achieved by careful planning, coordination, and collaboration between the restrictive placement and the regular classroom (of which the consultant teacher plays an instrumental role), or by providing the regular curriculum in the restrictive placement. Although generally not done, the regular classroom teacher might spend a small amount of time in the restrictive setting; or the consultant teacher might coordinate the use of materials and activities that are being used in the regular classroom.

> *We recognize that the mainstreaming issue imposes a difficult burden on the district court. Since Congress has chosen to impose that burden, however, the courts must do their best to fulfill their duty.*
>
> Roncker v. Walter
> 700 F.2d 1058 (1983), p. 1063

If a child is placed in a restrictive setting, the school district is nonetheless responsible for the student's IEP. If a child is able to participate in the regular classroom basal reading series, the need for a restrictive placement should not prevent the child from participating in the "curriculum that is used with nondisabled children" (which is how the general curriculum is defined in the regulations). If a child is able to participate in fifth grade mathematics, the child should be provided with all the necessary fifth grade mathematics materials, including textbooks, workbooks, quizzes, tests, etc. This is not an easy chore, but no one ever said that providing a child with a free appropriate public school education would be easy. The goal is not to make special education easy; the goal is to make special education **appropriate**.

Providing direct and indirect instruction in a restrictive setting is not uncommon for consultant teachers who have special expertise (e.g., deafness, visual impairments, autism, assistive technology). No matter how severe the disability, every child should have some access to the regular curriculum and input (viz., from the special education consultant teacher) concerning the extent of the child's participation.

> *This committee believes that the critical issue no is to place greater emphasis on improving student performance and ensuring that children with disabilities receive a quality public education. Educational achievement for children with disabilities, while improving, is still less than satisfactory.*
> -Senate Report 105-17

As shown in the below figure, the consultant teacher's responsibilities are far ranging and can include one-to-one teaching, working with nondisabled children, extensive planning, training and supervision, and developing and implementing the many possible classroom and curriculum accommodations that a child might need to participate in the classroom. The focal point, however, is to enable children with disabilities to participate in the regular classroom.

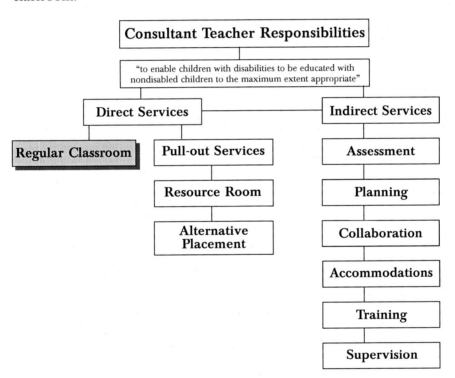

PRIOR WRITTEN NOTICE CHECKLIST

Special education is predicated on a partnership between the school and the parents. The special education consultant teacher might be required to explain to teachers, parents and administrators what procedural safeguards are available and the need to comply with the regulations . . . and the primary reasons are that it is a professional responsibility and the Supreme Court says that we should. Schools are required to "include a full explanation" relating to procedural safeguards, and what better way to meet this standard than to enlist the help of the consultant teacher. At a minimum, parents must be given a copy of the procedural safeguards, in an understandable language, upon initial referral for evaluation, each notification of an IEP meeting, reevaluation of the child, and receipt of a request for due process hearing under Sec. 300.507. Every consultant teacher should know the procedural safeguards; be able to explain the procedural safeguards to school personnel and parents; provide input concerning procedural safeguards that are considered prior to an action by the school; and provide input concerning IDEA compliance that might result in a due process issue.

For an initial referral, before the notification of an IEP meeting, for every reevaluation and when the school receives a request for a due process hearing, a copy of the procedural safeguards must be given to the parents. This notice must be given in an "understandable language." If the parents are non-English speaking, the notice should be given in the parent's native language. Some states achieve this by providing IEP-related documents in a variety of languages. For example, Massachusetts has IEP forms and documents translated in over 15 languages:

http://www.doe.mass.edu/sped/iep/tforms.html

In addition to non-English speaking parents, often everyone but a lawyer will have difficulty deciphering the legalese of the regulations. Solution: the consultant teacher should be able to translate the regulations from legal English to "understandable" English. The list of procedural safeguards required upon initial referral, notification of an IEP meeting, reevaluation or request for an impartial hearing are as follows:

Evaluation: An Independent Educational Evaluation (IEE) is provided at "public expense" upon request by the parents. Schools must indicate who provides IEEs.

Notice: Prior written notice must be provided by schools when considering an action or the refusal to initiate an action.

Consent: Parental consent must be given before an evaluation and upon the initial provision of services.

Records: Parents can inspect all educational records relating to evaluation, placement, and FAPE.

Opportunity: The opportunity to present complaints to initiate a due process hearing (see below).

Pendency: The child's placement during pendency of due process proceedings is the child's current educational placement.

Interim settings: Procedures for students who are subject to placement in an interim alternative educational setting.

Parent placements: Requirements for unilateral placement by parents of children in private schools at public expense.

Mediation: A method to resolve disputes that is less legalistic than an impartial hearing and is conducted by an impartial mediator.

Due process hearings: A formal (and often expensive) method for resolving complaints, including requirements for disclosure of evaluation results and recommendations.

Appeals: State-level appeals (if applicable in that State).

Courts: An option for both schools and parents when "aggrieved" by the results of an impartial hearing decision. The civil action can be "brought in any State court or in a district court."

Attorneys' fees: The State will not pay all attorney fees ("Reasonable attorney fees" is the key word here). If seeking advice from an attorney, read 34 CFR 300.513.

Complaints: The State complaint procedures under Secs. 300.660-300.662, including a description of how to file a complaint and the timelines under those procedures.

SUPPORTS FOR SCHOOL PERSONNEL

Each teacher and provider . . . is informed of (ii) the specific
accommodations, modifications, and supports that must be provided
for the child in accordance with the IEP.[10]

Support "refers to the personnel who will implement these accommodations and modifications." This could be an inclusion teacher, a special education teacher, a mainstreaming specialist or consultant teacher. Someone who is qualified must provide regular classroom support. South Dakota lists "Consultant service" and "Specialized material" as "Supports for School Personnel" in its IEP, but other service providers could be listed who provide direct and indirect services. Although an aide or paraprofessional might be assigned to the regular classroom to enable a child with a disability to participate, an aide is never responsible for specialized instruction and should never provide classroom support unless trained by qualified personnel, and unless under the supervision of a qualified special education teacher.

HOW THE CONSULTANT TEACHER CAN PROMOTE REGULAR CLASSROOM AND CURRICULUM PARTICIPATION

The statutory presumption in favor of mainstreaming has been construed as imposing a burden on the school district to prove that a child cannot be mainstreamed.[11]

1. Provide teachers with pre-referral strategies and interventions. One of the best ways to promote inclusion is to use school-wide resources to meet a child's needs.

2. Participate in the Child Study Team or other pre-intervention process to resolve classroom learning needs prior to referral for special education.

3. Be available to consult with regular classroom teachers concerning the evaluation process, IDEA-based disabilities, and the importance of regular classroom participation.

4. Determine the supports the regular classroom teacher will need to successfully participate in the classroom or the curriculum.

5. Make a determined effort to ensure that all school personnel realize that special education is a service and not a place.

6. Identify goals "to enable the child to be involved in and progress in the general curriculum."

7. Identify the "full range" of services and accommodations needed to participate in the regular classroom.

8. Systematically increase the amount of regular classroom participation.

9. Provide services so that special education does not become a "place."

LAWS, COURTS, AND MAINSTREAMING

Special education is about the civil rights of children with disabilities to be provided with an appropriate education. Case law can help the consultant teacher understand the "ins" and "outs" of exactly what is appropriate. It is often easy to do the right thing; it is not always easy to know what the right thing is. Case law can help understand what the right thing is . . . sometimes.

The primary law which guides the special education consultant teacher is the Individuals with Disabilities Education Act (IDEA) amendments of 1997 (Public Law 105-17) was signed into law June 4, 1997 by President Clinton. This is referred to as P.L. 105-17, IDEA, IDEA-1997, the IDEA amendments of 1997, the Law, or the Act (especially in court cases). **IDEAPractices** is an excellent site for laws, regulations, and all you need to know about IDEA:

http://www.ideapractices.org/law/law/index.php.

By far the best site for current laws and pending legislation is **Thomas**:

http://thomas.loc.gov/cgi-bin/query/D?c105:5:./temp/~c105aEi9pb::

When IDEA (the law) is cited, there are three methods for referencing a specific section of the law. The original text for IDEA uses the Title VI as the basic numbering system so that the section relating to IEPs is 614(d). This refers to Title VI of the Elementary and Secondary Education Act (ESEA) of 1965. After a law is passed, the law is codified in the United States Code (U.S.C.). In the U.S.C. IDEA is cited in Title 20 and begins at section 1400. Thus, the section in IDEA relating to IEPs is 20 U.S.C. 1414(d) (which is the same as the text at 614[d]). But there's more.

The Regulations: After the law is passed, regulations for the law are also issued Office of Special Education and Rehabilitation Services (OSERS), Department of Education. A complete copy of these regulations can be found online at **IDEAPractices**:

http://www.ideapractices.org/law/regulations/index.php

and at the U.S. Government Printing Office website via GPO Access:

http://www.access.gpo.gov/nara/nara005.html

Code of Federal Regulations

A regulation from the Code of Federal Regulations is cited as 34 CFR 300.347. This means that the entry is from title 34, part 300, section 347.

34 - the title for Education
part 300 - Subpart C dealing with Services
section 347 - details required IEP content

Sometimes the regulations merely repeat the law, and sometimes they explicate the law. The content for IEPs in the regulations (34 CFR 300.347) is basically a repeat of the law, but guidelines for parent participation (34 CFR 300.345) and IEP development (34 CFR 300.346) interprets the intent of the law. Many educators rely on the regulations for day-to-day guidance for compliance with the IDEA rather than the actual text for the law. Although hardly scintillating reading, the regulations are a must read for the consultant. At the very least the consultant teacher should read the following regulations.

Must-Read Regulations

Free Appropriate Public Education	34 CFR 300.300-313
Evaluations and Reevaluations	34 CFR 300.320-321
Individualized Education Programs	34 CFR 300.340-350
Procedural Safeguards	34 CFR 300.500-517
Discipline Procedures	34 CFR 300.519-529
Procedures for Evaluation and Determination of Eligibility	34 CFR 300.530-536
Least Restrictive Environment	34 CFR 300.550-556

State Code: Every state has regulations, a law, and/or rules relating to special education. Finding this information for a particular state is no easy task. Looking for state special education information? First, if you are unsure of the state website, go to a search engine such as Google and do a preliminary search. Second, select a site from the various options listed. Typical sites listed will be the U.S. Department of Education website which has an excellent listing of state departments of education.

http://bcol02.ed.gov/Programs/EROD/org_list.cfm?category_ID=SEA

or an easily accessible map-index guide to state departments of education from the Teacher Information Network.

http://www.teacher.com/sdoe.htm

To illustrate if you are looking for special education regulations/laws/guidelines for Illinois, go to the state department of education listed. For Illinois this is the Illinois State Board of Education website at:

http://www.isbe.state.il.us/teachers.htm

Third, find the special education home page by searching the website (simply enter special education in the search box) or find the special education address on the state department home page. Eventually you will find the special education home page for Illinois which is:

http://www.isbe.net/spec-ed/

or

http://www.isbe.state.il.us/spec-ed/default.htm

This page offers a potpourri of special education information (assistive technology, 504 complaint page, and more!) just waiting for the consultant teacher to *consult.* Under the Rules and Regulations entry you will find a 171-page PDF document listing the Illinois Administrative Code relating to special education.

The Courts: In 1975, the need for a special education law was prompted by what the courts considered a need to provide children in special education with an *appropriate educational program* (see *Pennsylvania Association for Retarded Children v. Commonwealth of Pennsylvania* [or *PARC v. Pennsylvania*[12]] and *Mills v. Board of Education of the District of Columbia.*[13] The IDEA should be a partnership between the school and parents but when the obligation of one of the partners is not met, the courts provide clarification (or at least an interpretation) of the law and the regulations.

Interpreting Legal Research

458 U.S. 176 (1982): Volume 458 of the United States Reports, beginning at page 176, decided in 1982.

874 F.2d 1036 (5th Cir. 1989): Volume 874 of the Federal Reporter (F), 2nd series (2d), beginning on page 1036, and decided by the 5th Circuit Court of Appeals in 1989.

789 F. Supp. 1322 (D.N.J. 1992), p. 1329: The District Court decision for Oberti v. Board of Education published in the Federal Supplement, in Volume 789, beginning at page 1322.

The procedural safeguards provided to parents include the right (in sequential order) to mediation, an impartial hearing, state-level appeal, and finally civil action. A civil action can be brought in a state court or a district court. A decision in a district court can be appealed to a United States Court of Appeals, and a United States Court of Appeals decision can be appealed to the United States Supreme Court. In short, there are several actions that a parent (or a school district) can do to resolve a misinterpretation in the basic partnership between school and parent.

THE VERMONT CONSULTING TEACHER

The Vermont Department of Education provides a licensing endorsement for the role of *consulting teacher.* The holder of this endorsement provides "comprehensive special education services to students in grades K-8 or 7 through age 21" and "leadership in the implementation of best practices in special education." An interesting feature of this endorsement is the ability to "provide instruction to students who are visually impaired or deaf, as those terms are defined in federal regulations pertaining to special education eligibility, in consultation with a Teacher of the Blind and Visually Impaired or a Teacher of the Deaf and Hard of Hearing."[14]

Vermont provides a very detailed outline of the consulting teacher's responsibilities, and considering the extent of regular participation of children with disabilities in Vermont classroom, the consulting teacher has been a great success. The following is the specific "performance standard" for the role of consulting teacher in Vermont:

Working in collaboration with teachers, parents/caregivers, the student, and other professional and paraprofessional personnel, the Consulting Teacher determines eligibility for special education services; develops, implements, case manages, and evaluates individual educational programs for students with special needs; identifies and implements accommodations of learning materials or environments in order to support inclusion; and provides direct instructional services, in order to enable students with special needs to meet Vermont's learning expectations for students. In addition, the Consulting Teacher provides professional and technical assistance to the Special Educator.

PROCEDURAL SAFEGUARDS

Why do we have procedural safeguards? Because children have not always been provided with an appropriate education and parents had no recourse to an action by a school. For children with disabilities, parents can file a complaint, request a hearing, appeal to the state, or initiate a civil action. For the consultant teacher this can be threatening. In some instances parents are heavy-handed, but a school will sometimes initiate an action that is in the best interest of the school and not the child. In most instances there is simply an honest disagreement between parent and the school. Most litigation is initiated on behalf of a child by the parents to compel a school to undertake a specific course of action. An administrator, a teacher, or a parent might dislike the procedural safeguard process, and no one really enjoys a contentious partnership (well . . .), but the very fact that IDEA allows for disagreements is the key to ensure that every child receives an appropriate education.

> ### Mediation
> ### 34 CFR 300.506
>
> (a) General. Each public agency shall ensure that procedures are established and implemented to allow parties to disputes involving any matter described in Sec. 300.503(a)(1) to resolve the disputes through a mediation process that, at a minimum, must be available whenever a hearing is requested under Secs. 300.507 or 300.520-300.528.
> (b) Requirements. The procedures must meet the following requirements:
>   (1) The procedures must ensure that the mediation process--
>   (i) Is voluntary on the part of the parties;
>   (ii) Is not used to deny or delay a parent's right to a due process hearing under Sec. 300.507, or to deny any other rights afforded under Part B of the Act; and
>   (iii) Is conducted by a qualified and impartial mediator who is trained in effective mediation techniques.

For the consultant teacher involved in a due process hearing, not to worry. The various procedural safeguards are an essential part of the special education process that ensures each child receives an appropriate education. If the consultant teacher has made a good faith effort to do the right thing, this is all that the consultant teacher can do. A mediator or impartial hearing officer might feel that a course of action other than yours is more appropriate. This is not only OK, this is a major purpose of the special education law. As a consultant teacher you are responsible for making a good faith effort to comply with the regulations and to help each child participate in the regular classroom. As a matter of fact, you (actually your school district) have a responsibility to ensure that parents understand all the procedural safeguard protections and what exactly can be done if dissatisfied with a school's action. Does this mean that school is required to provide information that might not be in the best interest of the school? Absolutely! This is the whole purpose for requiring schools to send a procedural safeguard notice to parents, and to explain these safeguards in an understandable language.

THE CONSULTANT TEACHER AND PROCEDURAL COMPLIANCE

...a court must first determine whether the State has complied with the statutory procedures, and must then determine whether the individualized program developed through such procedures is reasonably calculated to enable the child to receive educational benefits. If these requirements are met, the State has complied with the obligations imposed by Congress and the courts can require no more.[15]

1. Comply with the regulations.

2. Collect data to determine individual needs.

3. Communicate with teachers and parents all aspects of the special education process.

4. Consider all input from teacher and parents as extremely important and attempt to include this input in planning and implementation if at all possible.

5. Make decisions based on "need" and not "disability."

6. Ensure that the IEP is reasonably calculated.

7. Collect data to evaluate goal progress.

8. Develop an IEP to provide educational benefit.

9. Make what the regulations refer to as "a good faith effort to assist the child to achieve the goals and objectives or benchmarks listed in the IEP."

10. Help each child participate in the regular classroom to the maximum extent appropriate.

CERTIFICATION AND
THE CONSULTANT TEACHER

*Although several states do have consultant certification areas,
the only real requirement for providing special education consultant
teacher services is certification in at least one area of special education.*

The primary requirement for the special education consultant teacher is certification in an area of special education. These areas generally include special education, visual and hearing impairments, early childhood special education, and speech pathology. A special educator might have expertise for a specific disability such as learning disabilities consultant teacher, autism consultant teacher, or consultant teacher (or itinerant) for the hearing impaired of visually impaired. For areas involving special expertise, special certification is required (viz., teachers for speech and language impairments, visual impairments, hearing impairments). Specialty areas or teachers for low-incidence disabilities may or may not be called a consultant teacher but all invariably provide direct and indirect services and otherwise serve in a consultant teacher role.

Individual states might also have certification categories for other disabilities such as consultant teacher (e.g., Vermont), learning disabilities teacher consultant or autism consultant. Illinois provides certification for a Learning Behavior Specialist II/Curriculum Adaptation Specialist. The responsibilities of the LBS II/Curriculum Adaptation Specialist entail many of the direct and indirect services provided by the consultant teacher and include identifying the curriculum needs of students with disabilities, making curriculum modifications, and "understands models for co-teaching and consultation . . . collaborates with other educators concerning appropriate use of the different learning and instructional strategies for various students...provides direct assistance, when needed, to general educators, other special educators, and related service personnel as adaptations are implemented."[16]

Teachers of the visually and hearing impaired have historically provided consultant teacher services but on an itinerant basis because of the low incidence of these disabilities. Indeed, in Vermont the *consulting teacher* can collaborate with teachers of the deaf or visually impaired in providing services. For the special education consultant teacher two certification requirements are especially important:

First, certification in at least one area of special education in order to provide and supervise direct and indirect services.

Second, training relating to assessment, consultation, collaboration, instructional modifications, and curriculum accommodations.

The key requirement for a special education consultant teacher is certification in one or more areas of special education. The consultant teacher must be certified in special education but not necessarily certified as a consultant teacher. Certification in special education is required so that a child receiving services under IDEA is provided with specially designed instruction[17] by qualified personnel.[18]

Currently, few states have a consultant teacher certification category. New York state has a specific consultant teacher category as part of the continuum of services, but no specific consultant teacher certification. New Hampshire[19] consultant teacher certification is for "Assistant Superintendent and Teacher Consultant." Vermont, on the other hand, does not list consultant teacher services as part of the continuum of services (which includes instruction in regular classes, special classes, special schools, independent schools, home instruction and instruction in hospitals, and residential facilities) but does have a Consulting Teacher endorsement (5440-85 Consulting Teacher) which requires "procedural, consultation/collaboration, and case management knowledge and skills essential to implementation of an effective educational support program" and "the key roles of the special educator as teacher, advocate, consultant, facilitator, and collaborator within the educational support system."[20]

Often the resource room teacher or learning disabilities specialist will serve as a consultant teacher by providing direct and indirect services for including children with specific learning disabilities in the regular classroom and general curriculum. Because children with specific learning disabilities comprise over fifty percent of all children receiving services under IDEA, many schools employ a certified special education teacher to provide full time consultant teacher services to children with specific learning disabilities. New Jersey has a specific certification role to meet this need in the form of a Learning Disabilities Consultant Teacher (LDC-T).

California Standard 20
Collaboration and Consultation

The Level II program provides opportunities for each candidate to develop skills in communication, collaboration and consultation with teachers and other school personnel, community professionals, and parents. Each candidate is able to communicate relevant social, academic, and behavioral information in the areas of assessment, curriculum, behavior management, social adjustment, and legal requirements. Each candidate is prepared to serve in a coordination function before, during, and after special education placement has been made.

In California the Education Specialist Credential for mild/moderate disabilities authorizes the teaching of individuals with the labels of mental retardation, deaf-blindness, autism, serious emotional disturbance, and multiple disabilities.[21] This credential emphasizes many of the responsibilities of the consultant teacher providing direct and indirect services such as the need for collaborative teaming "in order to effectively educate students with moderate to severe disabilities within more inclusive settings, educators must be provided with a strong knowledge base in general education assessment, curriculum, and instruction . . . as well as collaboration and cooperation among general education and special education."[22] California recognizes the increasingly important role of consulting so that "in order to meet the needs of students in today's classrooms, the roles of all educators are changing, often requiring knowledge and skill sharing through consultation."[23] In New Hampshire the Exceptional Children certification requires consultation and communication skills "to assist in consultative functions necessary for educational programming" and "to interact and communicate with classroom teachers and specialists providing other services and programs to an individual pupil."[24] In Illinois, as part of the continuum of placements, regular classroom placements are supplemented by

- Additional or specialized instruction from the teacher;

- Consultation with the teacher by providers of special education and related services;

- Provision of special equipment, materials, and accommodations;

- Modification in the instructional services (e.g., multiage placement, expectations, grading, etc.);

- Modification of curricular content or educational methodology; or

- Other supplementary services, such as itinerant or resource services, in conjunction with the regular class placement.[25]

Certification in specific learning disabilities often requires specific skills relating to inclusion, collaboration, and the provision of the various direct and indirect services. In New Jersey the LDC-T involves certificate identifying specific learning needs and planning and implementing instructional programs.[26] Also, the Child Study Team is responsible for the "responsible for identification, evaluation, determination of eligibility, development and review of the individualized education program, and placement," a learning disabilities teacher-consultant (or LDT-C) is a required member of this team.[27]

The following is a great site for certification requirements from different states from the University of Kentucky College of Education:

http://www.uky.edu/Education/TEP/usacert.html

WHO IS A CONSULTANT TEACHER?

A consultant teacher is a professional who provides direct and indirect services "in regular education classes or other education-related settings to enable children with disabilities to be educated with nondisabled children to the maximum extent appropriate."

There is a distinction between a special education consultant teacher and school personnel who provide consultant teacher services. If a child is eligible for services under IDEA, the child must need special education[28] and therefore need specially designed instruction. Either directly or indirectly a child receiving consultant teacher services must also receive specially designed instruction. This means that the consultant teacher must be qualified to provide specially designed instruction. Other professional and paraprofessionals might provide direct services in the classroom and indirect services in the way of planning, curriculum accommodations, and consultation, but a child receiving service under IDEA must receive these services by or under the direct supervision of a special education teacher. An aide cannot independently serve as a consultant teacher, but a related service provider (e.g., a speech and language specialist) if the service is considered special education.

Consultant teacher services can be provided by a variety of school personnel to meet the specific or general needs of children with disabilities. Professionals other than certified special education teachers can sometimes provide specially designed instruction and function as consultant teachers but with certain restrictions. A reading teacher might provide consultant teacher services but these services are restricted to reading, and the reading teacher's caseload must be reduced in proportion to the consultant teacher services provided.

Personnel who provide consultant teacher services, or who might be called or employed in one capacity or another as a *consultant teacher* include:

• **Academic intervention service provider**

• **Autism consultant teacher**

• **Behavior intervention specialist**

• **Behavior therapists**

- Classroom consultant teacher

- Consultant teacher

- Consulting teacher

- Curriculum adaptation specialists

- Inclusion teacher

- Itinerant teacher

- Learning behavior specialist

- Learning disabilities consultant teacher

- Learning disabilities specialist

- Learning resource specialist

- Mainstreaming specialist

- Mainstreaming teacher

- Occupational therapists

- Parent counselor

- Physical therapist

- Reading and language arts consultant

- Reading consultant

- Reading teacher

- Resource room teacher

- Special education consultant

- Special education itinerant teacher

• **Speech and language teacher**

• **Teacher coach**

• **Teacher consultant**

• **Teacher for the deaf and hard-of-hearing**

• **Teacher for the visually impaired**

• **Transition specialist**

Many school districts employ a special education teacher as a consultant teacher to provide special education regular classroom services on a full or part-time basis. This does not mean that the position requires either special *consultant teacher certification* or that pull-out services are not possible, but that a qualified special education teacher is providing special education in the regular classroom or in support of regular classroom participation. In addition to special education, an experienced teacher might serve as a consulting teacher to provide individual consultation to improve teacher effectiveness by observation, feedback, collaboration, and one-to-one consultation. In California, the Peer Assistance Review program can assist tenured teachers needing help, teachers who volunteer for these services, and teachers with temporary permits. In this latter category, for teachers with temporary permits in special education who are not credentialed, a formal consultation program that assists inexperienced teachers in providing children with disabilities an appropriate education is absolutely essential for meeting the FAPE mandate.

There is considerable overlap between consultant services offered by special education teachers, related service providers, and remedial specialists. This is a good indication of a coordinated and collaborative plan to enable a child to participate in the regular classroom. The regular classroom teacher should reinforce related service provider interventions; the consultant teacher should help generalize resource room activities to the regular classroom; and all professionals and paraprofessionals should be working in concert to enable classroom success.

All professionals providing consultant teacher services will generally offer both direct and indirect services. The special education teacher might focus on behavior and content area performance in the regular classroom, the reading teacher on basic reading skills or reading in the content area, and the speech specialists on developing receptive or expressive language skills. All will likely provide indirect services in the way of collaborative planning with the classroom teacher, preparing materials for use in the regular classroom, and providing consultative services for the teacher, other teachers, and paraprofessionals, parents and the school administration (e.g., interpreting assessments, serving on the IEP team, evaluating performance).

The role of the special education consultant teacher is often more general and less defined than that of other professionals. The consultant teacher might be involved in reading, content area skills, behavior management, self-help skills, speech and language, and any and all other areas that are necessary to enable a child with a disability to participate in the regular classroom. With respect to indirect services, the consultant teacher will likely have a very large commitment of time and energy involving indirect services. Not only will the consultant teacher be engaged in extensive collaborative planning, but other important indirect service responsibilities will include monitoring and supervising classroom supports (e.g., special education aides and paraprofessionals), and developing classroom accommodations.

ITINERANT TEACHERS

Services provided to private school children with disabilities may be provided on-site at a child's private school, including a religious school, to the extent consistent with law.[29]

A special education teacher is often employed as a consultant teacher but with no clear description of what services should be provided. If you are a special education consultant teacher and feel alone and without collegial support and direction, contact the nearest itinerant teacher for the visually and/or hearing impaired in your district for excellent tips on direct and indirect services, scheduling, working in classrooms, working with parents, and most other consultant teacher services. Itinerant teachers are long-time consultant teacher providers and are an excellent source of information for everything from caseload to classroom support.

Itinerant services are described in the regulations as a supplementary service (along with resource room services) which are part of the continuum of alternative placements "provided in conjunction with regular class placement."[30] As is the case for the special education consultant teacher, itinerant teachers provide both direct and indirect services. In Iowa, students with visual impairments can receive direct services or consultation services which can include "parent conferences, pupil staffings, consultation, assessment, evaluation, observation, records, and correspondence . . . with students receiving direct services, time for professional development, and materials preparation."[31]

Depending on the size of the school district and number of children with disabilities, the special education consultant teacher might serve on an itinerant basis. For students receiving services in private schools who "may" receive special education on-site, the consultant teacher model is often an effective means for providing services. Likewise, when the number of students with a specific disability (low-incidence disabilities) is very small, an itinerant teacher is an important cost-effective method for providing services by qualified personnel. In 2000-2001, of the 5,762,935 who received IDEA services, 1.22 percent (70,662) were hearing impaired and .44 percent (25,927) were visually impaired. This is in contrast to 49.96 percent (2,879,445) who were identified as having specific learning disabilities.

Most states have specific certification categories for teachers of the visually and hearing impaired, but itinerant services are often provided or other low-incidence disabilities such as orthopedic impairments, traumatic brain injury, and autism. The Quality Services for the Autism Community (QSAC) in the New York provides services to persons with autism or PDD (pervasive developmental disorder) and their families. The QSAC provides a Special Education Itinerant Teacher (SEIT) program for children (ages 3 and 5) who are identified by a Pre-School Special Education (CPSE) as having a disability: "The objective of SEIT is to address all of the behavioral objectives and educational goals that are outlined in each child's Individual Educational Plan. In order to maximize the effectiveness of this program, all programmatic instruction is designed and implemented according to the principles and procedures of Applied Behavior Analysis."[32]

An itinerant teacher must schedule visits to multiple schools or even multiple districts to provide services. For the visually impaired, an itinerant teacher must not only service a wide area comprised of many schools and/or districts, but must discern the needs for each child and provide direct and indirect services when appropriate. A teacher for the visually impaired might work one-to-one with a child in School A, collaborate with a teacher in School B, consult with a teacher or paraprofessional in school C, and then attend an IEP team meeting in school D. This type of scheduling requires excellent organizational skills and the ability to engage in a variety of direct and indirect service activities. An itinerant teacher must serve many different roles and the varied types of activities can include any and all of the following:

Itinerant Teacher Activities

• Assessment	• Mainstreaming activities
• Assistive technology consultation	• Monitoring short-term objectives
• Classroom accommodations	• Observations
• Consultation	• Ordering (e.g., Braille materials)
• Curriculum modifications	• Overseeing Braille needs
• Determining equipment needs	• Overseeing transportation needs
• Determining vocational needs	• Paraprofessional training
• Developing alternate assessments	• Parent and teacher contacts
• Developing manipulatives	• Photocopying materials
• Developing behavior plans	• Planning
• Developing interventions	• Pull-out services
• Evaluating performance	• Regular classroom services
• Evaluating student work	• Report progress to parents
• Format modifications	• Scheduling
• IEP team participation	• Scheduling related services
• In-service training	• School-wide planning
• Language training	• Selecting materials

• Software/hardware acquisition	• Transcribing student work
• Standardized testing	• Transition service planning
• Taping lessons and tests	• Travel
• Test modifications	• Coordinating travel

Several sites for general information, guidelines, and strategies for the itinerant teacher of the deaf and hard-of-hearing include:

http://www.deafed.net/publisheddocs/tcnj%20itinerant%20strategies.ppt

http://www.deafed.net/publisheddocs/inclusion%20project(1).doc

http://www.fsdb.k12.fl.us/rmc/training/itinerant/eleven.html

The Texas School for the Blind and Visually Impaired provides a variety of excellent online instructional resources at:

http://www.tsbvi.edu/Education

ELIGIBILITY FOR
CONSULTANT TEACHER SERVICES

There are several views concerning who is eligible to receive consultant teacher services. From a mainstreaming standpoint, every child with a disability who participates in the regular classroom should have (and legally requires) supplementary aids and services (in the form of direct and indirect services) to enable participation with nondisabled children to the maximum extent appropriate. By this interpretation the consultant teacher is involved with every child with a disability to maximize regular classroom participation. Thus, the consultant teacher might work closely with the regular classroom teacher, with paraprofessionals, and with special education teachers in more restrictive settings to enable regular classroom and curriculum participation.

Another view of the consultant teacher's responsibility, one that is less inclusive, is that children who receive consultant teacher services should be able to participate in the regular classroom curriculum. When determining a child's eligibility for consultant teacher services, New York State United Teachers (NYSUT) has identified three factors for considerations:

> **First, academically students should have the basic knowledge to participate in the general curriculum, including "essential reading and math skills," and "learning rate should be consistent with the nondisabled students in the class."**

> **Second, students should be able to work in a regular classroom setting and exhibit appropriate behavior or behavior amenable to positive behavioral interventions.**

> **Third, students "should require minimal to moderate environmental modifications and human support services in order to benefit from instruction."[33]**

There is nothing wrong with a narrow interpretation of a consultant teacher's responsibilities that focuses on academically capable children, provided that all children with disabilities are provided with supplementary aids and services to maximize regular classroom participation. If the consultant teacher is responsible for academically capable students, a special education

47

teacher must be responsible for enabling regular classroom participation. Most importantly, the regular classroom is not restricted to children who are able to achieve at grade level; the regular classroom is intended for all children who are able to participate in academic and nonacademic activities to the maximum extent appropriate. To this end every child with a disability must receive supplementary aids and services to enable education with nondisabled children.

THE GENERAL CURRICULUM

The committee wishes to emphasize that, once a child has been identified as being eligible for special education, the connection between special education and related services and the child's opportunity to experience and benefit from the general education curriculum should be strengthened.
-Senate Report 105-17

Regular Classroom Expertise: The key to the general curriculum is the regular classroom teacher. The consultant teacher is the special education expert; the regular classroom teacher is the regular classroom expert and general curriculum expert. The consultant teacher should not recreate the wheel but use available expertise.

The consultant teacher must be knowledgeable about the general curriculum. And exactly what is this often-mentioned general curriculum? The general curriculum (or the regular classroom curriculum) is **"the curriculum that is used with nondisabled children."**[34] The consultant teacher enables participation in the regular curriculum if no attempt has been made to understand what that curriculum is. This is difficult for the consultant teacher. The consultant teacher might provide direct and indirect services for fifteen or even thirty children in a variety of settings and grade levels, yet there is an expectation that each child's general curriculum needs, both academic and nonacademic, are understood by the consultant teacher. As grade level increases, the ability to accommodate and modify the general curriculum becomes more difficult.

Special education is not a *special curriculum.* This misunderstanding of the purpose of special education dates back to a pre-1960 belief that children with disabilities needed a different classroom, a different curriculum and a different teacher. Depriving a child of the regular curriculum, preventing participation with nondisabled children or instruction by regular classroom teachers, and by offering a stale curriculum that is repeated every year, will result in an increasing inability to participate in the regular classroom and general curriculum.

General Curriculum – What the Consultant Teacher Should Know

• **If you are a consultant teacher, know the curriculum.**

- If you are a consultant teacher, know how to increase participation in the general curriculum.

- If you are a consultant teacher, know how to modify the general curriculum.

- If you are a consultant teacher, know that the academic focal point is the general curriculum.

- Most importantly, recognize that the regular classroom teacher is the curriculum expert. Use his or her expertise.

- Know: textbooks, workbooks, the regular classroom teacher's philosophy, regular classroom expectations, what is being taught in the regular classroom, regular classroom schedules, regular school nonacademic activities, curriculum modifications, instructional modifications, supplementary aids and services.

THE FUTURE AND THE CONSULTANT TEACHER (IDEA REVISIONS)

*In other words, although a handicapped child may not be able to absorb
all of the regular education curriculum, he may benefit from nonacademic
experiences in the regular education environment.*
-Daniel v. State Board, 1048

What does the future hold for the consultant teacher? The Individuals with Disabilities Educational Act is periodically revised (the last was in 1997) and the most recent bill passed by the House of Representatives (HR 1350) indicates several changes will be forthcoming. For the consultant teacher there will be an increased need to identify services that are based on scientifically-based instruction, to effectively communicate to parents the importance of services (the role of parents will increase), and to devote more time to providing services and (hopefully) less to paperwork (viz., benchmarks and short-term objectives). In addition, Senate bill (S. 1248) defines consultative services to mean "services that adjust the learning environment, modify instructional methds, adapt curricula, use positive behavior supports and interventions, and select and implement appropriate accommodations to meet the needs of individual children." Other proposed changes to IDEA:

Parents must provide consent for services: "If the parent of such child does not provide consent for services under clause (i)(II), or the parent fails to respond to a request to provide the consent, the local educational agency shall not provide special education and related services to the child through the procedures described in section 615."[35]

An emphasis on scientifically based instruction practices and programs: "In making a determination of eligibility . . . a child shall not be determined to be a child with a disability if the determinant factor for such determination is (a) lack of scientifically-based instruction practices and programs that contain the essential components of reading instruction (as that term is defined in section 1208(3) of the Elementary and Secondary Education Act of 1965); (b) lack of instruction in math; or (c) limited English proficiency."[36]

No more severe discrepancy for specific learning disabilities: "Notwithstanding section 607 of this Act, when determining whether a child has a specific learning disability as defined under this Act, the local educational agency shall not be required to take into consideration whether the child has a severe discrepancy between achievement and intellectual ability in oral expression, listening comprehension, written expression, basic reading skill, reading comprehension, mathematical calculation, or mathematical reasoning."[37]

How do we determine a specific learning disability? "In determining whether a child has a specific learning disability, a local educational agency may use a process which determines if a child responds to scientific, research-based intervention."[38]

IEP Measurable Annual Goals—Yes; Benchmarks or short-term objectives—No! "Until the beginning of the 2005-2006 school year, a description of benchmarks or short-term objectives, except in the case of children with disabilities who take alternate assessments aligned to alternate achievement standards, a description of benchmarks or short-term objectives shall continue to be included."[39]

Services based on research: "A statement of the special education and related services and supplementary aids and services, based on peer-reviewed research to the extent practicable, to be provided to the child, or on behalf of the child, and a statement of the program modifications or supports for school personnel that will be provided for the child."[40]

The regular education teacher and IEP meetings: "A regular education teacher of such child, but such teacher shall not be required to attend a meeting or part of a meeting of the IEP Team involving issues not related to the child's participation in the regular education environment, nor shall multiple regular education teachers, if the child has more than one regular education teacher, be required to attend a meeting, or part of a meeting, of the IEP team."[41]

Part II
Planning and the Consultant Teacher

Five minutes of direct instruction for a child with a disability by the consultant teacher can be very effective for meeting specific needs; spending five minutes convincing the regular classroom teacher to provide five minutes of direct instruction can be very effective for enabling overall classroom participation.

THE FIVE MINUTE CONSULTANT TEACHER

The regular classroom teacher and not the consultant teacher is the linchpin for special education.

Five Minute Listening: Consultant teaching services is about the regular classroom and regular classroom curriculum. Rule #1: Don't ignore the regular classroom teacher who has a child with a disability in his or her classroom. When working with classroom teachers, make a point of calling or meeting for at least five minutes (or even less) a week to *listen.* Of course you should devote more time to planning, but these five minutes go beyond formal planning and meetings. Five minutes to listen to ideas, thoughts, progress, complaints, whatever. Listen! If you are working with a small number of regular classrooms, set aside five minutes of quality *listening* time every day. No lectures, no pat answers, no legal guidelines or IEP mandates, but ask about the child's progress, what the child needs, and then listen. The goal is not to enable each child with a disability to participate in the regular classroom with the help of a consultant teacher; the goal is to enable each child with a disability to be educated with nondisabled children by the regular classroom teacher!

What the regular classroom teacher does, how the regular classroom teacher views each child with a disability, and the regular classroom teacher's willingness and ability to include children in the classroom and curriculum is the key for successful inclusion. Believing that skills necessary to participate in the regular classroom will magically generalize to the regular classroom without the participation of the regular classroom teacher is naïve. Recognize the singular importance of the regular classroom teacher, and you will have identified the most important ally and source of support that a child can have in the classroom.

What if the regular classroom teacher constantly complains, gripes about children, about services, about the consultant teacher (. . . that would be you)? Deal with it. The job description for the special education consultant teacher is not to have the regular classroom teacher say nice things and not complain. Consultant teacher services are about children with disabilities participating in regular classrooms, and not about children with disabilities participating in only those classes where teachers are committed to inclusion. The consultant teacher should not avoid regular classroom teachers who complain, who feel a lack of support, and who believe that the role of the regular classroom teacher is to be a regular classroom teacher and not a special education teacher. Address complaints, provide support, and deal with whatever concerns the teacher might have. When working with regular classroom teachers, listen and listen a lot! Listening is cheap, requires little energy, and is extremely effective.

We all know that children with disabilities are not placed in certain regular classrooms because of the classroom teacher. Ok, given a choice between teacher X who is energetic and accepting, and teacher Y who is harried and less than pleasant with children with needs, go with teacher X. But not if this results in an inordinate number of children being placed in teacher X's classroom. And not if teacher Y (our harried teacher) possesses certain expertise that a child needs. If a student needs biology, and is able to participate in biology with supplementary aids and services, but the student is not placed in this class because of the teacher, this student has been done a great disservice. The solution: listen and listen to every teacher who can enable a child with a disability to participate with nondisabled children. Listen to teacher complaints? Absolutely! This goes with the consultant teacher territory, but a few complaints is a small price to pay for successful inclusion.

Five Minute Planning: The question to be asked is what exactly does the child need to participate in the regular classroom? This is a very focused question for a very focused problem. This is not about what a child needs to be in the regular classroom 100 percent of the day or to participate in all aspects of the regular curriculum, but what is the first step, what is the current need, and what can be done *now* to enable some degree of regular classroom participation. Answer this question and the consultant teacher will know exactly what needs to be done to enable regular classroom participation. This is not time-consuming, but does require an understanding of what causes a child to not successfully participate in the regular classroom, and then addressing this need. Finally, the focus of the question, "exactly what does the child need to participate in the regular classroom," underscores the importance of the regular classroom and the regular classroom teacher. What *exactly* a child needs to participate in the regular classroom is never determined by a standardized test or a series tests (or an avalanche of tests), or by a group of professionals who may or may not have ever been in the classroom. Planning without input from the regular classroom teacher is counterproductive. No one has more expertise in the determination of classroom needs than the regular classroom teacher. When the regular classroom teacher can meet the needs of a child with a disability, the consultant teacher can do more. Well, maybe there might be more for the consultant teacher to do, but accomplishing this is really a good thing. Long-range planning might require a special meeting; special problems might require more extensive planning. But for meeting short-range objectives and providing services, five minutes to discuss needs and to plan services is a small investment for success.

Five Minute Services: We always think of direct services as services offered by the consultant teacher to a child with a disability. Five minutes of help provided by the consultant teacher can be good; five minutes of help provided by the regular classroom teacher to a child with a disability in the classroom can be even better. Over the course of the day **five minutes of direct services for a child with a disability by the regular classroom teacher** can be excellent step toward meaningful classroom inclusion. Should the regular classroom teacher devote more time than five minutes to child with a disability? Of course, just as the teacher might devote more time to a student without a disability who needed extra help.

One important goal for the consultant teacher is to provide opportunities for the regular classroom teacher to interact with a child with a disability. Direct services do not mean that an aide or a special education teacher provides all instruction in the regular classroom. This might be a step-up from a self-contained classroom, but there is really not much difference if the regular classroom teacher is not an active part of the instructional process. The regulations permit children who are not disabled to benefit from special education services. One important merit of this provision is that by allowing the special education teacher to work with nondisabled children, the regular education teacher has that often elusive support to provide individual attention to a child with a disability.

Five Minute Participation: Proponents of full inclusion sometimes disregard the concept of least restrictive environment and the continuum of services, and fail to realize that "participation" in the regular classroom means to be "educated with children who are not disabled." The consultant teacher should be committed maximizing the amount of time every child with a disability spends in the regular classroom, and committed to ensuring that every child actually participates in the regular classroom. Think of five minutes as the absolute minimum amount of time a child can "participate" in the regular classroom, and then focus on increasing that amount of real participation. Whether it is five minutes or 500 minutes, a commitment to classroom participation will provide focus for the consultant teacher in terms of the ultimate purpose of special education.

Five minutes of participation is especially important for all children with disabilities who are restricted from regular classroom participation by virtue of their placement (e.g., special school, residential facility). Inclusion and participation in the regular classroom does not cease to apply when a child is placed in a very restrictive alternative setting.

Five Minute Conferencing: A five-minute phone call to a parent every two weeks, once a month on a regular basis, will help the consultant teacher understand the child's progress, attitude toward school, and recent needs and concerns. There are parents whose only participation is the annual IEP meeting, in addition to the periodic progress reports. All of IDEA is predicated on the partnership between the school and the parents. Make this partnership real by establishing a regular contact during the school year by periodic meetings and phone calls. The contacts need not be extensive, but are intended to show a personal interest in both the child and the parents. Many parents of children with disabilities flinch when the school calls or sends a letter (registered mail no less). The news often centers about a concern, a behavior, or the plan for dealing with the concern or behavior. How nice it would be for a parent to receive a call from the school to learn that Fred or Nancy are doing just fine, progressing right on schedule, and there is no real concern or behavior that needs to be addressed, and the call is just to let the parents know how fine things are. The consultant teacher will often expend a considerable amount of time dealing with behaviors that are unpleasant and achievement that is less than adequate, so spread a little joy . . . let parents know how good things are!

Five Minute Assessment: One of the greatest deficiencies of many individualized education programs is not checking progress toward goals. We have all read the vacuous "to improve (put in a topic) to eighty percent accuracy as determined by teacher observation," and everyone knows that "eighty percent accuracy" is usually a pretend criterion (i.e., no one will ever measure this "80% accuracy"), and that the teacher will not systematically "observe" the child to determine this accuracy level. If goals are meaningful, it does not take a great deal of time or an extensive curriculum-based assessment to determine progress toward goals. If the goal is to increase sight words from twenty-five to fifty, presenting fifty index cards to a child can be done in minutes. If the goal is to improve writing ability, having the child write a paragraph on some topic once a month and then counting all errors, or specific errors (e.g., spelling), or the number of words written, or simply assigning a holistic grade (e.g., the paragraph is assigned a grade such as 70, 85, 95). What is important is that the behavior or skill cited in the child's IEP is evaluated. This can be done in a relatively short period of time; this does not require a battery of standardized tests; and doing so will result in an IEP that is truly designed to improve performance.

Five Minute Accommodations: Most IEPs have a section devoted to curriculum and test accommodations. These accommodations are often critical for participation in the curriculum but little time is given to ensure that the accommodations are (1) seriously considered by the IEP team; (2) are actually implemented; (3) are effective; or (4) are periodically evaluated. The consultant teacher should periodically monitor and evaluated the accommodations listed in each child's IEP. The consultant teacher must advocate for accommodations based on need (and data) at IEP team meetings, and must ensure that accommodations listed in the IEP are actually implemented and effective. If an accommodation is listed in the IEP, but is not being implemented, determine why. If an accommodation is unnecessary, request that the accommodation be modified or eliminated. If the accommodation is extra time, extra time might not be necessary, or more time might be required for certain curriculum activities or tests. Consider what is in each child's IEP, and eliminate what is unnecessary, change what needs to be changed, and add those accommodations that will enable classroom and curriculum participation. Spend a few minutes discussing the effectiveness of accommodations with the classroom teacher and then the child. Help make accommodations meaningful, and help the IEP become a useful document for providing an appropriate education rather than a list of recommendations that never change and have little impact on educational performance.

Five Minute Supervision: Classroom aides are an important part of special education and the importance of training and supervising aides cannot be understated. A great disservice to children with disabilities is to assign an aide with absolutely no training or supervision. No one has ever conceptualized a free appropriate public education as services provided by untrained and unsupervised school personnel. Aides need guidance; aides need training; and aides need supervision. For aides working with children with disabilities in the regular classroom, and especially full time aides in both regular and special education settings, help the aide become an integral part of the team. Five minutes not enough? Maybe not, but providing no training or supervision is simply wrong and inappropriate. As is the case for the consultant teacher, the task for an aide is simply not to keep children busy, or to keep themselves busy, but to enable participation in the regular classroom and curriculum. And this requires training and supervision from a qualified special education teacher and/or the consultant teacher.

The problem is not that aides are provided little supervision; the problem is that aides are often provided no guidance or supervision? Why does this occur? How could anyone remotely imagine that an unsupervised aide, often with no experience, would be able to provide a child with an appropriate education? The answer to this question is the incorrect belief that one-to-one assistance is tantamount to specially designed instruction. Or, even worse, a classroom aide is assigned to avoid the planning and services that specially designed instruction requires under the guise that the "individual attention" (sans training and supervision) provided by a classroom aide is sufficient.

Obviously five minutes of guidance and periodic supervision might far too little for a child with extensive needs, but this is only a problem if the aide is responsible for meeting all of the child's needs. A full-time aide might be necessary but the aide is not responsible for designing the curriculum, providing specially designed instruction, or ensuring that the child participates with nondisabled children to the maximum extent appropriate. In short an aide is allowed "to assist in the provision of special education" when appropriately trained and supervised. But when "assist" changes to "provides" special education, the aide must be trained and supervised like a special education teacher because that is exactly what the aide has become . . . and this takes a vast amount of time. Of course, when this happens, the classroom aide is usually abandoned (see below) and left to his or her own devices for meeting a child's individual needs.

Aides are invaluable; aides should be recognized for the important work they do; and aides should be contributing members to the team providing services. If an aide is an invaluable part of the team, there will be no need for constant supervision, training will be an everyday activity, and everyone will appreciate the help!

FIVE MINUTE CLASSROOM AIDE SUPERVISION MADE EASY

Plan what the aide will do. If you don't plan what the aide will do, the aide will do what the aide will do!

The morning visit. Set aside a few minutes every morning to discuss problems, needs and daily responsibilities.

Stop and chat. Don't abandon an aide for days or weeks on end. Part of this supervision business is to acknowledge what the classroom aide is doing is important, and input from the aide is essential for providing effective services.

Don't assume. Don't assume that an aide will know how to give a test, to design a quiz, to provide an accommodation. A few minutes clarifying task responsibilities, and creating an environment where aides know that understanding is expected, is important.

Give the classroom aide (or the regular classroom teacher) a break! Literally, give the aide a break for a cup of coffee, a walk around the block, whatever. One of the best ways to understand what someone is doing is to do what they are doing. The purpose of this is not to evaluate, to ask probing questions, but to spend a small bit of time doing exactly what the aide is doing.

Avoid "busy" work. The less important and meaningful the work performed by the classroom aide, the more planning and supervision required. Reason: keeping someone busy not only takes time, but doesn't really benefit anyone, and certainly does not benefit the classroom teacher, the regular education teacher or children with disabilities.

Welcome a new team member. Be sure that the classroom aide attends grade-level meetings, special education meetings, instructional support meetings, etc. Often the best training for a classroom aide is hearing what other professionals think, how problems are solved, and developing plans and providing services.

ESSENTIAL IEP FACTS FOR
THE CONSULTANT TEACHER

The consultant teacher plays an important role in the formulation of each child's individualized education program (IEP). The consultant teacher is often aware of classroom performance, the extent of regular classroom participation, and how classroom participation can be enhanced by direct and indirect services. This information is vital for an IEP intended as a plan to provide an appropriate education as opposed to constructing a document that is intended to show compliance (but not really a plan to provide for an appropriate education). The IEP will be effective when careful consideration is given to each child's needs, goals, and services. For many children the consultant teacher is able to evaluate specific classroom needs that will enable regular classroom performance, formulate relevant IEP goals, and select appropriate services and modifications.

1. **The classroom teacher and parents are an integral part of the IEP team;**

2. **The IEP is about services and not placement;**

3. **The IEP must identify measurable areas of needs;**

4. **The IEP provides a plan for achieving measurable annual goals;**

5. **The IEP enables participation in the general curriculum;**

6. **The IEP provides a plan for allowing a child to be educated with nondisabled children;**

7. **The IEP identifies services to allow participation in extracurricular and nonacademic activities;**

8. **The IEP addresses all other disability-related needs,**

9. **The IEP must be in effect at the beginning of each school year;**

10. **The IEP is in effect before services are provided;**

11. The IEP is implemented as soon as possible following the IEP meeting;

12. The child's IEP is accessible to each regular education teacher, special education teacher, or other service provider who is responsible for its implementation;

13. Each teacher and service provider is informed of his or her specific responsibilities related to implementing the child's IEP;

14. Each teacher and service provider is informed of the specific accommodations, modifications, and supports that must be provided in accordance with the IEP;[42]

15. The IEP is reviewed periodically or at least annually;

16. IEP goals are reviewed and modified at least annually.

"NONPARTICIPATION"

*This committee recognizes that every decision made for a child
with a disability must be made on the basis of what that
individual child needs. Every child is unique and so will be his
or her program needs. Nonetheless, when the decision is made to
educate the child separately, an explanation of that decision
will need, at a minimum, to be stated as part of the child's IEP.*
-**Senate Report 105-17**

The IDEA amendments of 1997 have underscored the importance of regular classroom participation. To this end IDEA includes a provision that has great purpose but, alas, has caused great confusion. Every IEP must include "explanation of the extent, if any, to which the child will not participate with nondisabled children in the regular class and in the activities" and in the general curriculum and nonacademic activities.[43] One purpose of this provision is to give pause for reflection when removing a child from the regular classroom. The specificity of this explanation is extremely important. The question is not why a separate location is preferable (e.g., so that a child can achieve his or her goals) but why participation in the regular classroom is not appropriate. Although goals might be achieved in a separate setting, if these goals can be achieved in the regular classroom with supplementary aids and services then the regular classroom is the appropriate setting.

The consultant teacher must emphasize the importance of the statement of nonparticipation to the IEP team in that when a child is removed from the regular classroom the team must explain why the regular classroom is an inappropriate setting, why supplementary aids and services cannot enable classroom participation, and why goals cannot be achieved in the regular classroom.

DANIEL v. STATE BOARD OF EDUCATION
874 F.2D 1036 (5TH CIR. 1989)[44]

Daniel concerns a six year old with Down's Syndrome. His parents wanted Daniel in a program with nondisabled children rather than a program devoted entirely to special education. The school initially provided a combined/special education program. Shortly after this the teacher noted Daniel's need for constant attention, a failure to master any skills, and the need to modify the curriculum beyond recognition. Daniel's placement was changed to just special education...but Daniel would eat lunch with nondisabled children if the mother were present to provide supervision and have contact with nondisabled children during recess. The impartial hearing officer agreed with the School, and the district court affirmed the school's decision.

The United States Court of Appeals, Fifth Circuit, considered the district court's decision and fashioned a two-part test for mainstreaming. First, can education in the regular classroom be achieved satisfactorily with the use of supplemental aids and services? If no effort has been made to accommodate the child in the regular classroom, the school is in violation of the Act's express mandate. If supplementary aids and services have been provided, a determination must be made whether these efforts are sufficient and "the Act does not permit states to make mere token gestures." Mainstreaming does not require the teacher to devote attention to one child "to the detriment of her entire class," or to modify the regular curriculum so that no skills normally taught in the classroom are not learned. When evaluating the effects of mainstreaming, both the academic and nonacademic benefits must be taken into account. Finally, the effect of a child with a disability on nondisabled children must be considered.

Second, if a decision is made that a child cannot be educated in the regular classroom satisfactorily, has the child has been mainstreamed to the maximum extent appropriate? "Thus, the school must take intermediate steps where appropriate, such as placing the child in regular education for some academic classes and in special education for others, mainstreaming the child for nonacademic classes only, or providing interaction with nonhandicapped children during lunch and recess. The appropriate mix will vary from child to child and, it may be hoped, from school year to school year as the child develops."

The appellate court affirmed the district court's decision and concluded that a special education placement was appropriate. A thoughtful decision but one that did not fully consider possible "intermediate steps" that the school might have implemented (not counting the highly inappropriate parent supervised lunch and "recess mainstreaming").

PLANNING SCHEDULES

An essential element of successful classroom participation is the
coordination of all services with regular classroom activities.

The IEP team and the consultant teacher should coordinate regular class-room participation with all direct, pull-out and resource room services. All too often services are provided with little or no regard for regular classroom activities. In some cases pull-out services exceed regular classroom partici-pation! "Regular classroom participation" means a meaningful attempt to be involved in the regular classroom and not use the classroom as a way-station for services provided in separate locations. The focal point of a child's sched-ule should be the regular classroom, and all other services are designed and scheduled to allow maximum participation in the classroom. A sure sign that scheduling has not been carefully considered is when the classroom teacher is unaware when, where, or why a child is pulled-out of the regular class-room. But even worse: a classroom teacher might believe that pull-out ser-vices are more important than regular classroom participation. Granted, a pull-out service might be of monumental importance, but this is no reason to dismiss regular classroom activities or how a pull-out service impacts the child's regular classroom performance. A well-coordinated schedule is essen-tial for successful classroom participation. The consultant teacher can increase classroom success by ensuring that:

- **The classroom teacher must be part of the scheduling process:**

- **Construct a matrix of services showing the frequency, location and duration of services,**

- **Coordinate pull-out services with regular classroom participa-tion,**

- **After the initial provision of services evaluated within one month the impact of scheduling on regular classroom perfor-mance,**

- **The location of service should be based on the child's needs and IEP and not dictated by the type of placement.**

A child with a disability should not be pulled-out of the regular classroom simply because they have a disability. The extent of resource room services, and all other pull-out services, should be based on need and the child's IEP. When need does mandate that a pull-out service is required, the scheduling of the service must be done in conjunction with the service provider, the regular classroom teacher and the consultant teacher. Pulling a child from the classroom for a service without consideration for the regular classroom is inconsiderate and disruptive, and will not promote regular classroom participation.

IEP TEAM MEETING RESPONSIBILITIES FOR THE CONSULTANT TEACHER

One purpose of the IEP meeting is to serve "as a communication vehicle between parents and school personnel, and enables them, as equal participants, to jointly decide what the child's needs are, what services will be provided to meet those needs, and what the anticipated outcomes may be."[45]

Even if consultant teacher services are not part of the State regulations for the continuum of services,[46] consultant teacher services can be specified as either a regular classroom special education service or as part of required supplementary aids and services. Because the IEP is the legal basis for services, and the school is required to provide the services specified in the IEP, the consultant teacher must advocate for IEPs that enable regular classroom participation.

IEP Meetings and the Consultant Teacher

1. Attend all IEP team meetings which involve consultant teacher services.

2. Attend IEP team meetings which "might" involve consultant teacher services.

3. Help identify specific levels of performance or behavior.

4. Help develop measurable annual goals.

5. Focus attention on the regular classroom and the general curriculum.

6. Ensure that required consultant teacher services are documented in the IEP.

7. Ensure that the extent of regular classroom participation is documented in the IEP.

8. Be sure that the IEP includes a schedule of services.

9. Help specify the related services that a child needs in the regular classroom.

10. Help identify needed curriculum and classroom accommodations.

11. Help identify all necessary supplementary aids and services "the full range" of services and accommodations necessary to be educated with nondisabled children satisfactorily.

12. Help to ensure that the regular classroom teacher is involved in determining regular classroom consultant teacher services.

13. Focus attention on the regular classroom and the regular classroom teacher at the IEP team meeting.

14. Be sure that the IEP team considers academic and nonacademic needs.

15. Be adamant that the regular classroom is the presumed placement, and that whatever placement is decided must be based on the child's IEP.

Consultant teacher services should be an integral part of the IEP process, and there are several ways in which consultant teacher services can be specified in a child's IEP by the IEP team. Just as an IEP is required prior to placement, individualized program goals must also be developed prior to the determination of IEP services. The IEP team should not begin with a prior determination that a child will receive consultant teacher services and then develop corresponding goals for the consultant teacher. Before any service is specified, two essential components of a child's IEP must be determined: Present Levels of Educational Performance and Measurable Annual Goals.

Based on observation, classroom work samples, and overall ability to participate in the regular classroom, the consultant teacher should ensure that each of these components addresses the ability to participate in the regular classroom and the general curriculum. All too often the IEP meeting resorts to a litany of test scores and not specific activities that the child does (or does not do) that causes the child to need specially designed instruction. The IEP team must focus on what a student needs to participate in the classroom and the curriculum. This is the heart of special education: providing specially designed instruction to change an ability, skill or level of behavior. When this is done, when legitimate areas of educational performance have been identified, a plan can be developed to address these needs in the form of measurable annual goals.

Present Levels of Educational Performance (PLEP): This basic component of a child's IEP should show "how the child's disability affects the child's involvement and progress in the general curriculum."[47] This section should indicate the extent of services needed to participate in the regular classroom. Identify specific classroom behaviors and specific skills that should be addressed to enhance classroom participation.

Present Levels of Educational Performance
34 CFR 300.347(a)

General. The IEP for each child with a disability must include--
(1) A statement of the child's present levels of educational performance, including--
    (i) How the child's disability affects the child's involvement and
      progress in the general curriculum (i.e.,); or
    (ii) For preschool children, as appropriate, how the disability affects
      the child's participation in appropriate activities.

Measurable Annual Goals: Based on beginning levels of performance, this section defines what annual goals will allow a child to participate in the general curriculum (and meeting other disability-related goals). Measurable annual goals can be written to increase regular classroom participation (e.g., from 10% to 50%), to improve regular classroom learning skills, to improve reading comprehension from ten percent to sixty percent, sight words from five to fifty, to decrease off-task behavior from thirty per day to five, etc.

After the levels of educational performance have been identified and measurable annual goals developed, special education, related services, supplementary aids, and services are specified. This section of the IEP identifies the type of special education services that a child will require in order to achieve the measurable annual goals. A child might require five hours of direct special education services per week, and three hours of resource room help. This is not *the placement decision* but a determination of the scope of services needed to achieve the measurable annual goals. If a child requires five hours of daily specialized instruction, exactly where this instruction is provided is determined after the principal components of the IEP have been developed.

The following is a list of the services that the IEP team should consider after the levels of performance and measurable annual goals have been determined:

- Special Education
- Direct and Indirect Services
- Related Services
- Supplementary Aids and Services
- Support Services
- Full Program Options
- Accommodations and Modifications
- Test Accommodations
- Assistive Technology

Each of the above services is first considered within the context of the regular classroom. Regardless of the disability, the first placement considered, the presumed placement, is always the regular classroom. Three important considerations for the consultant teacher:

First, consider how each service could be provided in the regular classroom.

Second, consider when services are not sufficient to allow a child to be educated in the regular classroom, an alternative placement is considered.

Third, if an alternative placement is necessary, consider how each service can be provided to enable participation in the regular classroom and general curriculum.

THE "GOOD IEP" CHECKLIST

Although the IEP repeatedly incants these phrases-"teacher observation,"
"80% success"-because there is little indication of what Frank's level of
success was when the IEP was written, it fails" to measure progress
and identify effective teaching strategies.[48]

The Supreme Court is clear about what is a "good" IEP or at least an appropriate IEP:[49] **compliance with the statutory procedures, and reasonably calculated to enable a child to receive educational benefits.**

Each child's IEP should be a roadmap to enable participation in the regular classroom and general curriculum to the maximum extent appropriate. If a child's IEP is noncompliant, or worse, the IEP does not provide a real plan for an appropriate education, services will be lacking at best or woefully inappropriate. Many factors contribute to a good (meaning "appropriate") IEP, but every IEP should meet the following criteria:

The IEP is not completed before the IEP team meeting: An IEP is developed by the IEP team and if an IEP is pre-prepared, despite the rejoinder that "it can be changed," there is a good likelihood that it will not be changed to any substantial degree. Be especially skeptical about computer generated IEPs which often substitute minutia for meaningful IEP content, and the sheer bulk of the IEP inhibits meaningful implementation or change.

The parents contribute to the IEP development: The IEP process is about a partnership between the school and parents, and if one of the partners does not participate there is a problem.

The regular classroom teacher contributes to the IEP development: How can an IEP that emphasizes regular classroom participation be effective if the regular classroom teacher does not contribute? It can't.

The IEP has beginning levels of performance: If the beginning levels of performance for an IEP are not specific, determining end of year measurable annual is unlikely. Look for vague statements such as "inappropriate behavior" or "poor comprehension" as a sign that beginning levels of performance have not been assessed as opposed to specific levels: "twenty classroom interruptions (e.g., calling out, jumping out of seat) per day, able to comprehend thirty percent of grade level reading material."

The IEP has measurable annual goals: Don't be fooled by pretend goals that are blithely included in the IEP as meaningful measurable annual goals. For example, "improve classroom behavior to eighty percent as determined by teacher observation" is a pretend goal because not only is classroom behavior not defined, but the venerable eighty percent (or seventy-five percent) is meaningless . . . eighty percent of what?

No prior IEP-goal evaluations: If you want to know whether goals are taken seriously, simply review "how the child's progress toward the annual goals was measured; and how the child's parents were informed (through such means as periodic report cards), at least as often as parents are informed of their nondisabled children's progress, of (a) their child's progress toward the annual goals; and (b) the extent to which that progress is sufficient to enable the child to achieve the goals by the end of the year."[50] Often goals are not measured to evaluate progress, and reports to parents are wholistic (e.g., "making progress toward achieving the goal") rather than reports of specific measures used to evaluate progress.

Supplementary aids and services are considered: The IEP should include specific services and modifications necessary for including the child in the regular classroom. In addition, the IEP should indicate what accommodations are necessary in the restrictive setting to increase participation in the regular classroom.

Modifications are based on needs: Don't feel compelled to check modifications simply because a long list of modifications is presented. Every modification listed in the IEP should be based on need. No modifications should be included because they are available or "seem like a good idea."

The focus is on services and not the placement: If the IEP meeting begins with the placement consideration, the entire IEP process is flawed. The placement is based on the IEP.

The child is placed after the IEP has been written. This basic tenet of the IEP process that a child's placement is based on the IEP. You know that

> The Child's Placement
>
> (1) Is determined at least annually;
>
> **(2) Is based on the child's IEP;** and
>
> (3) Is as close as possible to the child's home.

the entire process is askew if the IEP meeting begins with determining the child's disability, assigning the child to a special education classroom, and then considering the IEP or, even worse, assigning the IEP task to the special education teacher. A variation of this scenario is to assign the IEP to the special education teacher, who brings the completed IEP to the IEP meeting. The requirement that "each public agency is responsible for initiating and conducting meetings for the purpose of developing, reviewing, and revising the IEP of a child with a disability"[51] is disingenuously ignored by stating that the IEP is not permanent, that it can be changed, that it is not the final IEP, etc. Don't believe any of this. When an IEP is brought to a meeting, the intent is that this is indeed the final IEP for the child, and the IEP does not reflect that much talked about partnership between school and parent.

Suspicious IEPs: As previously mentioned, be especially suspicious of computer-generated IEPs which contain a long list of easily generated goals from a bank of goals. These goals are often generated by an individual and not by the team, often do not reflect individual need but an actually hodgepodge of activities, and are often measured by that incantation (see *Evans v. Board of Education*) "teacher observation." Also, be suspicious of IEP meetings where a complete IEP is presented before the meeting, when the IEP is void of goals but that "goals will be developed at a later time." If there is no IEP, there is no placement in that the IEP is should be incorrectly based on the placement.

ACCOUNTABILITY AND
THE CONSULTANT TEACHER

*Part B of the Act does not require that any agency, teacher, or
other person be held accountable if a child does not achieve the growth
projected in the annual goals and benchmarks or objectives. However,
the Act does not prohibit a State or public agency from establishing
its own accountability systems regarding teacher, school, or agency
performance.[52]*

The task of the consultant teacher is to enable regular classroom participation which is difficult, and success is not assured. How is the consultant teacher held accountable? What if goals are not achieved? What if classroom performance is not successful? There is a provision in the regulations that states IDEA "does not require that any agency, teacher, or other person be held accountable if a child does not achieve the growth projected in annual goals and benchmarks or objectives."[53] Schools and teachers are required to "provide special education and related services to a child with a disability in accordance with the child's IEP" and to "make a good faith effort to assist the child to achieve the goals and objectives or benchmarks listed in the IEP."[54]

THE IEP AND PLACEMENT

"The law and this bill contain a presumption that children with disabilities are to be educated in regular classes. Therefore, the legislation requires that the IEP include an explanation of the extent, if any, to which a child with a disability will not participate with nondisabled children in the regular class and in the general education curriculum including extra-curricular and nonacademic activities."

-Senate Report 105-17

If there is one belief the consultant teacher should promote among all who will listen (and those who won't) it is the need to reconceptualize the purpose of special education placements. School personnel, from administrators, to teachers, to aides, often regard a special education placement as the purpose of special education. After a child has been determined to have a disability, the child is automatically assigned to a special education class or resource room to receive help. This is not the law and never has been the law. If anything, this is an atavistic practice that relates more to segregation and the reason why IDEA was first passed (P.L. 94-142) rather than providing children with disabilities a free and appropriate public education.

Special education is first and foremost about services. The first placement that is always considered by the IEP team is always the regular classroom. Unless services cannot be achieved in the regular classroom satisfactorily, the regular classroom is where special education is provided.

The order for developing a child's IEP and the placement to best implement the IEP is absolutely critical when selecting an appropriate placement. The order is as follows:

First, a child is determined to have a disability under IDEA;

Second, the child is determined to need special education;

Third, an IEP is developed;

Fourth, the child is placed in the least restrictive environment based on the IEP.

When Schools Fail to Comply
Sec. 300.587 Enforcement.

If a school fails to comply with the regulations (e.g., horribly
inappropriate IEPs the Office of Special Education Programs (OSEP) is not
without authority:

(b) Types of action. The Secretary, after notifying the SEA (and any LEA or
State agency affected by a failure described in paragraph (a)(2) of this section)--
    (1) Withholds in whole or in part any further payments to the State under
        Part B of the Act;
    (2) Refers the matter to the Department of Justice for enforcement;
    (3) Takes any other enforcement action authorized by law.

Before anything, before the thought of a placement is considered, an independent determination must be made that the child has a disability and needs special education. If the child does not have a disability under IDEA or does not need special education, IDEA services are not possible and no placement should be made (although services might be possible under Section 504).

After a child has been determined to have a disability under IDEA and needs special education, an IEP is developed. If the IEP is developed after the placement, the placement is not appropriate and not compliant with IDEA. Reason: **the placement must be based on the child's IEP**. If an IEP has not been developed, a placement cannot be based on the IEP.

After a child's IEP has been developed, the least restrictive placement is determined. For all children, regardless of the severity of the disability, the first placement considered is the regular classroom with supplementary aids and services, accommodations, test modifications, and assistive technology. If supplementary aids and services are not successful for enabling a child to participate in the regular classroom, the extent of regular classroom and curriculum participation possible is considered. Last, the least restrictive alternative placement from the continuum of placements is determined.

Common errors made when making placements: the IEP is not completed, supplementary aids and services are not considered, the IEP meeting begins with the placement, and regular classroom participation is considered a right earned by children rather than a presumption of every child.

The Daniel two-part test for determining compliance with the mainstreaming provision of IDEA is important because the emphasis is not only on the regular classroom (and this case was decided in 1989), but for providing a clear guideline for implementing the least restrictive environment provision. The first test cited in Daniel is whether the child can be educated in the regular classroom with supplementary aids and services. If not the second test determines the extent the child can be educated in the regular classroom. **If the child cannot be educated in the regular classroom with supplementary aids and services, the IEP team must determine to what extent the child can be educated in the regular classroom.**

> If we determine that education in the regular classroom cannot be achieved satisfactorily, we next ask whether the child has been mainstreamed to the maximum extent appropriate. The EHA and its regulations do not contemplate an all-or-nothing educational system in which handicapped children attend either regular or special education. Rather, the Act and its regulations require schools to offer a continuum of services.55

The continuum of services is the vehicle for allowing a child to participate in the regular classroom to the maximum extent possible. For one child regular classroom participation might be ten percent of the day, for another fifty percent and for a third child ninety percent of the day might be spent in the regular classroom. The amount of time a child spends in the regular classroom is a function of regular classroom success with supplementary aids and services. If a child is successful for ten percent of the day in the regular classroom with supplementary aids and services, this is the least restrictive environment. Likewise, if a child can be successful for fifty percent of the day or ninety percent of the day with supplementary aids and services, then these are the parameters for the least restrictive environment.

☞ **The least restrictive environment is the mix of settings in which a child can participate to the maximum extent appropriate.**

The following table illustrates various combinations of settings (regular classroom, resource room, and self-contained) and the maximum time a child can participate in each. Children A and B are regular classroom placements (more than 79% of the day in the regular classroom), although Child B receives resource room support. Children C receives resource room but the time outside of the regular classroom qualifies as a resource room placement (between 21% to 60% of the day outside of the regular classroom). Child D receives extensive resource room services and because more than sixty percent of the day is spent outside of the regular classroom, this is considered a separate placement. Children E and F are both separate placements, but child E receives services in both the regular classroom and the resource room.

Setting/Child	A	B	C	D	E	F
Regular	100	90	50	35	10	5
Resource	0	10	50	65	20	0
Self-contained	0	0	0	0	70	95

The disability does not determine the placement; the extent the child can successfully function in the regular classroom with supplementary aids and services is the guiding factor. When a child's disability determines the placement, the placement is clearly not in compliance with IDEA. All children

> *Placement mechanisms for E.M.R. classes operate with a discriminatory effect that to paraphrase Lau, effectively forecloses a disproportinate number of black children from any meaningful education.*
>
> Larry P. v. Riles
> 496 F. Supp. 926 (1979), p. 965

with autism cannot automatically be placed in School X; all children with mental retardation cannot automatically be placed in special classes; all children with developmental disorders cannot automatically be placed in residential settings; and all children with specific learning disabilities cannot automatically be placed in resource rooms. For every child with a disability, the placement is always a function of the extent each child can participate in the regular classroom with supplementary aids and services.

The regulations concerning placements are contained in Section 34 CFR 300.552 of the regulations and 1412(a)(5) of the United States Code. Note that these regulations emphasize the important of the IEP and the Least Restrictive Environment (LRE).

> The Regulations and Placements
> 34 CFR 300.552
>
> In determining the educational placement of a child with a Disability, including a preschool child with a disability, each public Agency shall ensure that

(a) the placement decision--
   (1) Is made by a group of persons, including the parents, and other persons knowledgeable about the child, the meaning of the evaluation data, and the placement options; and
   (2) Is made in conformity with the LRE provisions of this subpart, including Secs. 300.550-300.554;

(b) The child's placement is determined at least annually;
   (1) Is Determined at least annually;
   (2) Is based on the child's IEP; and
   (3) Is as close as possible to the child's home;

(c) Unless the IEP of a child with a disability requires some other arrangement, the child is educated in the school that he or she would attend if nondisabled;

(d) In selecting the LRE, consideration is given to any potential harmful effect on the child or on the quality of services that he or she needs; and

(e) A child with a disability is not removed from education in age-appropriate regular classrooms solely because of needed modifications in the general curriculum.

THE MICHIGAN CONSULTANT TEACHER

The Michigan Department of Education provides a teacher consultant approval for teachers "with a valid Michigan teaching certificate and full endorsement in one of the following areas: learning disabled, emotionally impaired, mentally impaired, visually impaired, hearing impaired, physically and otherwise health impaired and autistic."[56] The candidate for teacher consultant approval must demonstrate competencies in all of the following areas:

- **Interpersonal relations.**

- **Consultation skills.**

- **Specialized instructional methods.**

- **Effective time and classroom management techniques.**

- **Educational diagnostic techniques.**

- **Problem solving/conflict resolution techniques.**

- **Team planning and implementation processes.**

- **Organizational theory and group dynamics.**

The responsibilities for the consultant teacher in Michigan entail instructional services to students who are enrolled in special education programs which are supportive of the general education or special education teacher. However, a teacher consultant shall not grade, give credit for, or teach a general education or a special education subject, class, or course. The caseload for the consultant teacher is not more than twenty-five students with disabilities, and factors such as instructional services, evaluation, consultation with special and general education personnel, report writing, and travel are considered when determining caseload. Finally, in Michigan the "the teacher consultant shall not serve in supervisory or administrative roles."[57]

IEP: DIRECT AND INDIRECT SERVICES

*...funds provided to an LEA under Part B of the Act may be used for
...services and aids that also benefit nondisabled children.*[58]

The IEP team is responsible for specifying all special education direct and indirect services in each child's IEP. Because indirect services provide the foundation for direct services in the way of planning, support, and organization, these services should be considered first. The difficulty with specifying IEP indirect services concerns the varied nature of these services and location or where the services are provided. For indirect services the location of the services might be varied. Planning might take place in the regular classroom, library, conference room, or teacher's lounge. In addition, indirect service might be offered in off-campus locations (e.g., private school, home, work location). With experience the IEP team, with consultation from the consultant teacher and parents, will be able to approximate direct and indirect services that best meet a child's needs. If the services need to be adjusted, the annual review is a perfect time to modify the IEP and reconsider a child's changing needs and, hopefully, growing classroom independence.

After specifying needed accommodations (e.g., curriculum modifications), planning and classroom supports, the IEP team can identify needed direct services such as direct instruction by the consultant teacher, collaborative activities, resource room support, or aide support (under the direct supervision of the consultant teacher).

IDENTIFYING IEP
CONSULTANT TEACHER SERVICES

1. Determine necessary indirect services (e.g., making modifications to the curriculum, developing materials, classroom accommodations).

2. Approximate the extent of planning, meetings, parent conferences, training aides, travel, etc.

3. Determine the amount of direct services provided in the classroom. This should be a relatively easy task. The IEP team must determine whether the child needs one period a week, daily consultant teacher help, or a schedule when and for how long the consultant teacher will be in the classroom. This should be reviewed at least annually or more if necessary.

4. Identify supports for the regular classroom teacher (e.g., team teaching, working with children who are not disabled, resource room support, assistant teacher, AT specialist, translator, classroom aides, etc.).

5. Provide a weekly schedule showing when direct services will be provided and approximate times for indirect services (e.g., scheduled meetings, time required for making curriculum accommodations).

6. Indicate in the IEP the frequency and duration of direct services.

7. If the location of a direct consultant teacher service is not the regular classroom, indicate the location, frequency, and duration of the service.

8. Indicate in the IEP the approximate frequency and duration of the various indirect services (e.g., three 30-minute periods of indirect services per week).

9. In all likelihood, the location for many of the indirect services will be "various school settings." If the indirect service is provided in a

nonschool setting (e.g., home, private school, etc.), indicate the setting in the IEP.

TIME TO PLAN

Of all the indirect services provided by the special education consultant teacher none is more important than collaborative planning between teachers, paraprofessionals, related and remedial services providers, parents, and the consultant teacher. The consultant teacher should plan and plan collaboratively as much as possible.

• **Actually plan**

• **Plan with the IEP team**

• **Plan with parents**

• **Plan with the regular classroom teacher**

• **Plan**

According to NYSUT teachers need to "negotiate assurances that administrators support general education and special education teachers in their efforts to implement consultant teacher services." In addition to the need for professional development NYSUT also recognizes that:

> release time for teachers from instructional responsibilities has been identified by those participating in this program as the most important factor for ensuring a student's success in the general education class. Participating general education and consultant teachers must be provided ongoing scheduled planning and consultation time in which to review the student's past performance and to plan the necessary instructional approaches to meet the individual needs of the students. This time must be in addition to the teachers' regular planning time.[59]

IEP PLANNING

*The IEP is intended as a partnership between the parents and the
school, and not a legal proceeding to resolve disputes.*

A poorly planned IEP is a recipe for failure, and a well-planned IEP
requires planning by the entire IEP team. The inappropriateness of IEPs
prepared prior to the IEP meeting compromises the entire special education
planning process. The purpose of having the child's regular education
teacher as part of the IEP team, as well as an individual knowledgeable about
the general curriculum, a person with expertise in special education, and
someone who can interpret evaluation results as IEP team members is to better plan for a child's needs.[60] Furthermore, "the concerns of parents and the
information that they provide regarding their children must be considered in
developing and reviewing their children's IEPs."[61]

Meaningful planning requires a "good faith effort" to involve the entire
IEP team in the planning process. The IEP team meeting is not intended to
be adversarial where the parents and the school vie for services and
resources. The Senate Report for IDEA states "that the IEP process should
be devoted to determining the needs of the child and planning for the child's
education with parents and school personnel."[62]

The planning essential to the IEP is about the school and the parents and
"the bill specifically excludes the payment of attorneys' fees for attorney participation in IEP meetings, unless such meetings are convened as a result of
an administrative proceeding or judicial action."[63] However, when the parent
is the prevailing party "the court, in its discretion, may award reasonable
attorneys' fees as part of the costs to the parents of a child with a disability."[64]
Not great news for the consultant teacher but certainly motivation for attorney's to successfully litigate a parent's case.

A partnership between the school and parents? Too good to be true.
Maybe a large part of what consultant teacher services are really about concerns that elusive partnership between the school and parents, and finding
that balance between what is good for the school, what is good for the parents, and, most importantly, what is appropriate for the child.

PLANNING GUIDELINES FOR THE CONSULTANT TEACHER

- Schedule a specific time to plan with the regular classroom teacher.

- Find the time to meet and plan! There is always a reason not to meet to plan and not to plan when meeting.

- The classroom teacher should know what you are doing in the classroom, and vice versa.

- Plan to support the regular classroom teacher to enable a child with a disability to be educated with nondisabled children to the maximum extent appropriate.

- Plan to work with children who are not disabled to promote classroom participation, and to provide opportunities for regular classroom teacher to work directly with children with disabilities in a supportive and collaborative environment.

- Identify behaviors and skills that will enable regular classroom participation.

- Create measurable annual goals that enable regular classroom participation.

- Plan to achieve IEP measurable annual goals in the regular classroom.

- Plan to increase the level of regular classroom and curriculum participation.

- Plan to collaborate; plan responsibilities; plan for success in the regular classroom.

STRATEGIC PLANNING AND COLLABORATION

*Strategic planning is a coordinated effort among all professionals
and paraprofessionals providing services to enable regular classroom
and regular curriculum participation.*

There is not a single plan for the consultant teacher which lists lessons, activities, and accommodations that will enable regular classroom participation. What is unique about the role of the consultant teacher is the responsibility to provide services and accommodations that will enable each child to participate in the regular classroom and the regular curriculum. This requires strategic planning or a logical and focused plan which enables a child to participate in the regular classroom.

Planning has always been recognized as the basic element for providing a free appropriate public education. The basis for planning in special education is the Individualized Education Plan or IEP. Without planning to determine a child's needs, to design an individualized program, and to plan for progress, there is little likelihood that a child will receive an appropriate education. Planning is a critical skill for the consultant teacher, but this does not mean planning a series of activities, but planning with focus and purpose. Areas of planning to be considered by the consultant teacher include:

- Pre-referral planning

- Planning time

- Planning assessments

- Strategic planning

- Collaborative planning

- Planning goals

- Planning classroom participation

- Planning services

- Parent planning

88

- **Planning pull-out and related services**

- **Planning support services (the role of the aide)**

- **Planning nonacademic participation**

- **Planning accommodations**

- **Planning assistive technology**

Planning is the foundation for all consultant teacher services. Before a child is referred for special education, teacher, parents and school specialists should plan and implement interventions to address learning and behavioral problems. If a child is referred for special education, an assessment plan should be devised to coordinate input and assessments (e.g., work samples, curriculum-based assessments, standardized assessments, observational data) from teachers, parents, and other professionals involved in the full and individual evaluation.[65]

The IEP is the cornerstone of special education and provides the overall plan for all services, supports, and accommodations. Before P.L. 94-142 in 1975 specified the need for an IEP for every child with a disability, the Senate conceptualized an individualized planning conference which convened "at least three times a year for the purpose of developing, reviewing, and when appropriate and with the agreement of the parents or the guardian, revising a written statement of appropriate educational services to be provided for each handicapped child."[66] The reason for suggesting an individualized planning conference rather than a written document (the IEP used today) was to allow all the principals an opportunity to participate in the planning process. Although the House version of the bill which advocated an individualized education program was eventually included in the law, planning has always been the basis for special education services.[67] The IEP focuses on planning: measurable annual goals must be planned to address individual needs, services must be planned and coordinated, accommodations must be thoughtfully considered, and regular classroom participation must be the focus of all planning.

The consultant teacher will be engaged in many activities and services, but none is more important than collaborative and strategic planning to enable regular classroom participation.

RELUCTANT PLANNERS

Not every parent will be available to plan; not every teacher will want to plan. The consultant teacher might feel that there is not time to plan. But for the consultant teacher planning is essential. Because parent participation at the IEP meeting is so important, schools must make considerable and documented efforts to ensure parent participation. To ensure parent participation in the IEP planning process schools must notify "parents of the meeting early enough to ensure that parents can plan to attend, schedule meetings at a mutually agreed-on time, and inform parents of the purpose, time, and location of the meeting and who will be in attendance."[68]

But what to do if the parents can't, don't, or refuse to attend an IEP meeting? The regulations are emphatically clear that the school must make a well-documented effort to ensure parent participation by

- Providing sufficient notification,

- Clearly stating the purpose of the meeting,

- Ample notification of time and location of the meeting,

- Considering meeting alternatives (e.g., conference calls),

- Finding a mutually agreeable meeting place (which may not be the school),

- Using individual or conference telephone calls,

- Providing, if necessary, an interpreter for the parents,

- Documenting attempts to ensure parent participation. If parents cannot attend the IEP meeting the school can conduct the meeting but must record detailed records of telephone calls made or attempted and the results of those calls; copies of correspondence sent to the parents and any responses received; detailed records of visits made to the parent's home or place of employment and the results of those visits.[69]

An IEP meeting can be conducted without a parent in attendance, but overall planning will suffer. Special education is built on planning between the school and parents and no matter how well-intentioned a school is, the parent of a child with a disability should be the best advocate for the child.

What to do if parents will not or cannot participate in the planning process? *Persist.* Persist when calls are unanswered. Persist when appointments are not kept. Persist when notes and correspondence are ignored. Most parents are excellent advocates for their children; all parents can contribute to the planning process. Don't give up on parents and whatever success is achieved by increasing parent participation will be reflected in regular classroom participation and success.

There are very definite provisions for ensuring parent participation in the planning process, IEP team participation,[70] and assisting in the determination of program modifications and supports.[71] However, providing an opportunity to participate is a far cry from actually being an integral and contributing IEP team member. Ensuring that the classroom teacher is an important part of the planning process lays the foundation for successful classroom participation.

A classroom teacher cannot openly refuse to allow a child with a disability to participate in the regular classroom but there are teachers who, to be kind, are "reluctant" to include children with disabilities in the regular classroom. This might be because of an incorrect belief that children with disabilities require special placement so that "to help" a child with a disability is to place a child in a setting where this help can be provided. This is a restatement of the antiquated view that special education is a place and not a service, and that the goal of special education is not regular classroom participation but a different curriculum, in a different place by a different teacher. In some instances regular classroom teachers are not inclined toward including children with disabilities because of previous mainstreaming or inclusion experiences where children with disabilities have been placed in classes with little or no support. These teachers have a point. Solution for the consultant teacher: provide support for the regular classroom teacher and you will encourage active planning rather than reluctant planners.

MEASURABLE ANNUAL GOALS

Classroom success is based on focused, systematic and measurable annual goals.

Every child with a disability must have an IEP, and every IEP has measurable annual goals. If there are no goals for the child in the regular classroom, there will be nothing to guide and measure progress. For the consultant teacher meaningful measurable annual goals require measuring specific levels of performance such as the number of classroom interruptions, aggressive behaviors, sight words, identified, percent of problems correctly answered, performance of tests and quizzes, the amount of time spent in the regular classroom, the number of assignments completed. If a child's disability affects educational performance, measurable annual goals should be developed that focus on skills and behaviors which eliminate or mitigate the affects of the disability on educational performance.

The sequence is to **Identify** → **Develop** → **Provide**:

→ **Identify** specific levels of performance.

→ **Develop** goals based on these beginning levels of performance.

→ **Provide** services to achieve these goals.

If there is uncertainty as to relevant measurable annual goals, there is not a clear understanding of either the child's disability or the need for special education. A child is said to have a disability under IDEA because the child's disability impacts educational performance. The task is to identify areas of educational performance that need improvement, and then to develop measurable annual goals to achieve this improvement. First identify the relevant behavior or skill. Next, measure the behavior or skill. Last, develop a goal that can be accomplished over the course of the school based on the beginning level of performance. The following are several examples of goals based on beginning levels of performance:

Measureable Annual Goals
34 CFR 300.347(a)(2)

A statement of measurable annual goals, including benchmarks or short-term objectives, related to--
   (i) Meeting the child's needs that result from the child's disability to enable the child to be involved in and progress in the general curriculum (i.e., the same curriculum as for nondisabled children), or for preschool children, as appropriate, to participate in appropriate activities; and
   (ii) Meeting each of the child's other educational needs that result from the child's disability.

- **Increase sight words from 10 to 50**

- **Correctly identify 80% of primary subtraction facts**

- **Complete 90% of classroom assignments**

- **Receive a grade of at least 50% for classroom quizzes in mathematics**

- **Improve reading comprehension with grade level material from 0 to 60%**

- **Decrease loud classroom comments from 20 to 5 per day**

- **Attend school 10 consecutive days**

- **Be on-task for 30 minutes**

- **Be on time for class 5 consecutive days**

- **Receive a grade of 70 in English**

- **Improve homework assignment completion from 0 to 10 per month**

The consultant teacher can eliminate much of the criticism of IEP goals (and much of this criticism is justified) by the following:
Focus on measurable goals: A vague goal to improve reading, develop self-esteem, or respect others might be useful for indicating general concerns,

but these are not measurable as stated. If reading is to be improved, how is reading measured? How is self-esteemed measured? And what exactly is used to determine respect for others?

Use "real" assessments: An easy way to identify nonmeasurable goals is to see what assessment is said to be used to collect data. Pay particular attention to the phrase "said to be used." When IEPs for a school or district are each filled with "as determined by teacher observation" this usually means that data is not collected to measure performance. At the very best a teacher might be required to check a progress rating (no progress, some progress, adequate progress, goal complete), but this is a sorry excuse for actually measuring goal progress. Parents must be sent progress toward achieving goals but this is not the same as actually measuring progress. "Measurable" means that reading, behavior, or whatever is actually measured.

Collect data: Look at a child's IEP. If there is no actual data to show progress, the goals are virtually meaningless and were never intended to be measured. If the goal is to identify 100 primary arithmetic facts, and three assessments over the course of a year reveal scores of 12, 26, 41, and 63, this clearly indicates that primary fact ability was assessed. True, the goal of 100 was not achieved, but the progress from 12 to 63 seems excellent. Now, consider this same goal when there is no beginning level of performance and the only assessment information (if that is what it is) is a statement that the student is "making progress toward achieving the goal." If the beginning level of performance is 98, an annual goal of 100 is hardly appropriate or a "high expectation." On the other hand, if the beginning level of performance is 0, a goal of 100 might be unrealistic. In either case, a goal without a beginning level of performance is not measurable in that there is no beginning level form which to measure progress. The test for a measurable annual goal is whether data exists for showing progress; the test is not simply to say that there is or is not progress.

Create inclusion goals: Determine the amount of time a child is able to participate in the regular classroom with supplementary aides and services, and increase this amount over the year.

Create direct service goals: If a child requires sixty minutes of one-to-one instruction a day, a goal might be to decrease this amount while maintaining or increasing successful classroom performance. When appropriate, a goal should be to reduce direct services so that the child can participate in the regular classroom the same way nondisabled children participate.

> *A public agency is not required to include in an IEP annual goals that relate to areas of the general curriculum in which the child's disability does not affect the child's ability to be involved in and progress in the general curriculum.*
>
> IDEA Regulations, Appendix A

PLANNING: AT DEVICES AND SERVICES

*In developing each child's IEP, the IEP team, shall consider whether
the child requires assistive technology devices and services.*[72]

Assistive technology (AT) devices and services must be made available to
children as part of special education or related services, and as supplementary
aids and services to enable a child to participate with nondisabled children
to the maximum extent appropriate.[73] Also, during the development of
the IEP, assistive technology is one of the special factors that must be considered
by the IEP team.[74] The consultant teacher, working with parents, regular
classroom teachers, and related services providers (e.g., speech, physical
and occupational therapy), is often able to develop a coordinated AT plan
for the effective use of devices and services. All too often AT is provided on
a hit or miss basis, and services become fragmented and important AT
devices that will enhance regular classroom participation are not considered.
The consultant teacher must be aware of available AT devices and services
used in the school or district, and be able to assist the IEP team when considering
"whether the child requires assistive technology devices and services."[75]
This is not to say that the consultant teacher must be an AT expert,
although this might well be the case, but the consultant teacher must be able
to identify AT needs and qualified personnel who can meet these needs.

AT Guidelines for the Consultant Teacher

- **Identify AT devices and services to enable classroom participation.**

- **Meet with the classroom teacher and parents to discuss AT needs.**

- **Consider low- and high technology to enable classroom participation.**

- **Ensure that AT needs are identified in the IEP.**

- **Identify and collaborate with persons having AT expertise.**

AT Expertise: Assistive technology is a vast domain that involves something
as simple as a felt tip pen to highly sophisticated augmentative com-

munication devices. The consultant teacher will not have the time (or probably the inclination) to re-invent the wheel with respect to assistive technology. Utilize the expertise of other professionals and persons knowledgeable about AT. The regular classroom teacher might have ideas about devices or services that will facilitate writing, parents might be aware of devices that are used as home successfully (e.g., special chairs), and a speech pathologist or vocational rehabilitation professional might have expertise relating to computer technology or augmentative communication. Finally, for children with hearing and visual impairments, and for children with serious multiple disabilities, qualified teachers must be consulted when considering AT services and devices.

> ☛ **"assistive technology device means any item, piece of equipment, or product system, whether acquired commercially off the shelf, modified, or customized, that is used to increase, maintain, or improve the functional capabilities of a child with a disability."[76]**

The Any-item Rule: Assistive technology is not synonymous with computers or augmentative communication devices but encompasses "any item, piece of equipment," etc. "that is used to increase, maintain, or improve the functional capabilities of a child with a disability." This means that special pencils, scissors, rulers, page turners, magnifiers, amplification devices, humidifiers, air purifiers, language boards, special lamps, furniture, tape recorders, hand calculators, computers, and Braille readers are all AT devices. Bold lined paper might be just as effective for enhancing writing ability, and maybe even less restrictive for teaching handwriting, than a sophisticated software package. The measure of the quality of an AT item is not technological complexity, but the degree an item meets a need to enable classroom participation.

Identify AT Needs: Before making decisions concerning a device or services discuss the possible need for AT with parents, the regular classroom teacher, and related service providers. Parents are often aware of the AT history in terms of what has been tried, what has been successful, and what might be useful. The regular classroom teacher can provide insights as to what is being used in the classroom and what might be needed. At the IEP meeting, if AT is thought to be an important factor, qualified AT personnel should attend the meeting. Because AT encompasses everything from computer technology to bookstands and simple magnification devices, the question before the IEP team is whether there is any device or service a child might need. Several AT areas to consider include (1) computer technology,

(2) augmentative communication, (3) vision enhancement, (4) Braille, (5) hearing enhancement, (6) environment (e.g., humidity, air quality), (7) recreation, (8) academic aids (e.g., special scissors, pencils, etc.), and (9) transportation. These areas are not mutually exclusive so that the driving force for providing AT devices and services does not begin with a checklist but is based on what AT devices and services will best meet a child's education and disability-related needs.

AT Planning: One reason why AT plans are not successful, or not as successful as they should be, is because services are not offered as part of a carefully considered plan. For example, an augmentative communication device (e.g., language board) is used by one teacher or by one service provider but is not an integral part of all the various everyday activities. This is why the regular classroom teacher should be aware of what AT devices are being used and services provided in the classroom. The regular classroom teacher is not expected to become an AT specialist, but an awareness of what is being used and why can facilitate the generalization of AT proficiency to a variety of school-related activities. Besides, AT can be fun! The use of AT should not end when the child leaves school. As is the case for the regular classroom teacher, parents need to become AT specialists but using AT devices at home can provide many opportunities for developing and generalizing AT skills. Although the consultant teacher may or may not have experience with many AT devices and services, the consultant teacher should be able to identify qualified personnel, and be willing to assist the classroom teacher and parents in the implementation of AT. On a case-by-case basis, the use of school-purchased assistive technology devices in a child's home or in other settings is required if the child's IEP team determines that the child needs access to those devices in order to receive FAPE.[77]

AT Services: Services that might be necessary to benefit from AT services includes evaluation, selecting and purchasing devices, preparing and modifying AT devices and materials, AT implementation, preparing and training. Every service is important but for the consultant teacher training others to use AT in the classroom, and receiving training is critical if a child is to function as independently as possible in the regular classroom. AT services include

- **The evaluation of the needs of a child with a disability, including a functional evaluation of the child in the child's customary environment;**

- **Purchasing, leasing, or otherwise providing for the acquisition of assistive technology devices by children with disabilities;**

- Selecting, designing, fitting, customizing, adapting, applying, maintaining, repairing, or replacing assistive technology devices;

- Coordinating and using other therapies, interventions, or services with assistive technology devices, such as those associated with existing education and rehabilitation plans and programs;

- Training or technical assistance for a child with a disability or, if appropriate, that child's family; and

- Training or technical assistance for professionals (including individuals providing education or rehabilitation services), employers, or other individuals who provide services to, employ, or are otherwise substantially involved in the major life functions of that child.[78]

AT Resources: The internet offers a wealth of information relating to AT resources, manuals, services, devices, and manufacturers. For links to AT resources consider:

ABLEDATA (a comprehensive resource):
                    http://www.abledata.com/Site_2/assistiv.htm

Closing the Gap (computer technology in special education and rehabilitation):
                    http://www.closingthegap.com

Center for Assistive Technology at the University of Buffalo:
                    http://cat.buffalo.edu/

Virtual Assistive Technology Center:
                    http://www.at-center.com/

Assistive Technology and Environmental Access:
                    http://www.assistivetech.net

Part III
Indirect Services and the
Consultant Teacher

Indirect services provide classroom and curriculum support, but indirect services can also support the transition from intensive direct-services to independent classroom functioning. The goal is not to provide more specially-designed instruction, but sufficient specially-designed instruction so that a child can be educated satisfactorily with children who are not disabled. This requires support in the form of indirect services.

THE PEOPLE BUSINESS

Your generic consultant provides technical advice or opinions relating to his or her area of expertise. Well, for the most part. A consultant might be hired to write a report, to edit a report, to solve a problem, to help understand a problem, to be a devil's advocate, or simply to observe and comment. Likewise, the consultant teacher not only provides direct services when necessary, but will also engage in services that require a variety of generic consulting skills.

Consultant teaching is about working with regular classroom teachers, working with parents, working with related service providers, aides, and paraprofessionals. The goal is not to "be in charge," the goal is not to "consult," and the goal is not to demand inclusion. The goal is to enable children with disabilities to be educated with nondisabled children to the maximum extent appropriate, and this goal is achieved by collaborating with parents, teachers, and other school personnel, and providing support and indirect services so that this goal can be achieved.

The consultant teacher is often expected to help solve a problem, when the actual task is understanding what the *problem* is. A functional behavioral assessment (FBA) is a case in point. An FBA is only required in the regulations when a change of placement is considered but an FBA is essential for every child when behavior is a variable because this type of assessment helps to clarify the problem rather than selecting very restrictive solutions (viz., a change in placement).[79] The consultant teacher helps clarify!

There is a time to listen, a time to talk, and always a time to communicate. Less advice; more communication! The task is to engage the regular classroom teacher in the process of specially designed instruction. The consultant teacher wants the regular classroom teacher to provide information, offer suggestions, make criticisms. Do this by asking questions. Ask questions to clarify, ask questions to understand the problem or a behavior, ask questions to understand feelings, and ask questions to learn about academic performance or about academic needs, and ask questions for ideas, suggestions, recommendations. *Ask questions.*

An essential consultant skill is simply listening. No problem solving; no expert advice or solutions, just listening and encouragement so you can listen more. What does the regular classroom teacher need? Like most, the regular classroom teacher needs someone to talk to, make sure that they are on the right track, to complain, to vent, and to receive a little support. Like everyone else the regular classroom teacher needs a periodic sanity check (although meeting this need is not listed as one of the many indirect services provided by the consultant teacher). Once-a-week listening will accomplish much with so little effort.

Be honest, but don't confuse honesty with being hurtful. A teacher says that child A should not be in the classroom because the child is mentally retarded and the child needs a special *place*. What is the appropriate feedback? "What you are saying is wrong, noncompliant with the law, and Child A should be in your classroom to the maximum extent appropriate." This may be absolutely right, but will saying this actually compel a teacher to help a child with a disability participate in the classroom? Doubtful. Feedback should be honest but also considered and mindful of the fact that the goal is not to reprimand or admonish, but to ensure that a child with a disability is able to participate in the regular classroom to the maximum extent appropriate. This is not to say that a time will not come when the consultant teacher will need to provide very heavy-handed feedback, a time cite to the law section by section, but feedback should be supportive and collaborative and not directive and contentious.

Most important, don't dismiss or ignore what the regular classroom teacher says. When you do something, anything, as result of a request, the effort will not go unnoticed. Everyone understands that there is just so much that you can do, just so much time in the day. But if you say you are going to provide an accommodation, provide it; if you say you are going to spend more time co-teaching or providing direct services, don't renege.

The business world is certainly aware of customer importance, and the consultant teacher should be aware of the regular classroom teacher's and parent's viewpoint. This does require an ability to suspend assumptions about what a teacher or parent *might* want and actually determining what is wanted. In many ways the consultant teacher should view the regular classroom teacher and parents (and, of course, the child) as valued customers. We want satisfied customers; we want regular classroom teachers who are satisfied with the quality and quantity of direct and indirect services, parents who are satisfied with their child's progress, and children who are satisfied to be able to participate in the regular classroom. If the teacher or parents are not satisfied, there is a reason and a viewpoint. And to show that we truly value our customers, the consultant teacher must understand the reason for dissatisfaction with services or results. Maybe nothing can be done, but before something can be done, the consultant teacher must understand the problem or the perceived problem.

BEST PRACTICE FOR CONSULTANT TEACHERS

The fourth procedural failure raised by Evans is the District's failure, when developing the 1994-95 IEPs, to include Frank's classroom teacher in the evaluation team, to conduct a classroom observation of Frank, and to prepare a written report that included a statement of the basis for the determination that Frank was learning disabled.[80]

Best practice, the law, and regulations suggest the following guidelines for the special education consultant teacher when providing services.[81]

1. The consultant teacher provides direct "and/or" indirect services to students with disabilities.

2. Consultant teacher services are for students enrolled in regular education classes, including career and technical education, and other educational settings.

3. Consultant teacher services might be necessary for children in more restrictive settings to participate in the regular classroom or curriculum.

4. Consultant teacher services are provided by a "qualified" special education teacher.

5. Direct classroom services are not provided by individual aides unless trained and under the direct supervision of a qualified/certified special education teacher.

6. Consultant teacher services should be as least restrictive as possible.

7. Consultant teacher services should enable regular classroom participation.

8. Consultant teacher services are based on the child's needs.

9. Consultant teacher services are recommended by the IEP team to meet specific needs of students.

10. Consultant teacher services are clearly specified in the child's IEP.

11. The IEP should specify the frequency and duration of direct and indirect services.

12. Consultant teacher services are consistent with all other elements of the child's IEP (e.g., goals, accommodation).

13. The IEP should show the child's weekly schedule for regular classroom participation and all other pull-out or nonregular classroom services.

14. The consultant teacher caseload must reflect the number of children served and the extensiveness of direct and indirect services.

15. The classroom teacher and parents must be part of the determination that a child needs consultant teacher services.

16. The regular classroom teacher should plan and collaborate with the consultant teacher to enable a child to successfully participate in the classroom.

17. Support for the classroom teacher must be specified in the IEP.

18. Regular classroom teachers should have a copy of the student's IEP in order to implement the supplementary aids and services necessary to enable participation in the regular classroom and regular curriculum.[82]

19. Regular classroom teachers are "informed of his her responsibilities related to implementing the child's IEP."[83]

20. Release time is provided to regular classroom and consultant teachers for planning and collaboration.

21. The goal of consultant teacher services is successful and independent classroom performance.

EASY-TO-DO LISTENING SKILLS

There is a tendency to believe that the primary responsibility of the consultant teacher is to advise and consult. Listening is probably even more effective...and appreciated! There are certainly occasions when special expertise is important, but the most important indirect consultant teaching service, bar none, is listening. To this end the following lists several ways to improve "regular classroom listening:"

- **Focus on the content of what is being said (and not on what you are going to say),**

- **Ask questions (shows interest and helps clarify),**

- **Be interested and attentive (if you are not, it will show); look at the speaker,**

- **Encourage your speaker "Right," "OK," 'I see," "uh, huh;" nod,**

- **Be patient,**

- **Talk less . . . talk a lot less!**

- **Don't overlook nonverbal messages,**

- **Don't interrupt to lecture, inform, or criticize,**

- **Don't be sarcastic, insulting, or belittle the speaker's message,**

- **Avoid "Yes, but . . ." responses,**

- **Be supportive and accepting,**

- **Paraphrase to avoid misperceptions; summarize what was said.**

- **Focus on the key points, primary issues, and concerns,**

- **Don't rehearse your response while listening.**

INDIRECT SERVICES

Although sometimes regarded as secondary to direct services, indirect services are an integral component of the consultant teacher model. Without indirect services there would be no consultant teacher services. Indeed, the consultant teacher can provide indispensable direct services in the regular classroom, but indirect services provide the independence by which children with disabilities can truly participate in the regular classroom to the maximum extent appropriate with nondisabled children.

The Arkansas Department of Education interprets indirect services to mean "services provided by a qualified professional, commonly termed 'consulting teacher,' whose primary role is to consult with general and/or special education teachers regarding the modification and/or adaptation of instruction for specific students with disabilities" and "the special education professional provides special education services by assisting and problem solving with the student's general education teacher/s on a regular basis."[84] Here, the emphasis is clearly on indirect services, while "the consulting teacher may provide limited direct instruction to students."[85] In Vermont indirect services are designated as services "delivered directly to the student by another person (e.g., a paraprofessional) under the direct supervision of a qualified professional."[86] A somewhat similar definition is provided by West Kentucky Special Education Cooperative where "indirect services are defined as services not related to a specific student and are considered to be training or technical assistance which impacts a number of school staff or students."[87]

Indirect services can have a dual role. First, indirect services are often inextricably related to direct services. Not only must the consultant teacher provide direct teaching services in the regular classroom, but this cannot occur without planning, curriculum accommodations, and providing regular classroom support which are all indirect services. Second, indirect services can be viewed as less restrictive than direct services in that these services provide the support that allows for the gradual decrease of direct teaching services. A child might need a constant level of indirect support, but the goal is enable a child to be successful in the classroom using resources available to all children.

Indirect services are necessary to enable participation in the regular classroom and to provide the regular classroom teacher with suitable support (e.g., planning, materials, etc.). Just as direct services include all forms of teaching to enable a child to participate in the regular classroom, indirect services include all nonteaching activities that enable participation in the regular classroom.

GENERAL CLASSROOM ACCOMMODATIONS

When the IEP team meets to discuss a child's needs, general accommodations to the classroom will be considered as part of necessary supplementary aids and services and/or as part of the "consideration of special factors" which includes a consideration by the IEP team of required assistive technology devices and services. Before the IEP team meets, the regular classroom teacher and the consultant teacher might spend a few moments considering the general classroom environment with respect to the following general areas:

- Lighting (e.g., current lighting, natural lighting)

- Sound (e.g., acoustics, amplification needs)

- Environment (e.g., heat, humidity)

- Accessibility (e.g., within the classroom)

- Location (e.g., accessibility to the classroom)

- Equipment (i.e., available and needed)

- Furniture (e.g., tables, chairs, adaptive)

- AT Devices (which are currently available)

CURRICULUM FORMAT ACCOMMODATIONS

An appropriate accommodation allows a child to participate with nondisabled children on a fair playing field.

Accommodations are not about giving a child an advantage; accommodations are not made because a child has a disability. Every accommodation is based on need and is provided to enable a child to receive an appropriate education.

When accommodations are discussed at the IEP meeting, the consultant teacher and regular classroom teacher should consider the need and practicality for each accommodation. 'This seems like a good idea," is not a justification for an accommodation. Large print or having material read might be "a good idea" for all students, but these accommodations should only be used if there is a need and then support is provided to actually make the accommodations. An IEP might indicate that sentences should be printed on a single line to facilitate reading, but consideration must be given to who will make these accommodations, with what material, and how will the accommodations be made. Most importantly, although this might seem like a "good idea," and an idea that might be helpful to some students who are not disabled as well, what **need** suggests that this is an appropriate accommodation?

Many students will require accommodations to either the format or the substance of the curriculum but never select an accommodation simply because an item is included in an IEP accommodation checklist. "Calming music" as an accommodation? This is mentioned in the Washington Assessment Program Accommodation Checklist but this accommodation requires a little thought. Would this be "calming music" for the entire class? Would the student use ear phones? And what if the music is hard rock or very, very loud?

The consultant teacher cannot expend all of his or her time modifying curriculum content and text, especially when the need for the accommodation is not clear. If paraprofessional support is provided to make the necessary adaptations, appropriate training and supervision must be provided. The responsibility of the consultant teacher is to enable participation in the general curriculum, and not to re-do the curriculum or to create a curriculum that is unlike the general curriculum.

Examples of Format Accommodations

• Abbreviated assignments	• Functional content
• Abbreviated concepts	• Highlighting
• Additional time	• Interpreter
• Alternative test format	• Language simplification
• American sign language	• Large print
• Assignment modifications	• Modified grading
• Auditory aids	• Multiple-choice format
• Behavior/performance contracting	• One sentence per line format
• Bold/color font	• Oral questions
• Bold-lined writing paper	• Oral responses
• Braille	• Paraphrasing
• Calculator	• Peer tutoring
• Colored transparencies	• Providing copies of notes
• Computer aids (e.g., spell check)	• Reader
	• Reading windows
	• Recorders
• Computerized content	• Reduced material per page
• Content deletion	• Sign language
• Content enhancement	• Signing directions
• Content reduction	• Single-switch format
• Content substitution	• Study guide
• ESL accommodations	• Synthesized content
• Extra credit	• Taped materials
• Extra grade opportunities	• Total communication
• Flexible scheduling	• Translator
• Flexible setting	• Word bank

If needed and if effective, highlighting text can be a useful classroom accommodation. Highlighting accommodations include reading windows (a cardboard slit that exposes several words or a sentence at a time), colored transparencies, text markers (e.g., a stop-sign symbol to indicate important text), large bubble multiple-choice answer, bold-lined writing paper, reformatting text (e.g., one sentence per line, line spacing, reduced material per page), modifying font characteristics, and the font size.

As with all IEP accommodations the key words are **need** and **effectiveness**. In addition to being a potentially labor intensive activity for the consultant teacher (or for an aide under the direction of a consultant teacher), providing accommodations that are not based on need or have questionable effectiveness will likely muddle an already muddled curriculum strategy. Reformatting text so that each sentence is on a single line, or all material is in

18 point might be useful but IEP accommodations should not be selected because they might be useful; accommodations are selected because of need and to mitigate the effects of the disability. If children in the regular classroom use text with 10 point type, 18 point type should not be used with a child simply because the child has a disability. If a child can manage as nondisabled children without an accommodation, the accommodation is probably not necessary.

Before the IEP meeting, at the IEP meeting, and when implementing accommodations, the consultant teacher should always focus on the need and effectiveness for each accommodation. This is accomplished by evaluating any and all accommodations before they are used on a regular basis. The evaluation of necessary accommodations begins with the classroom teacher. The consultant teacher should always interview the classroom teacher to determine the following:

Are there any special accommodations that the student currently uses in the classroom?

Are there any accommodations that seem to be especially useful?

Are there any teaching strategies or techniques that seem to improve performance?

Do you know of any test accommodations that the student requires?

Are there any accommodations that should be considered to improve performance?

At the very least there should be some data, observation, test report, or report from the classroom teacher supporting the need for every accommodation listed in the IEP. If extended time is listed in the IEP, there should be information showing the time needed to complete tasks or how the extended time is provided (e.g., multiple sessions, extra periods, etc.). A child with an orthopedic impairment might need extended time, just as a child reading Braille will require extra time, or a child using an assistive technology device to communicate. What should not be done is to assume that because a child has a disability, that extended time or any other accommodation appropriate.

MODIFYING THE CURRICULUM

If the state is providing supplementary aids and services and is modifying its regular education program, we must examine whether its efforts are sufficient. The Act does not permit states to make mere token gestures to accommodate handicapped students; its requirement for modifying and supplementing regular education is broad.

-**Daniel v. State Board of Ed.**

Modifying curriculum content must always be done with great care. Curriculum modifications can be essential for providing access to the curriculum, but also, if not based on need and thoughtfully provided, can severely restrict access to the curriculum and ability to be educated with nondisabled children. This is the reason why schools are reluctant to exempt a student from state or district-wide tests because doing so can potentially deprive a student from future participation. If third grade mathematics is thought to be too difficult and the curriculum is modified, fourth grade mathematics and beyond will be even more difficult. However, for a child with severe disabilities reducing the scope and difficulty of the curriculum might be the appropriate way to access the curriculum.

If the curriculum content must be modified, the consultant teacher should attempt to make only those modifications absolutely necessary to enable the student to participate in the curriculum. In addition, if the curriculum is modified, personnel (e.g., an aide) should be adequately trained. An interpreter should know that his or her role is to translate and not to teach or to re-interpret what the teacher says or what the student might feel. The regular classroom teacher might have little experience concerning the role of an aide, interpreter, or paraprofessional in the classroom, but the consultant teacher should provide supervision and guidance to ensure that a student participates in the curriculum to the maximum extent appropriate. If an aide is reading content or recording/writing content dictated by a student, very clear guidelines should be established concerning spelling (e.g., is the student asked to spell difficult words), embellishing content, syntax, and vocabulary.

Many low-assistive technology aids have virtually no effect on test content other than making the content more accessible (e.g., slant boards, special lighting, markers, special scissors, visual and auditory amplification devices). On the other hand, an accommodation that modifies content (e.g., simplifying text) should be used in such a way that access to curriculum content is maximized. A calculator might be used in some instances, but not when the curriculum goal is to learn a specific computational skill; or a computer might be useful for developing writing skills but not if the goal is to teach spelling.

If curriculum content is modified, the consultant teacher must ensure that access to the regular curriculum is not restricted. This requires focus on making changes that are absolutely necessary; training aides, paraprofessionals, and other school personnel and providing appropriate supervision; and to focus on those accommodations identified by the IEP team. If the IEP stipulates extended time, clearly indicate to the classroom teacher or aide what exactly this means (e.g., 50% more time, 20 minutes). If the IEP states preferential seating, indicate whether this means seating near the test proctor, near the door, near a window, or wherever. If the IEP requires enhanced instructions, extra sample items, or abbreviated concepts, what this means to the test proctor, aide, or classroom teacher must be clear.

Curriculum content can be impacted by how the curriculum is accessed and by actually changing or modifying the curriculum content. Format accommodations can impact the curriculum, depending on the format. Large print has little effect on the curriculum, Braille might require some slight modifications (e.g., with charts, graphs, etc), while sign language, American Sign language (ASL) and fingerspelling can substantially modify vocabulary and syntax, depending on the use of signs and fingerspelling.

Calculators and computers can impact the curriculum if the device replaces important skills. For advanced tests in mathematics calculators are often allowed when the skill being assessed is problem solving rather than computational skill. However, using a hand calculator to answer primary fact problems for a workbook activity would teach, apparently, calculator usage rather than primary fact skills.

Assistive technology accommodations can be very labor-intensive in terms of preparation, but often essential for allowing a child to participate in the curriculum. Consider a student who has limited speech and limited mobility to use a traditional keyboard effectively. This student might respond to curriculum content by using a computerized multiple-choice format to scan possible choices. For example, if the question **What is the capital of North Dakota?** is presented via computer, possible responses could be scanned sequentially by highlighting each possible choice until the student engages a switch to indicate a response: Chicago, Bismarck, Springfield, St. Paul.

The nature and type of format accommodation can indirectly affect curriculum content, but accommodations can also directly and intentionally affect the difficulty of the curriculum. This is not to say that accommodations that sometimes radically modify curriculum content are not necessary, but that changing the level of difficulty or meaning of the content is very restrictive in that doing so prevents access to material which might be necessary for other more advanced study. The curriculum content can be substantially modified by deleting (e.g., only doing a limited number of problems), enhancing (e.g., adding notes or highlighting important ideas), or reducing the amount of curriculum content, paraphrasing, content substitution (e.g., using a functional content) and language simplification.

Changing the language or substance of curriculum content is not only exceedingly difficult and time-consuming, but often arbitrary. If at all possible, the language of text should not be changed. If this is a necessary option and participation in the regular curriculum requires language simplification, consider other alternatives before specifying a change in the difficulty or content of the curriculum. Consider this sentence from *The Red Badge of Courage* by Stephen Crane: **The cold passed reluctantly from the earth, and the retiring fogs revealed an army stretched out on the hills, resting**. If the IEP specified a simplification of the curriculum or the difficulty level of text, the readability of this sentence could be reduced by **The ground became less cold. The fog lifted. The army could be seen resting**. This might provide access to the curriculum, but this is not Stephen Crane's *Red Badge of Courage*. Even more importantly, consideration must be given to the practicality of making this type of content accommodation on a regular basis to all elements of the curriculum.

Many IEP teams would be more effective in the designation of curriculum accommodations if they were aware of content accommodations entailed from the standpoint of labor, implementation, and effectiveness. And who better to inform the IEP team than the consultant teacher?

The consultant teacher can prevent or at least limit many of the inconsistencies and problems associated with test accommodations by providing in-service training. This is especially important for readers, recorders and scribes, translators, and interpreters. Even though the consultant teacher might have limited sign language skill, if an interpreter is used in the classroom, the role and responsibilities of the interpreter must be clearly defined. This is also the case for readers and scribes. A reader must be able to read material at a rate that is understood, ask questions without indicating the answer; a scribe must have guidelines for spelling, how to record punctuation, making changes, and otherwise enhancing what is being recorded.

Accommodation Selection Guidelines

1. **What exactly is the accommodation?** Indicating that a computer can be used is virtually meaningless, and says nothing about exactly how a computer will be used.

2. **Who will make the accommodation?** Curriculum accommodations might be needed, but they can be labor-intensive. Consider the work required for the accommodation, and who will provide this work.

3. **When is the accommodation permitted?** With all classroom material, with some material, with workbooks, classroom tests and quizzes, basal readers? A checklist rarely provides the detail necessary for the effective and fair use of an accommodation. For the consultant teacher attending the IEP meeting, if this detail is not included, ask for clarification and take notes!!

4. **Is the accommodation needed?** As already said, *need* and *not disability* should guide the selection of curriculum accommodations.

5. **Is the accommodation effective?** If a child is able to perform as nondisabled children without the accommodation, the accommodation should not be used.

6. **Is the accommodation the least restrictive?** Determine whether the accommodation is the least intrusive for mitigating the effects of the disability.

ALTERNATE ASSESSMENT

Not all children with disabilities will be able to participate in state and district-wide standardized assessments. However, there is a reluctance to deprive a student the opportunity to demonstrate his or her skills via standardized testing. And for good reason! Not participating in a testing program in which nondisabled children participate "solely by reason of his or her disability" would be an exclusion and denial of benefits and thus discriminatory under Section 504.

Alternate Assessment
34 CFR 300.347(a)(5)(ii)

If the IEP team determines that the child will not participate in a particular State or district-wide assessment of student achievement (or part of an assessment), a statement of--

(A) Why that assessment is not appropriate for the child; and
(B) How the child will be assessed.

If a student is participating in the regular classroom via consultant teacher services, and the student is not able to participate in a state or district-wide assessment, the consultant teacher has a responsibility to explain to the IEP team why that assessment is not possible and how the student will be assessed. There are several approaches for conducting an alternate assessment, including portfolio assessment and alternate standard assessment. The Kentucky Alternate Portfolio assessment is designed for students unable to complete a regular diploma program even with modifications and accommodations and "it is comprised of student products and work samples, the portfolio may include peer and teacher notes, data and graphs, video/audiotapes, and photographs."[88] Alaska's alternate assessment is developed by a "working portfolio" and is an important element of Alaska's Comprehensive System of Student Assessment (CSSA). The modification for the English/Language Arts standard that "a student should be able to speak and write well for a variety of purposes and audiences" is to "use functional written communication (includes writing in pictures, words, or symbols)."[89] Although not necessarily responsible for the development of an alternate assessment, the consultant teacher should provide guidance as to how regular classroom and curriculum performance can be included in an alternate assessment. The consultant teacher can increase the effectiveness of alternate assessments by the following:

- **Give examples of the student's current classroom work.**

- **Identify and evaluate behaviors, skills or abilities that interfere with classroom or curriculum participation.**

- **Identify classroom skills, behaviors and abilities which can be included in the alternate assessment.**

- **Evaluate measurable annual goals in terms of classroom performance.**

- **Develop a regular classroom rating survey that can be used to evaluate classroom participation.**

- **Discuss ways in which the alternate assessment should be modified to enable participation in the general curriculum.**

- **Integrate the alternate assessment with state standards and state assessments.**

- **Consider who will develop, conduct, and score the alternate assessment.**

- **Develop an objective system for evaluating the portfolio or alternate assessment. For example, the special education teacher might develop the portfolio but the consultant teacher scores the assessment or vice versa.**

- **If the consultant teacher is responsible for developing and administering alternative assessments, time must be provided to accomplish this task.**

EXAMPLES OF CONSULTANT TEACHER
INDIRECT SERVICE ACTIVITIES

❑ Administrative support
❑ Aide supervision
❑ Aide training
❑ Assessment interpretation
❑ Assistive technology implementation
❑ Assistive technology need assessment
❑ Assistive technology training
❑ Behavioral intervention planning
❑ Child Study Team participation
❑ Classification consultation
❑ Classroom accommodations
❑ Classroom management supervision
❑ Classroom observations
❑ Classroom participation analysis
❑ Collaborative planning
❑ Collect classroom participation data
❑ Collect teacher-based data
❑ Coordinate transition services
❑ Coordinating interventions
❑ Coordination of services
❑ Curriculum accommodations
❑ Curriculum evaluation
❑ Curriculum materials procurement
❑ Curriculum modifications
❑ Curriculum-based assessments
❑ Declassification review
❑ Declassification services
❑ Developing intervention plans
❑ Developing section 504 plans
❑ Developing teaching materials
❑ Dispute resolution
❑ Due process issues
❑ Ecological evaluations
❑ Procuring equipment

❑ Evaluating curriculum materials
❑ Evaluating classroom participation
❑ Functional behavioral assessment
❑ Goal identification
❑ IEP development
❑ IEP management
❑ IEP meetings
❑ IEP monitoring
❑ IEP progress evaluation
❑ IEP Reports
❑ IEP team meetings
❑ Individual consultation
❑ In-service training
❑ Developing instructional materials
❑ Instructional modifications
❑ Interpreting classroom performance
❑ Interpreting district-wide assessments
❑ Learning environment evaluation
❑ Materials procurement
❑ Modifying classroom activities
❑ Modifying classroom tests
❑ Monitoring classroom participation
❑ Monitoring nonacademic activities
❑ Monitoring student work
❑ Paraprofessional supervision
❑ Paraprofessional training
❑ Parent conferences
❑ Parent consultation
❑ Parent correspondence
❑ Peer tutoring
❑ Physical education planning
❑ Planning time
❑ Portfolio assessment
❑ Pre-intervention consultation
❑ Preparing text formats

❑ Private school consultation	❑ School-wide training
❑ Procuring equipment and materials	❑ Section 504 consultation
❑ Progress checks	❑ Section 504 services
❑ Progress reporting	❑ Section 504 supervision
❑ Providing learning aids	❑ Service management
❑ Referral consultation	❑ Special education consultation
❑ Regular classroom consultation	❑ Supervising services
❑ Reporting to parents	❑ Identifying supplementary aids and services
❑ Resource room consultation	
❑ Review student performance	❑ Teacher meetings
❑ Annual reviews	❑ Team meetings
❑ Rules and regulations	❑ Technical assistance
❑ Scheduling	❑ Test modifications

THE DO'S AND DON'TS OF ASSESSMENT

Tests are selected and administered so as best to ensure that if a test is administered to a child with impaired sensory, manual, or speaking skills, the test results accurately reflect the child's aptitude or achievement level or whatever other factors the test purports to measure, rather than reflecting the child's impaired sensory, manual, or speaking skills (unless those skills are the factors that the test purports to measure).[90]

The consultant teacher is often instrumental in collecting curriculum-based data, standardized test information and ratings and observational data for the following five reasons:

First, to determine whether a child has an IDEA disability,

Second, to determine whether the child needs special education,

Third, to determine present levels of performance,

Fourth, to develop a child's IEP,

Fifth, to evaluate progress.

When using and interpreting assessments, the consultant teacher should be aware of the following:[91]

Assessments have been validated for the specific purpose for which they are used:

- Don't read a reading test to a child.
- Don't spell words for a child when giving a spelling test.
- Don't allow an aide to provide answers.

Assessments are administered by trained and knowledgeable personnel in accordance with any instructions provided by the producer of the tests:

- Do read the test manual and test instructions.

119

• Do attempt to follow all test instructions.

A variety of assessment tools and strategies are used to gather relevant functional and developmental information about the child, including information provided by the parent, and information related to enabling the child to be involved in and progress in the general curriculum:

- Do consider standardized **and** curriculum-based tests.
- Do consider parent and teacher reports, rating scales, etc.
- Do interview the regular classroom teacher.
- Do review classroom grades, reports, work samples, etc.

The child is assessed in all areas related to the suspected disability, including, if appropriate, health, vision, hearing, social and emotional status, general intelligence, academic performance, communicative status, and motor abilities:

- Do conduct a comprehensive evaluation.
- Don't rely on a single score, especially an IQ score.

If an assessment is not conducted under standard conditions, a description of the extent to which it varied from standard conditions (e.g., the qualifications of the person administering the test, or the method of test administration) must be included in the evaluation report:

- Do attempt to administer tests under standard conditions.
- Do list departures from test instructions (e.g., extended time was given).
- Do indicate who administered the test (e.g., teacher, consultant teacher, aide).
- Don't make unnecessary or unfounded modifications.

The purpose of a full individual evaluation is to determine (1) whether the child is a child with a disability under Sec. 300.7; (2) whether the child needs special education, and (3) the content of the child's IEP:

- Do consider the disabilities listed under 300.7.
- Do consider the need for special education.
- Do determine present levels of educational performance.
- Do determine beginning benchmarks for possible measurable annual goals.

• Do consider the need for test accommodations.

The IEP must include "a statement of any individual modifications in the administration of State or district-wide assessments of student achievement that are needed in order for the child to participate in the assessment."[92]

• Do determine the need for test modifications before and during testing.
• Do not invalidate a test by a test modification.
• Do not use test modifications to give a child an advantage.
• Do not wait until the IEP meeting to first consider test modifications.

Test accommodations for state-wide tests generally have very specific criteria as to what is or is not permitted. The consultant teacher should be aware of state guidelines concerning accommodations, and should provide guidance for the inclusion of test accommodations which consider the panorama of a child's test needs. For children who are not able to participate in assessments, the consultant teacher will often provide guidance as to why a particular assessment is not appropriate and how the child should be assessed.[93]

Before a referral is made for special education and an individual evaluation conducted, much time and effort could be saved if the regular education teacher (or whoever is making the referral) understands that a child must have an IDEA disability and must need special education before a child can receive services.

The need for IDEA services is described as a disability that "adversely affects a child's educational performance." If educational performance is not affected, the child might have a disability but would not require special education or specially designed instruction. For example, a student might have an emotional disturbance that requires serious intervention but if this disability had no affect on the student's educational performance, the student would not need specially designed instruction. Of course, an adverse affect on educational performance is not simply a matter of test scores, but also includes the ability of the teacher to teach and the effect on other students in the classroom.

> *The SEA or LEA must ensure that their assessments are valid, reliable, and consistent with professional and technical standards, particularly for assessments that will have important consequences for the student or the school.*
>
> -Memo from Michael Cohen and Judith E. Heumann
> January 12, 2000

TEST ACCOMMODATIONS

*If an assessment is not conducted under standard conditions, a
description of the extent to which it varied from standard conditions
(e.g., the qualifications of the person administering the test, or the
method of test administration) must be included in the evaluation report.*[94]

The consultant teacher can play an extremely important role in the planning, documentation, and implementation of test accommodations by collaborating with the school psychologist and regular classroom teacher to coordinate the determination of test accommodation needs. Test accommodations should reflect a student's need to participate in district-wide tests, classroom tests and quizzes, and accommodations that are used on a regular basis to participate in the classroom and the curriculum.

**Test Accommodations
34 CFR 300.347(a)(5)**

(i) A statement of any individual modifications in the administration of state or district-wide assessments of student achievement that are needed in order for the child to participate in the assessment; and

(ii) If the IEP team determines that the child will not participate in a particular state or district-wide assessment of student achievement (or part of an assessment), a statement of--

  (A) Why that assessment is not appropriate for the child; and
  (B) How the child will be assessed.

The basic rule to follow when making test accommodations is that every accommodation must be based on the need to allow students with disabilities to participate on a fair basis with children who are not disabled. Test accommodations should never be made gratuitously, to give an advantage, or because a child has a disability. The basic principles that the IEP team should consider include test accommodations that

- **are based on need,**

- **are as least restrictive as possible,**

122

- mitigate the effects of the disability,

- are reviewed at least annually,

- are correlated with curriculum accommodations,

- are considered within the guidelines provided by the test publisher,

- are used so as not to negate a test's validity,

- are documented if the test differs from a standard administration.

Every IEP is required to indicate modifications to state and district-wide assessments (e.g., the Stanford Achievement Test). The Arkansas IEP offers a wide variety of accommodations for tests (reduced length, taped tests, color-coding, alternate locations). Tennessee makes a distinction between **classroom testing modifications, assignment modifications, classroom modifications**, and state and district-wide **assessment modifications**. The modifications for **classroom testing modifications** can be very permissive (or restrictive) and include modified grading, oral testing, additional time, modifying the test content (e.g., using multiple choice format or a word bank), and abbreviated concepts; **assignment modifications** include abbreviated assignments, additional time, study guide, extra grade opportunities (re-do items missed, extra credit) and compacting; and **classroom modifications** include preferential seating, provide copies of material to be copied from book to board, providing copies of notes (from another student), peer tutoring, behavior/performance contracting, highlighted textbook (student), and taped materials. State assessments include No Modifications, Revised Format, Flexible Scheduling, Alternative Test Format, Flexible Setting, Recording Answers, Signing Directions and Auditory Aids (special permission).

Consultant Teacher Test Accommodations Guidelines

1. **Need:** Test accommodations must be based on need. If a child is able to complete tests in a time frame comparable to children who are not disabled, extra time would be an inappropriate test accommodation. If a student is able to take tests in the regular classroom, removing the student to a separate location simply because the student has a disability and not based on need would be restrictive.

2. **Data:** Collect data from classroom testing to show that accommodations are needed. Use information provided by the parents, data based on classroom-based assessments and observations, observations by regular classroom teachers and related service providers when determining test accommodation needs.[95]

3. **Test:** If necessary, *test* for needed test accommodations. Observe the child's performance during an assessment, during quizzes and classroom tests to determine the effectiveness of a specific accommodation and the need for potentially effective test accommodations.

4. **Discuss:** Discuss the need for possible test accommodations with regular classroom teachers, parents, and other related service providers what accommodations are being used, and what accommodations are effective or what might be effective.

5. **Curriculum:** Attempt to coordinate accommodations to state and district-wide tests with daily accommodations to the curriculum. If a student does not need large print or have content *read* for daily work and classroom tests and quizzes, a very sound rationale would be needed to include these accommodations for state or district-wide tests.

6. **IEP team decisions:** How not to make test accommodations is to march into an IEP meeting and then select test accommodations from a list that seems "helpful" without regard for need or implementation. Given a test with no accommodations and the same test with X test accommodation, the former (no test accommodations) would be appropriate if the test accommodation had no impact on test performance. More is not better when making test accommodations. Enabling a child to participate in school testing means enabling participation as children without disabilities participate in testing to the maximum extent appropriate.

7. **Independence:** Provide a foundation for real success in the classroom by encouraging independent behavior. The goal is not to provide a child with every conceivable accommodation, but only those accommodations needed that will allow the child to function independently and on what some in testing refer to as a "fair playing field."

8. **Test instructions:** A common error made by IEP teams is to completely disregard (or ignore) test instructions. The IEP team must be aware what is permissible and what is not. If the state requires that a particular test must be administered in one day, an IEP team that ignores this would run afoul of the requirement that tests are administered "in accordance with any instructions provided by the producers of the test" by permitting testing over a period of days.

9. **Resources:** Be prepared to discuss the resources necessary to provide accommodations. If given over several periods, where and when will the testing take place? If two hours is given to complete a one-hour test, will

the student remain in the room after other students have completed testing, go to the library, etc.? Who will proctor the test? Is a proctor required for all tests or just district-wide tests? State tests? The IEP team is not responsible for every detail involving the implementation of test accommodations, but some thought must be given accommodations that impact the classroom teacher, the consultant teacher, other children being tested and students.

10. **Personnel:** An essential question about test accommodations concerns who will be administering the test and who will be making the accommodation. If a test is to be read, or responses recorded by a recorder or scribe, who will perform these tasks (e.g., consultant teacher, classroom teacher, aide)?

11. **Training:** Simple accommodations do not require a high level of expertise (e.g., providing extended time, preferential seating during a test), but many other accommodations require at least some degree of preparation. To indicate that "test instructions can be simplified" or that "sample items" are permitted are too open-ended. How much time should be spent simplifying instructions? How many sample items are permitted? How does the test proctor determine if a child understands the instructions or needs sample items? Most important, training and/or guidelines must be provided to all readers, scribers, interpreters, and translators so that each understands his or her responsibility to enable classroom participation.

12. **Proctors:** The effective use of a proctor is more a matter of preparation than training. If a proctor is used to administer a test, the consultant teacher should meet with the proctor to ensure that permitted accommodations are understood. The proctor should know what accommodations are required or what to do (or not do) if a student suddenly leaves the room, uses a calculator, or requests to sit in the front row. Students are often aware of what accommodations are permitted, but should not be expected to explain permitted accommodations to the proctor. Students are often less assertive when explaining the need for accommodations, but even if this is not the case a proctor should have formal direction before permitting test accommodations. A word or two from the consultant teacher prior to testing ensures that all necessary accommodations will be implemented and clarifies any confusion concerning the role of the proctor during testing.

13. **Special testing:** In addition to the use of proctors for general testing, a special proctor might be necessary if a student is tested separately. If the proctor for the special testing is a special education teacher, this is not a problem. However, if the proctor for the special testing is not a special educator, the proctor should understand the role of the interpreter, scribe, reader, and their own role with respect to instructions, answering ques-

tions, time restraints, and any other factors that differ from normal test administration procedures.

14. **Validity:** Providing test accommodations for a student that also invalidates a test helps no one and results in a very restrictive assessment in that the student is deprived from participating in the curriculum as a nondisabled student would. Deleting test items or sections of a test, explaining or simplifying the language of test items, providing clues, and providing extra time would all undermine a test's validity.

15. **Implementation:** Decide who will make and/or provide the test accommodations, what tests the accommodations will be provided, and where and when the testing will take place. If a test is read to a child, the regular classroom might be disruptive to other children being tested. In this situation scheduling becomes important because if the child must be tested at a different time, participation in other classroom activities (as well as the scheduled testing time) might be disrupted.

16. **Documentation:** The consultant teacher should be aware of the IEP format for providing test accommodations. One IEP might simply require that all necessary accommodations be listed in the required space. In this situation the consultant teacher might be required to "consult" with IEP team members concerning what a child needs in the way of test accommodations and how these accommodations should be stated in the IEP. Not only can the consultant teacher help clarify specific accommodations but also reinforce the idea that accommodations should be as least restrictive as possible and that the purpose of an accommodation is not to give a child with a disability an advantage but to allow the child to participate in assessments on an equal footing with nondisabled students. Last, the consultant teacher should convey to the IEP team that test accommodations are not a *sine qua non* for every child's IEP; if no accommodations are necessary, the IEP team should **not** check one or two to make the IEP look as if it were better meeting a child's needs. There is nothing wrong with checking the NO ACCOMMODATION NEEDED category if no accommodations are needed. What is inappropriate is to impose test accommodations when none are needed because this restricts participation in the curriculum as nondisabled children would participate. Giving a student extra time to complete a task, when extra time is not warranted, is misconstrued altruism rather than an attempt to provide a free appropriate public education.

IEP Test Accommodation Checklist

- ❏ No test accommodations
- ❏ Adaptive responses
- ❏ Amplification
- ❏ Assistive communication
- ❏ Braille
- ❏ Breaks during testing
- ❏ Classroom accessibility
- ❏ Classroom lighting
- ❏ Climate (e.g., Air purifier)
- ❏ Communication device
- ❏ Enhanced instructions
- ❏ ESL accommodations
- ❏ Extended time
- ❏ Extra sample items
- ❏ Individual testing
- ❏ Large print
- ❏ Magnification aids
- ❏ Modified response
- ❏ Morning/afternoon testing
- ❏ Multi-day testing
- ❏ Noise reduction
- ❏ Nonverbal responses
- ❏ Oral responses
- ❏ Practice testing
- ❏ Preferential seating
- ❏ Reading aids
- ❏ Reading test items
- ❏ Recorder
- ❏ Reduced test time
- ❏ Scribe
- ❏ Signing instructions
- ❏ Signing test items
- ❏ Simplifying instructions
- ❏ Special location
- ❏ Taped tests
- ❏ Translator
- ❏ Using a calculator
- ❏ Using a computer
- ❏ Writing aids
- ❏ Other:

CURRICULUM ACCOMMODATIONS

Very often, regular education teachers play a central role in the education of children with disabilities (H. Rep. No. 105-95, p. 103 (1997); S. Rep. No. 105-17, p. 23 (1997)) and have important expertise regarding the general curriculum and the general education environment.

-Senate Report 105-17

All classroom and curriculum accommodations should be well considered and planned. The consultant teacher should play an important role in planning, implementing and evaluating curriculum accommodations. Although the decision to use an accommodation is made by the IEP team (and the parents), possible accommodations should be evaluated and discussed before the IEP meeting. The first consideration for needed accommodations should not be at the IEP meeting, but in the classroom. The classroom and consultant teacher can inventory existing (if any) and needed accommodations that will allow the child to participate in the regular classroom. The regular classroom teacher should be aware of and/or involved in classroom accommodations provided in the classroom. This is achieved by the active participation of the classroom teacher in the identification, planning, and implementation of classroom and curriculum accommodations.

For the consultant teacher at the high school level, or whenever a student has multiple teachers, the consultant teacher plays an even more important role in the determination of needed classroom accommodations. At least one of the student's classroom teachers will attend the IEP meeting but input concerning needed curriculum accommodations in *all* regular educational environments is essential. This does not require a lengthy two-week survey but several minutes discussing curriculum needs with each regular education teacher.

Considering accommodations before the IEP meeting does not mean that this portion of the IEP document is completed before the IEP meeting but that the determination of needed curriculum accommodations is an important part of the full and individual evaluation process. The individual evaluation is not simply the administration of several standardized tests but entails "a variety of assessment tools and strategies that are used to gather relevant functional and developmental information about the child, including information provided by the parent, and information related to enabling the child to be involved in and progress in the general curriculum (or for a preschool child, to participate in appropriate activities)."[96]

As is the case with all planning, the parents of the child should not only be aware of all curriculum accommodations being considered, but parents might have important input for accommodations that will enable classroom participation. An important responsibility of the consultant teacher is to develop an understanding of what classroom services and accommodations will enable successful participation. This is achieved by evaluating the need for accommodations based on classroom performance, and input from regular classroom teachers, parents and all other persons knowledgeable about the needs of the child.

> *Thus, in collaboration with the family, a school district must make a threshold determination as to what special services a child with a disability needs and must then determine whether those needs can be met within the matrix of a regular classroom setting with the provision of supplementary aids and services.*
> -Oberti v. Board of Ed.
> 789 F. Supp 1322 (D.N.J. 1992), p. 1328

LEAST RESTRICTIVE ACCOMMODATIONS

Every service and accommodation that will enable an appropriate education should be provided, but every service and every curriculum accommodation should be as least restrictive as possible.

Curriculum accommodations should not be gratuitous. This frequently occurs when an IEP is generated by computer, when accommodations are not based on need (or data), and when the IEP team is presented with a long list of accommodations to check. Nothing contravenes the planning of relevant curriculum accommodations more than ill-considered accommodations that may or may not be based on need, that may or may not be restrictive, and may or may not enable regular classroom participation. The concept underlying the least restrictive environment provision is the dictum to enable a child to participate with nondisabled children "to the maximum extent appropriate,"[97] and "the maximum extent" is participation in the regular classroom with no services and no accommodations. Every service and every accommodation imposes a restriction on a child's participation so that the IEP team must balance the need to mitigate the effects of the disability by appropriate accommodations and providing access to the curriculum similar to that provided to nondisabled students.

As is the case with all accommodations, the goal should be to provide the least restrictive accommodation that will enable a child to successfully participate in the curriculum. The curriculum accommodations that a child needs should be based on observed classroom performance or other data that substantiates the need for the accommodation. In this respect, input from the regular classroom teacher is vital concerning how an accommodation impacts classroom performance.

The first step in making the least restrictive accommodations is to clearly state

- **What is the exact nature of the accommodation?**

- **Who will make the accommodation?**

- **When is the accommodation permitted?**

- **Will the accommodations conflict with IEP goals?**

The IEP might indicate that curriculum text should be provided in an easy-to-read and uncluttered format but no indication what this means, who will actually do this, whether this accommodation is permitted for all curriculum and testing activities, and whether the accommodation will conflict with other components of the IEP. Of course, if an accommodation is needed to provide an appropriate education, the accommodation must be provided. However, the IEP team must realize that needless, excessive or ill-considered accommodations can impact the appropriateness of the education for the student. An accommodation that is ostensibly intended to help can impact the services for all children receiving consultant teacher support.

If an accommodation for a student is the responsibility of the consultant teacher, school personnel must realize that the consultant teacher's time is not endless and that expending a considerable amount of time making curriculum format accommodations might detract from other important consultant teacher responsibilities.

Finally, the IEP should be logically constructed so that the various elements provide a reasonably calculated plan to provide an appropriate education. If IEP goals address the need to develop certain reading skills, but an accommodation requires an aide to read tests and curriculum content to the child, then some thought must be given to the compatibility of goals and accommodations. This is not to say that either the goal or accommodation is inappropriate, but an attempt should be made to clarify or reconcile potential IEP logical inconsistencies before the IEP is implemented.

The restrictiveness of curriculum accommodations depends on the format and difficulty of the content. Converting text to 18 point large print has little effect on the curriculum, while converting material to Braille might impact certain areas involving graphs and charts. Likewise, the degree a translator using sign language departs from the curriculum depends on the degree of fingerspelling and how the translation corresponds to what was actually said.

One area in which the consultant teacher can provide valuable input (especially to the IEP team) concerns time accommodations that a child might need to complete tasks. At the IEP meeting *extended time* is often automatically checked for students but this accommodation can be not only inappropriate but counterproductive for some students. For a child with ADHD extended time might be very inappropriate whereas taking breaks or presenting the curriculum in small-time units might be very effective. The consultant teacher, based on classroom observations and input from the classroom teacher, should present to the IEP team time needs based on observed behavior, samples of work, and other data. Not only is this important for making necessary accommodations to the curriculum, but this also provides a basis for making necessary test accommodations.

☞   The consultant teacher should collect data for the IEP team showing the need and effectiveness before an accommodation is listed in the IEP.

Low Impact ("least restrictive") Accommodations

❏ Accessibility - tables, seating, shelving, materials
❏ Calming music[98]
❏ Concept chart (page, card)
❏ Developing study skills
❏ Essential vocabulary primer
❏ Examples
❏ Extra practice
❏ Flow charts
❏ Graphic organizers
❏ Isolate key concepts
❏ Key concept chart
❏ Learning devices (KWHL: Know, What, How, Learned)
❏ Medication during class time
❏ Metacognition (organizers)
❏ Modeling instructions
❏ Noise buffer
❏ Note-taking skill

❏ Organizational skills, aids
❏ Overview content
❏ Peer tutoring
❏ Permission to bring in snacks
❏ Pre-activity tasks (e.g., pre-reading)
❏ Providing outlines
❏ Readiness activities
❏ Resource room
❏ Review content
❏ Self-assessment of skills or behavior
❏ Self-monitoring skills
❏ Study guides
❏ Target key skills (e.g., Note taking)
❏ Task demonstration
❏ Task instructions
❏ Task/topic/text outline
❏ Using study aids
❏ Written step-by-step instructions

CURRICULUM ACCOMMODATION GUIDELINES

The task is not to modify the curriculum beyond recognition but to make adaptations and accommodations only when needed. The consultant teacher should discuss with the classroom teacher needed and potentially useful curriculum accommodations, and observe firsthand how the child participates in the curriculum with and without the accommodation.

For the consultant teacher an important task is the coordination of test and curriculum accommodations. If a test accommodation specifies large print, some thought must be given to large print and the regular curriculum. Indeed, providing a student with a test accommodation but providing no experience with using that accommodation might be more of a burden than a help. For example, reading content test questions to a student (e.g., science, social studies) might be the only feasible way to assess the content and not reading, but if the student is never given practice using this assessment technique, the technique itself might be less effective than desired.

The following provides several guidelines for consultant teachers when making accommodations to the curriculum:

Curriculum Accommodation Guidelines for the Consultant Teacher

1. **Seek input from classroom teachers, parents, related service providers and paraprofessionals concerning needed curriculum accommodation.**

2. **Base curriculum accommodations on observed need or other data.**

3. **"Test" the usefulness of accommodations.**

4. **Provide the least restrictive accommodations so that the accommodation enhances rather than restricts access to the curriculum.**

5. **Assign responsibility for making and implementing the accommodations.**

6. Provide supervision and training for paraprofessionals to implement accommodations when appropriate.

7. Make a distinction between curriculum accommodations and skill accommodations.

8. Coordinate curriculum accommodations with test accommodations when possible.

9. Actually implement IEP accommodations.

10. Evaluate the ongoing effectiveness of accommodations at least annually.

11. Add or delete IEP accommodations, as necessary, at least annually.

12. Always consider the possibility that "no accommodations" might be appropriate.

COORDINATING CURRICULUM AND
TEST ACCOMMODATIONS

Curriculum and test accommodations are not necessarily one and the same. Accommodations to the curriculum can include modifications to accessibility, assignments, books, classroom location, content difficulty, curriculum content, extracurricular activities, grading homework, lectures, physical education (e.g., adaptive physical education), technology, tests, textbooks, workbooks, etc. The list is endless. Making the classroom accessible, preferential seating, improving classroom lighting, air quality, temperature, and humidity can all enhance the ability of a child to participate.

For the most part test accommodations should replicate curriculum accommodations. However, test accommodations are usually more restrictive in that the purpose of the test is to determine a level of performance. Furthermore, unlike the general curriculum, many tests have specific test administration guidelines. A reading test should not be *read* to a student, but a science test or biology test might be read if reading prevented a student from demonstrating his or her knowledge of the content.

The least restrictive accommodations are those that enable a child to participate in the curriculum yet encourage independent behavior. Pre-reading material is less restrictive than providing an aide to offer reading assistance during the lesson; reviewing math facts is less restrictive than allowing the student to use a calculator to determine answers; reviewing key concepts or vocabulary is less restrictive than allowing a student to use a dictionary during an activity.

Before considering modifications to the actual curriculum, the consultant teacher should spend time in the classroom identifying and evaluating classroom needs, discussing the need for accommodations with teachers and parents, and considering the effectiveness of existing accommodations. At the IEP meeting, based on all information and reports, determine needed accommodations to the curriculum. Next, use necessary curriculum accommodations as a basis for identifying needed test accommodations while taking into consideration the requirements for specific tests.

GOOD TEACHING AND GOOD ACCOMMODATIONS

The consultant teacher's task is to identify those skills that will enable participation in the curriculum, to collaborate with regular classroom teachers and paraprofessionals to develop these skills, and then to generalize these skills to actual regular classroom situations.

Before recommending an IEP accommodation, help make the IEP manageable by including accommodations that are based on observed need and effectiveness such that the accommodation is considered essential for enabling classroom success. The Chicago Public Schools has a publication entitled Curriculum, Accommodations & Modifications (Volume II) which lists a variety of excellent teaching strategies and suggestions for adapting and modifying the curriculum. One set of accommodations suggests that students

- **May engage in think-aloud paired problem solving with another student.**

- **May illustrate a major theme in the story rather than do a written essay.**

- **May use a computer and dictionary with grammar and spellcheck.**

- **May write their essays during resource period or at home.**[99]

The above strategies provide excellent ideas for participating in the curriculum, but not every curriculum strategy will be listed in the IEP as an accommodation. Many strategies and techniques are simply good teaching. Developing study skills, remedial help and practice skills are certainly activities that could benefit all students.

"May engage in think-aloud paired problem solving" might be useful for all students, and not just for a student with a disability; "May illustrate a major theme in a story rather than do a written essay" might be appropriate but this is tantamount to an exemption from writing an essay or even an alternative assessment. Likewise, using a computer with grammar and spellcheck might be appropriate for some but not all activities (e.g., when spelling is what is being measured). Finally, achieving the content goal (e.g., writing an essay) by providing alternative times (or completion dates) is the type of accommodation that can enhance participation.

The need to accommodate or manage classroom behavior is often the one single factor that will provide access to the regular classroom and curriculum. The Arkansas IEP has a section relating to behavior management and includes items such as clearly defined limits, rules and consequences, model appropriate behavior, frequent reminders of rules (verbal and/or nonverbal prompts and cues), praise appropriate behavior immediately, intervene and redirect inappropriate behavior immediately, and frequent eye contact/proximity control/teacher circulation around room. Excellent ideas, but many of these come under the heading of good teaching rather than IEP accommodations.

ESSENTIAL CLASSROOM ASSESSMENT DATA

Child find: The State must have in effect policies and procedures to ensure that all children with disabilities residing in the state, including children with disabilities attending private schools, regardless of the severity of their disability, and who are in need of special education and related services, are identified, located, and evaluated.[100]

When a child is identified as possibly having a disability, the first reaction is to test the child as if no information existed concerning the child's classroom performance. Every child must be "assessed in all areas related to the suspected disability including, if appropriate, health, vision, hearing, social and emotional status, general intelligence, academic performance, communicative status, and motor abilities."[101] One important function of the full and individual assessment is to determine the need for special education. In this regard much information concerning classroom performance is often ignored. Always consider existing data before automatically giving a child a barrage of tests. Always begin the full and individual evaluation with input from the regular classroom teacher and the parents. The following are several data sources which can be essential for determining the need for specially designed instruction.

- **Teacher observations**

- **Parent observations**

- **Work samples**

- **Curriculum-based assessments**

- **Grades**

- **Classroom participation**

- **Ratings**

- **Checklists**

- **Questionnaires**

- **Behavioral reports**

- **Behavior records**

- **Inventories**

- **Attendance**

- **Completed assignments**

- **Homework**

- **Classroom quizzes**

- **Diagnostic evaluations**

- **Classroom tests**

- **Standardized tests**

- **State tests**

The evaluation process has long been associated with testing. For the consultant teacher the key words are **collecting** and **interpreting** data. The goal is to collect existing relevant classroom information, and to interpret this data to formulate goals to enhance classroom participation.

As part of an initial evaluation (if appropriate) and as part of any reevaluation the IEP team is required to review existing evaluation, including evaluations and information provided by the parents of the child, current classroom-based assessments and observations, and observations by teachers and related services providers.[102] Part of the motivation for this is not to subject a child to unnecessary tests and assessments. Standardized testing is important, or, at least, can be important. But we must not lose sight of the fact that the most important assessment concerns exactly how a child's disability impacts educational performance so as to require specially designed instruction.

> *If there is no need to collect additional information about a child's continuing eligibility for special education, any necessary evaluation activities should focus on collecting information about how to teach and assist the child in the way he or she is most capable of learning.*
>
> -Senate Report 105-17

CLASSROOM ASSESSMENT PORTFOLIO

Of all the rules and regulations involving special education, of all the techniques and practices, of all the theories and programs, the heart of special education, the very essence of the entire special education process is the determination of what a child does or does not do that affects involvement and progress in the general curriculum. For the consultant teacher useful classroom data is essential for developing a successful individual education plan and for successful classroom participation. The regulations are abundantly clear that a single score or procedure is not used to determine whether a child is a child with a disability. However, standardized assessments are useful for determining the extent of a child's need and the impact of a child's disability on educational performance; and curriculum-based assessments are useful for determining specific levels of performance and to provide beginning benchmarks for measurable annual goals.

The consultant teacher can determine important classroom and curriculum needs, and progress toward meeting these needs, by maintaining a portfolio of classroom performance for each child. An assessment portfolio is useful for all children, can be invaluable for identifying important classroom needs, and can serve as an alternative assessment when a child is not able to participate in state or district-wide assessments.

The classroom assessment portfolio combines standardized, nonstandardized assessments and evaluations, samples of student work, descriptions of activities, projects, classroom reports, interview summaries with classroom teachers, quizzes, curriculum-based assessments. The standardized assessments show the need for special education and the impact of the child's disability on educational performance; the nonstandardized assessments show specific and measurable classroom needs. The entire portfolio should provide a clear indication of a child's classroom progress, classroom needs, and the effectiveness of services for improving progress and addressing needs. Items should be added to the assessment portfolio that provide insight and direction concerning a child's classroom progress. Also, a useful practice is to date each item added to the portfolio. This will be useful when evaluating annual progress, and for discerning academic and/or behavioral regressions in performance. Possible items to include in the portfolio are:

- **Anecdotal reports**

- **Inventories of classroom work**

- **Work samples (e.g., homework, quizzes, workbooks, etc.)**

- **Classroom observational reports**

- **Self-assessments**

- **Measurable annual goal progress reports**

- **Curriculum-based assessments**

- **Quizzes and classroom tests**

- **Standardized test results**

Every child will not need a complete classroom assessment portfolio, especially if the measurable annual goals are very specific. However, for children with very diverse needs, a classroom assessment portfolio often provides a viable method for understanding classroom performance as opposed to interpreting different data, skills and behavior in relative isolation. Classroom performance can be complex, and sometimes we need a portrait of that complexity: this is the **portfolio**.

FONT MODIFICATION GUIDE

1. **Font Style:** Less stylistic fonts (san serif) such as Arial, and Verdana are usually preferred to highly stylistic fonts.

2. **Font Size:** Font size is measured in *points* where 12 point is 12/72 of an inch, 18 point is 18/72 of an inch, and 36 point is 36/72 or an inch or one-half an inch. 18 point or larger is usually considered *large print*.

3. **Font Width:** Variable-width fonts provide a book-like quality (e.g., Times Roman, Arial) while fixed-pitch fonts are useful for aligning text and math problems.

4. **Font Color:** Black is generally easy to read, other colors can be useful for highlighting, and light shades can be difficult to read.

5. **Font format:** Underlining and italic can increase reading while bold may or may not be preferred depending on the font, font size and individual need. For Free Fonts online (e.g., cursive) see **http://desktoppub.about.com/library/fonts/bl_schoolfree.htm**

6. **Shading:** Useful highlighting technique but be sure that the shading does not blur the text (this is 5% gray).

7. **Highlighting:** This can be useful for identifying important content vocabulary of concepts. If color highlighting is used, be sure that the highlighting does not interfere with the readability of the text.

8. **Background:** A blackboard effect can be generated by selecting a black background and white font; other background font color combinations must be carefully considered so that the text is not blurred or obscured by similarity between background and font color.

9. **Proportionality** (see font width above): There are two types of fonts: proportional (variable width) and nonproportional (fixed-width or fixed-pitch). Times New Roman and Arial are examples of proportional fonts (each letter is proportional to its size), and Courier and Monaco are examples of nonproportional fonts (the width for each letter is the same and is not proportional to its size). Variable-width fonts are also called proportional-pitch fonts or proportional space fonts because the pitch or cell for each character is proportional to the width of the actual font character

(e.g., the character cell for the letter **i** is smaller than the cell for the letter **w**).

10. **Font usage:** Times Roman is a very popular proportional serif font. Arial is also proportional but is a sans serif font. Courier New is a non-proportional serif font and is useful for math problems and when aligned text is needed. Monaco is a nonproportional sans serif font.

Font and Point Size	Font Example
Times New Roman, 18	The Red Badge of Courage by Stephen Crane
Courier New, 18	24 + 26 = 12 − 18 =
Arial, 18	The Red Badge of Courage by Stephen Crane

Part IV
Direct Services and the
Consultant Teacher

Success for the consultant teacher is not how much time is spent providing direct services in the classroom, or the amount of time providing indirect services, but the extent to which a child with a disability is able to function successfully in the regular classroom. If a child is able to participate ten percent or one hundred percent in the regular classroom, and the extent of participation is the maximum extent appropriate, the consultant teacher has been successful . . . and the child is successful!

DIRECT SERVICES

For the consultant teacher direct services means teaching/remedial services provided to a child or on behalf of a child to enable the child to participate in the regular classroom or curriculum. These direct teacher services can involve on-to-one, remedial, small or large group instruction, co-teaching, team teaching, collaborative teaching, etc., and can be provided to children with and without disabilities.

There are several reasons for providing direct services and include the following:

First, to provide specially designed instruction,

Second, to enable participation in the classroom,

Third, to enable participation in the general curriculum,

Fourth, to provide support for the regular classroom teacher to include children with disabilities in the classroom and curriculum,

Fifth, to enable education with nondisabled children to the maximum extent appropriate.

Many professionals and paraprofessionals provide direct services, but the consultant is qualified to provide special education. A classroom aide will provide many direct (e.g., instructional activities) and indirect (e.g., curriculum modifications) services, but these are provided under the supervision of a special education and regular classroom teacher.

As is the case placements, direct services are not based on disability but on a child's needs. The consultant teacher's purpose is not to provide special education in the regular classroom, but to enable a child to participate in the classroom and in the curriculum. A child might need one hour of direct instruction on a daily basis, but small group instruction, team teaching or medial teaching might be appropriate for enhancing classroom participation for another child. Individual need should guide instructional methodology and not the belief that one instructional methodology is appropriate for all children.

For the consultant teacher team-teaching, in and of itself, is not the goal of direct instruction. The ability of the consultant teacher to collaborate with the regular classroom teacher to provide services that benefit disabled and nondisabled children has several purposes. Direct services in the classroom allow the consultant teacher to

- **Create opportunities for classroom participation.**

- **Provide opportunities for participation in the curriculum and academic activities.**

- **Modify and adapt materials that enable participation.**

- **Provide support for the teacher to meet individual learning needs.**

- **Identify and respond to specific classroom needs.**

- **Provide training for classroom aides to support the classroom teacher.**

- **Coordinate all services to ensure effective classroom participation.**

One of the major changes in the IDEA amendments of 1997 is the ability of special education personnel to provide services that benefit nondisabled children.[103] This change in the permissive use of funds no longer creates a self-contained setting in the regular classroom but encourages special education personnel to become a more integral part of the regular classroom. This can result in increased participation of a child with a disability, and provide a source of classroom support that will allow the regular classroom teacher more opportunities to engage in direct service activities. As much as possible, the consultant teacher should involve the regular classroom teacher in all direct services provided in the classroom.

Time in the regular classroom for the consultant teacher is not simply about providing direct instruction to a child with a disability. If the consultant is able to manage the entire class, to act as the regular classroom teacher, while the classroom teacher provides remedial support and functions as the "consultant teacher," the benefits to a child might be immeasurable in terms of daily classroom participation when the consultant teacher is not available. Whether the consultant teacher is training an aide, coordinating a variety of classroom and pull-out services, or using specially designed curriculum adaptations, the ultimate goal is the same: successful classroom participation.

LEAST RESTRICTIVE DIRECT SERVICES

If the State uses a funding mechanism by which the State distributes State funds on the basis of the type of setting where a child is served, the funding mechanism may not result in placements that violate the requirements" the least restrictive environment and continuum of services provisions.

-34 CFR 300.130(b)(1)

As is the case with the restrictiveness of placements, direct services have several dimensions which define the extent a service restricts access to the regular classroom and regular curriculum.

Type of direct service: There is a wide range of direct services that can be offered including one-to-one, homogeneous small group, heterogeneous small group instruction, remedial services, large group instruction, etc. Although one-to-one teaching is generally more restrictive than small group instruction, and small group instruction more restrictive than large group instruction, this is not the case if, for example, large group instruction is simply not possible because of behavior or skill level. In this case, one-to-one might be restrictive when compared to small or large group instruction, but the least restrictive direct service when considering what teaching strategy will allow the child to participate.

Place of direct services: The regular classroom is the presumed placement for services, and the regular classroom is the preferred location for services provided by the consultant teacher. However, just as specialists in other areas might require a separate location for providing services, the consultant teacher might also need a separate location to develop the behaviors or skills necessary to participate in the regular classroom. Unlike resource room services, pull-out consultant teacher services must

- **focus on regular classroom or curriculum participation,**

- **be evaluated in terms of the affect on regular classroom performance,**

- **be as minimal as possible,**

- **and end when the direct services can be provided in the regular classroom.**

149

The continuum of restrictiveness: Restrictiveness often has a negative connotation which is probably due to the fact that special education has historically been associated with self-contained settings which are often unduly restrictive. In the below sequence, a consultant teacher might work with a small group of children in the regular classroom with similar needs, or the regular classroom teacher might work with a small group while the consultant teacher works with the entire classroom. There might be occasions when the consultant teacher must provide one-to-one service, when a pull-out service is necessary, or when resource room support is necessary to enable regular classroom participation. In all cases the goal is not a particular teaching strategy or placement, but to provide direct services that meet individual needs and are as least restrictive as possible. If a child is able to function successfully with only indirect support, providing one-to-one instruction would hardly seem appropriate. Likewise, if a child with a specific learning disability is able to function in the regular classroom with consultant teacher services, resource room support would be unnecessary and restrictive.

The benchmark for restrictiveness: Involvement in the regular classroom, in the general curriculum, and with the regular classroom teacher provide benchmarks for the restrictiveness, and the least restrictiveness, of direct services. If a child receives all teaching services via a special education teacher or an aide in the regular classroom with little or no involvement from the special education or regular classroom teacher, the child might not be involved in the classroom to the maximum extent appropriate. A full-time aide or one-to-one teaching might be necessary, but this is not the same as being educated *with* nondisabled children where "being educated as nondisabled children" means instruction provided by the regular classroom teacher involving the regular curriculum.

Success: Success for the consultant teacher is not how much time is spent providing direct services in the classroom, or the time providing indirect services, but the extent to which a child with a disability is able to function successfully in the regular classroom. If a child is able to participate ten percent or one hundred percent in the regular classroom, and the extent of participation is the maximum extent appropriate, the consultant teacher has been successful.

Many different models and techniques exist which can be used to provide direct services in the regular classroom by the consultant teacher. The various direct teaching services can be viewed as representing a relative continuum of restrictiveness but the restrictiveness of each technique depends on the needs of the child and the impact the service has on classroom participation, curriculum participation, and independent classroom functioning. For example, direct remedial instruction in the regular classroom might be viewed as far more restrictive than, say, collaborative teaching. However, if the remedial instruction is for thirty minutes a day while the collaborative teaching results in the special education teaching being in the regular classroom the entire day, the restrictiveness of each technique is not easily compared.

The ultimate goal for the consultant teacher is for a child with a disability to function with no direct or indirect services. Special education is not about dependence and the success of special education is not gauged by the extensiveness of services provided. The goal of special education is not team teaching, not collaboration, not one-to-one services but to enable a child to be successfully educated with nondisabled children to the maximum extent appropriate in the least restrictive environment.

All services, whether direct services in the classroom or providing aide support or resource room services, should be viewed as constituting a continuum of services. If the consultant teacher must work with a child in the classroom individually or in very small groups, a goal should be to increase the child's participation in regular classroom activities; a full-time aide is more restrictive than an aide who provides occasional classroom support; and one hour a day in a resource room is less restrictive than two or three hours a day. The goal is not to embrace a single teaching philosophy, but to provide services that will enable regular classroom participation.

One problem with a full-time aide assigned to a child with a disability in the regular classroom is the mistaken belief that this is the solution (i.e., simply assigning the aide solves all problems) rather than a service which should be designed to increase independent classroom performance. Obviously, if an aide is responsible for a child's education (which, of course, is contrary to the law and regulations) and is provided with no training or supervision, this is the epitome of a restrictive environment. Having a full-time aide serve as an intermediary between a child with a disability and the regular classroom teacher is far more restrictive than an aide who allows the child to participate in the classroom and curriculum as independently as possible.

DIRECT SERVICE CHECKLIST

In a case where the segregated facility is considered superior, the court should determine whether the services which make that placement superior could be feasibly provided in a non-segregated setting. If they can, the placement in the segregated school would be inappropriate under the Act.[104]

✓ **Provide the least restrictive direct services:** If a child is able to function without an aide fifty percent of the day, do not provide an aide one hundred percent of the day. If a child is able to function satisfactorily in group activities, don't provide additional remedial instruction simply because all children with disabilities receive a set amount of remedial instruction. To some the requirement of a "satisfactory education" seems to suggest that we want to do what is minimally required for a child with a disability rather than all that we can do. The goal of successful classroom participation is not achieved by restricting participation with nondisabled children, especially when that participation can be successful.

✓ **Plan all direct services with the regular classroom teacher:** If the regular classroom teacher has no idea what the consultant teacher is doing, other than providing direct services, this is hardly a model for increasing the ability of the child to participate in the regular classroom and regular curriculum. All direct services should be carefully planned between the regular classroom teacher and the consultant teacher, and the regular classroom teacher should participate, as much as possible, in the provision of direct services.

✓ **Direct services should focus on classroom needs:** The special education consultant teacher must focus on regular classroom needs. The consultant teacher must meet "the child's needs that result from the child's disability to enable the child to be involved in and progress in the general curriculum" and "meeting each of the child's other educational needs that result from the child's disability."[105] If all children require the same type of service, the same level of services, the services are likely inappropriate and based on disability rather than need.

✓ **Collaborate:** An important provision in the regulations is that "for the costs of special education and related services and supplementary aids and services provided in a regular class or other education-related setting to a child with a disability in accordance with the IEP of the child, even if one or more nondisabled children benefit from these services."[106] The regular classroom teacher can assume the role of consultant teacher (and the consultant teacher the role of lead teacher) thus allowing the regular classroom teacher an opportunity to provide remedial and instructional support. One of the benefits of collaboration and co-teaching is the ability to focus on individual needs, and to enable a child to participate in the regular curriculum. In this sense collaboration is effective because classroom support is provided by the consultant teacher to enable the classroom teacher to better understand and address a child's individual learning needs. Provide the regular classroom teacher with all the skills that you have as a consultant teacher, and your success as a consultant teacher will be great! Finally, note that services provided by the regular classroom teacher are less restrictive than services provided by the consultant teacher in the regular classroom. Every contribution by the regular classroom teacher in the way of direct services, accommodations, or adaptations enhances classroom participation.

✓ **Direct service should nurture independence:** Remember that the goal is not to be successful in one-to-one situations but to be successful in the regular classroom and regular curriculum as independently as possible. This is especially important when pull-out services are provided. If a pull-out service is necessary, considerable thought should be given to how the skills or knowledge acquired as a result of the pull-out service will be generalized to the regular classroom.

✓ **Systematically decrease services:** The goal is to decrease direct services. A situation might reveal that more direct services are needed, or that pull-out services are required. Once the extent for direct services has been determined, the goal should be to systematically reduce the level of services. As a child's participation in the regular classroom increases, there is often a corresponding decrease in the direct services provided. Likewise, as the need for direct services decreases, there might be a greater need for indirect services, especially as a student progresses from one grade to the next. If a child requires three hours of direct services a day, experiment with 2.5 hours, then 2.0 hours, etc.

✓ **Select relevant direct services:** Rather than doing busy work, don't do anything. Don't waste your time; don't waste the regular classroom teacher's time; don't waste the child's time. Each direct service provided in the regular classroom should be selected to impact classroom participation. Don't team teach because team-teaching is all the rage. Team teach because it will impact a child's ability to participate in the classroom.

NEW JERSEY LEARNING DISABILITIES TEACHER-CONSULTANT (LDT-C)

In New Jersey, certification as a Learning Disabilities Teacher-Consultant is an endorsement of the standard New Jersey instructional license, plus three years of successful teaching experience, a master's degree from an accredited or approved institution, and the completion of an approved graduate or twenty-four semester hour graduate credits which include the following required areas:[107]

- Education of the handicapped

- Learning theory

- Physiological bases of learning

- Orientation in psychological testing

- Remediation of basic skills

- Diagnosis of learning disabilities

- Correction of learning disabilities

- College supervised consultant level practicum in diagnosis and remediation of learning disabilities in school and clinical situations. The practicum should provide for a minimum of 90 clock hours of college supervised experience.

TEAM TEACHING

The benefits of team teaching and collaboration are many and include

1. **shared planning,**

2. **shared commitment,**

3. **high expectations for all students,**

4. **collegial feedback,**

5. **providing different instructional perspectives to enhance learning.**

For the consultant teacher there are additional benefits of team teaching and collaboration: providing the regular classroom teacher to engage in direct service consultant teacher activities. The ability of the consultant teacher to engage the entire class or a large group in a lesson, affords the regular classroom teacher opportunities to provide individual assistance and to evaluate, firsthand, a child's individual needs and to implement effective instructional strategies. But, as is the case with all teaching strategies, the consultant teacher must remember that the goal is not team teaching but to enable regular classroom participation.

> ### The Benefits of Co-Teaching for the Consultant Teacher
>
> - Encourages regular teacher participation,
> - Provides opportunities for student participation,
> - Directly involves the special education teacher in the general curriculum,
> - Integration of specially designed instruction with regular classroom instruction,
> - Enables a "child to be involved in and progress in the general curriculum" (see 34 CFR 300.347,
> - Creates opportunities to evaluate regular classroom participation and needs.

BROWN v. BOARD OF EDUCATION
347 U.S. 483 (1954)[108]

BROWN v. BOARD OF EDUCATION
347 U.S. (1954)

The famous *Brown* decision is actually a consolidation of four cases from the states of Kansas, South Carolina, Virginia, and Delaware. In each case race had been used to deny admission to schools on a nonsegregated basis. The rationale for the segregation was doctrine of "separate but equal" established by Plessy v. Ferguson (163 U.S. 537). The civil right of children with disabilities to be educated with children who are not disabled is the heart of special education. Paradoxically, some children might require a segregated environment in order to provide a free appropriate public education (FAPE). Thus, removing a child who is disabled from a regular classroom is, indeed, a very serious matter.

The Court reasoned that "Today, education is perhaps the most important function of state and local governments. Compulsory school attendance laws and the great expenditures for education both demonstrate our recognition of the importance of education to our democratic society. It is required in the performance of our most basic public responsibilities, even service in the armed forces. It is the very foundation of good citizenship. Today it is a principal instrument in awakening the child to cultural values, in preparing him for later professional training, and in helping him to adjust normally to his environment. In these days, it is doubtful that any child may reasonably be expected to succeed in life if he is denied the opportunity of an education. Such an opportunity, where the state has undertaken to provide it, is a right which must be made available to all on equal terms."

The Court then stated "We come then to the question presented: Does segregation of children in public schools solely on the basis of race, even though the physical facilities and other 'tangible' factors may be equal, deprive the children of the minority group of equal educational opportunities? We believe that it does."

The Court concluded "that in the field of public education the doctrine of "separate but equal" has no place. Separate educational facilities are inherently unequal. "

WHO RECEIVES CONSULTANT
TEACHER SERVICES?

There are over 5,000,000 children with disabilities under IDEA, and every child receiving services must be educated with nondisabled children to the maximum extent appropriate. How many children receive consultant teacher services in one form or another? Many. How many children should receive consultant teacher services? Probably many more. Every special education teacher, every teacher in every self-contained classroom, residential setting, and resource room must attempt to enable each child served to be educated with nondisabled children to the maximum extent appropriate.

Every child with a disability under IDEA must receive specially designed instruction, and must be educated with nondisabled children. Because the goal for every child with a disability is to be included in the regular classroom and curriculum to the maximum extent appropriate, every special education teacher will, to some degree, provide consultant teacher services.

Although there are specific categories of consultant teachers for specific disabilities (depending on individual states and school districts) such as autism, hearing and visual impairments, the majority of children receiving special education involve what are referred to as the high incidence disabilities. These include Specific Learning Disabilities (49.96%) which represents the largest number of children served, followed by Speech or Language Impairments (18.95%), Mental Retardation (10.61%), and Emotional Disturbance (8.20%). From 1992-1993 to the 2000-2001 data there has been a slight decrease in the number of high incidence disabilities, and a corresponding increase in Other Health Impairments from 1.43 percent (1992-1993) to 5.05 percent (2000-2001) which can be attributed to the inclusion of ADHD/ADD in the OHI category. These four high-incidence disabilities account for 87.7 percent of all children receiving services under IDEA. Table 1 shows the number and percent of children served by IDEA for children between the ages of 6 to 21.

Table 1: Number and Percent of Children Ages 6-21 Served Under IDEA (1987-1988 to 2000-2001) [109]

Disability[110]	1987-1988		1992-1993		1999-2000		2000-2001	
	N	%	N	%	N	%	N	%
SLD	1,942,304	47.68%	2,366,487	51.16%	2,871,966	50.53	2,879,445	49.96
Speech	953,568	23.41%	998,049	21.58%	1,089,964	19.18%	1,092,105	18.95
MR	598770	14.70%	532,362	11.51%	614,433	10.81%	611,878	10.61
ED	372,380	9.14%	401,652	8.68%	470,111	8.27%	472,932	8.20
OHI	46,056	1.13%	66,063	1.43%	254,110	4.47%	291,474	5.05
Multiple	79,023	1.94%	103,279	2.23%	112,993	1.99%	121,954	2.11
Autism		0.00%	15,580	0.34%	65,424	1.15%	78,717	1.36
Orthopedic		0.00%	52,588	1.14%	71,422	1.26%	73,011	1.26
Dev. Delay.		0.00%		0.00%	19,304	0.34%	28,683	0.49
Visual	22,821	0.56%	23,544	0.51%	26,590	0.47%	25,927	0.44
TBI		0.00%	3,960	0.09%	13,874	0.24%	14,829	0.25
Hearing	56,872	1.40%	60,616	1.31%	71,671	1.26%	70,662	1.22
Deaf-Blind.	1,454	0.04%	1,394	0.03%	1,845	0.03%	1,318	0.02
All	4,073,248	100%	4,625,574	100%	5,683,707	100%	5,762,935	100%

In addition to the more than 5,000,000 children who have high incidence disabilities, children who are suspected of having a disability, children who have a disability but do not need special education, and children who are no longer considered to have a disability under IDEA will benefit from consultant teacher services.

As one might expect the type of disability can influence the degree of participation in the regular classroom. Although the majority of children classified as having a specific learning disabilities (49.96%) receive services in the regular classroom or resource room services to supplement the regular classroom, 45.32 percent are in regular classroom placements and receive "supplemental resource room support", 37.85 percent are in resource room placements (21 to 61% of the time is outside of the regular classroom), and 15.78 percent receive services outside of the regular classroom. As shown in Table

2 children with speech and language impairments receive the majority of services (87.47%) in the regular classroom, followed by visual impairments (49.1%), specific learning disabilities (45.32%), other health Impairments (44.91%) and orthopedic impairments (44.35%). The children spending the least amount of time in the regular classroom are multiple disabilities (11.19%), mental retardation (14.05%), deaf-blindness (14.86%), autism (20.64%), and emotional disturbance (25.78%).[111]

Table 2: Where Children Receive Services for IDEA Disabilities

Time Outside the Regular Classroom					
Disability	0-21%	21-60%	>60%	Separate	Resident.	Home/Hosp.
Speech&L	87.47	6.75	5.27	0.4	0.06	0.05
Visual	49.1	19.5	17.69	5.7	7.38	0.63
SLD	45.32	37.85	15.78	0.68	0.18	0.18
OHI	44.91	33.22	17.24	1.62	0.33	2.67
Orthopedic	44.35	21.93	27.72	4.14	0.27	1.59
Dev. Delay	44.31	29.92	24.4	0.98	0.08	0.31
Hearing	40.33	19.31	24.5	7.05	8.59	0.23
TBI	31.06	26.61	31.6	7.17	1.26	2.3
ED	25.78	23.42	32.8	13.03	3.47	1.51
Autism	20.64	14.45	49.91	13.3	1.25	0.45
Deaf-Blind	14.86	10.17	39.37	17.35	16.56	1.69
MR	14.05	29.48	50.5	4.94	0.6	0.43
MD	11.19	18.7	43.07	21.86	2.68	2.5

INCLUSIVE SUPPORT

Classroom support is good; classroom support is necessary; and often the lack of support is the reason why participation in the regular classroom is not successful. But an essential element of support is the goal of successful classroom participation. To this end the consultant teacher must be aware of when support encourages dependence, and when that lofty goal of high expectations is lost by an excess of support, and help and assistance.

1. Aides: Aides must be aware that the task is to nurture independent behavior. Doing tasks for a student that the student can accomplish prevents classroom participation and can be more restrictive than a self-contained classroom.

2. Resource Room: Time assigned to a resource should not be automatic but based on need. The goal is to develop skills so that resource room support is not necessary.

3. Related Services: If possible, provide related services in the regular classroom.

4. Indirect Services: The goal is not for the consultant teacher to do everything; the goal is to develop school-wide support so that consultant teacher services are not needed.

5. Direct Services: Teaching services provided in the regular classroom should be focused and designed to enable participation in the classroom and curriculum.

6. Amount of services: When services are sufficient to allow successful participation, the level of services provided is appropriate. If a child can participate in the classroom satisfactorily with no direct services, then that is the correct amount.

AND MORE "TO DO" FOR
THE CONSULTANT TEACHER!

*Direct and indirect service responsibilities provided by the consultant
teacher will include children receiving pre-service interventions,
services under IDEA, and Section 504 services.*

The responsibilities for the special education teacher are many and
include direct teaching responsibilities, planning, providing indirect and support services, supervision of paraprofessionals, training and professional
development, overseeing assistive technology needs, IEP monitoring, evaluating progress, enabling children to participate in the regular classroom
and/or regular curriculum to the maximum extent appropriate, and providing the various supplementary aids and services required to achieve this
objective.

The consultant teacher might be responsible for ensuring aides are appropriately trained and supervised, determining the need for classroom support,
and developing a coherent and managed plan that enables a child to participate in the regular classroom to the maximum extent appropriate. But there
is more! There are three additional areas linked to IDEA services which can
actually increase the consultant teacher's responsibilities and include the following:

Pre-referral interventions: One way to ensure that a child is not needlessly excluded from the regular classroom is identify children using IDEA
guidelines. In other words, don't misidentify children as having a disability
when the causative factor is cultural, environmental, socioeconomic, or lack
of instruction. Special education is not intended to be the answer to every
learning/instructional problem. The consultant teacher should be an advocate for school-wide remedial approaches, pre-referral intervention planning,
and other school-based solutions (e.g., remedial reading) for addressing academic and behavior needs without special education.

Section 504: A child might not have a disability under IDEA or not need
special education, but every child is entitled to accommodations and services
if the child has a disability as defined by Section 504, has a record of such an
impairment,[112] or is regarded as having such an impairment. Although a separate group, team, or committee might oversee Section 504 services, the IEP
team is usually the best situated group to determine, provide and monitor
Section 504 services and accommodations. To this end, the consultant

teacher is often the ideal person to ensure that the accommodations and services a child requires to prevent discrimination are being provided. Every child with a disability, as defined in Section 504, is entitled to any and all services that are necessary to receive an appropriate education, regardless of whether the child has a disability under IDEA.

Declassification: Not only must the special education consultant teacher attempt to increase the extent of classroom and curriculum participation, but the consultant teacher will often be instrumental in declassifying a child when IDEA services are no longer needed. Even when a child no longer has a disability under IDEA or no longer needs IDEA services, the child is entitled to all necessary support services and other accommodations as per Section 504 (see above).

THE CALIFORNIA CONSULTING TEACHER

The California Department of Education has what is called Peer Assistance and Review (PAR) program which provides funding and release time for experienced teachers with "substantial" classroom experience who have "demonstrated exemplary teaching ability, as indicated by, among other things, effective communication skills, subject matter knowledge, and mastery of a range of teaching strategies necessary to meet the needs of pupils in different contexts."[113] The PAR consulting teacher serves as a "coach" for teachers referred by an evaluation process, emergency permit teachers, and other teachers who volunteer for PAR services, to observe classroom performance, provide clinical supervision, offer consultation on a on-to-one basis, guide curriculum development, and work collaboratively with the PAR participating classroom teachers to improve teaching performance. Unlike the special education consultant teacher the PAR consulting teacher provides one form of indirect service, consultation for teacher performance, rather than direct classroom services and curriculum-based (e.g., classroom modifications and adaptations) indirect services.

The PAR program is designed to assist teachers but the program is also critical for "the large numbers of uncredentialed teachers who have taken positions in special education classes, says Laurie Schneider, a consulting teacher in the PAR program for the Westminster School District. She works with emergency permit teachers in that field. 'They need everything in the way of help to work with special needs children. I want to support these people from start to finish, so they get their credentials and stay with us. It's a very wise investment.'"[114]

163

IDEA DISABILITIES AND
THE CONSULTANT TEACHER

*If it is determined . . . that a child has one of the disabilities identified
. . . but only needs a related service and not special education, the
child is not a child with a disability under this part.*[115]

Whether or not a child has a disability under IDEA is determined by considering the thirteen disabilities listed in the regulations. The criteria for each of these disabilities range from the relatively objective to the very subjective. Identifying a child with a hearing, visual, deaf-blindness, traumatic brain injury, speech or language, or orthopedic impairment is often less difficult than identifying a specific learning disability or less severe forms of mental retardation.

IDEA Disabilities
34 CFR 300.7

1. Autism
2. Deaf-blindness
3. Emotional disturbance
4. Hearing impairment
5. Mental retardation
6. Multiple disabilities
7. Orthopedic impairment
8. Other health impairment
9. Specific learning disability
10. Speech or language impairment
11. Traumatic brain injury
12. Visual impairment
13. Developmental delay (for children aged 3 through 9)

Although the consultant teacher will encounter a wide variety of disabilities, the following definitions listed in the regulations account for over ninety-four percent of children receiving services under IDEA:[116]

Specific Learning Disability: Specific learning disability is defined as follows:

164

(i) General. The term means a disorder in one or more of the basic psychological processes involved in understanding or in using language, spoken or written, that may manifest itself in an imperfect ability to listen, think, speak, read, write, spell, or to do mathematical calculations, including conditions such as perceptual disabilities, brain injury, minimal brain dysfunction, dyslexia, and developmental aphasia.

(ii) Disorders not included. The term does not include learning problems that are primarily the result of visual, hearing, or motor disabilities, of mental retardation, of emotional disturbance, or of environmental, cultural, or economic disadvantage.

Speech or language impairment: Speech or language impairment means a communication disorder, such as stuttering, impaired articulation, a language impairment, or a voice impairment, that adversely affects a child's educational performance.

Mental Retardation: Mental retardation means significantly subaverage general intellectual functioning, existing concurrently with deficits in adaptive behavior and manifested during the developmental period, that adversely affects a child's educational performance.

Emotional Disturbance: Emotional disturbance is defined as follows:

(i) The term means a condition exhibiting one or more of the following characteristics over a long period of time and to a marked degree that adversely affects a child's educational performance:

   A. An inability to learn that cannot be explained by intellectual, sensory, or health factors.
   B. An inability to build or maintain satisfactory interpersonal relationships with peers and teachers.
   C. Inappropriate types of behavior or feelings under normal circumstances.
   D. A general pervasive mood of unhappiness or depression.
   E. A tendency to develop physical symptoms or fears associated with personal or school problems.

(ii) The term includes schizophrenia. The term does not apply to children who are socially maladjusted, unless it is determined that they have an emotional disturbance.

Other Health Impairment: Other health impairment means having limited strength, vitality or alertness, including a heightened alertness to environmental stimuli, that results in limited alertness with respect to the educational environment, that—

(i) Is due to chronic or acute health problems such as asthma, attention deficit disorder or attention deficit hyperactivity disorder, diabetes, epilepsy, a heart condition, hemophilia, lead poisoning, leukemia, nephritis, rheumatic fever, and sickle cell anemia; and (ii) Adversely affects a child's educational performance.

Autism: (i) Autism means a developmental disability significantly affecting verbal and nonverbal communication and social interaction, generally evident before age three, that adversely affects a child's educational performance. Other characteristics often associated with autism are engagement in repetitive activities and stereotyped movements, resistance to environmental change or change in daily routines, and unusual responses to sensory experiences. The term does not apply if a child's educational performance is adversely affected primarily because the child has an emotional disturbance, as defined in paragraph (b)(4) of this section, and (ii) A child who manifests the characteristics of "autism" after age three could be diagnosed as having "autism" if the criteria in paragraph (c)(1)(i) of this section are satisfied.

SPECIALLY DESIGNED INSTRUCTION

*For the consultant teacher teaching methodology centers about
developing skills, abilities and behaviors that will enable regular
classroom participation.*

Special education under IDEA is necessary when a child has one of the thirteen **IDEA disabilities,**[117] and **needs special education** because educational performance has been impacted. When these two conditions have been met (**disability** and **need**), specially designed instruction is provided so that the child can receive an appropriate education. The primary responsibility of the special education teacher is to adapt the content, methodology, and delivery of instruction so that a child can receive an appropriate education.

**Specially Designed Instruction
34 CFR 300.26(b)(3)**

Specially-designed instruction means adapting, as appropriate to the needs of an eligible child under this part, the content, methodology, or delivery of instruction:

(i) To address the unique needs of the child that result from the child's disability; and
(ii) To ensure access of the child to the general curriculum, so that he or she can meet the educational standards within the jurisdiction of the public agency that apply to all children.

Methodologies for special education and the delivery of instruction abound in special education. There are general methodologies (e.g., precision teaching, applied behavioral analysis), disability-specific methodologies (e.g., Braille, total communication, sign language, oral communication), and techniques that are controversial (e.g., facilitated communication). The consultant teacher will often have several responsibilities with respect to teaching methodology:

First, to provide specially designed instruction in the form of direct and indirect services,

Second, to enable participation in the regular curriculum,

Third, to enable a child with a disability to benefit from regular classroom instruction.

If the consultant teacher has expertise in a methodology deemed necessary for a child, considerable time might be devoted to providing this service. Regardless where these services are provided, the consultant teacher is functioning as special education teacher because the primary task is to enable a child to develop whatever skills or abilities the child needs. A good example of this is the time required by a teacher for students with visual impairments. Often the primary role for a teacher of students with visual impairments is that of consultant, but the expenditure of time for a child learning Braille increases greatly because of the special expertise and extent of direct services required for Braille instruction. Likewise, a teacher for a child with a severe hearing impairment might expend far more time providing direct instruction than for a student with a mild hearing loss. In the area of assistive technology, providing a simple service or device might require hardly no time at all, but meeting the augmentative communication needs of a child might necessitate modifying how the curriculum is presented, providing and supervising direct AT instruction, and AT training for school personnel.

The consultant is first and foremost a special education teacher who provides specially designed instruction to a child. This could be developing expressive language, alternative or augmentative communication skills, regular classroom academic skills, classroom behavior, etc. to meet a child's classroom needs. However, the consultant teacher is also concerned with generalizing and applying skills and behavior acquired by the child to the regular classroom.

One of the problems with special education, especially when provided in a separate environment, is not generalizing what has been developed to the regular classroom. Whether a child receives resource room services or direct consultant teacher services in the classroom, the child must be given the opportunity to generalize the skills acquired in more restrictive settings to the regular classroom. This is the test for consultant teacher: How well can a child with a disability be educated with children who are not disabled? The consultant teacher can ensure the effectiveness of specially designed instruction by:

• **Select teaching methodologies tailored to meet a child's needs.**

• **Integrating specially designed instruction in the regular classroom.**

- Generalizing skills and behaviors developed through related services.

- Training other professionals and paraprofessionals who provide specially designed instruction.

- Generalizing specially designed instruction skills and behavior to regular classroom situations.

- Using independent classroom behavior as a test for the effectiveness of specially designed instruction.

- Being flexible and changing instruction to accommodate a child's needs.

ADAPTING DELIVERY OF INSTRUCTION

Adapting the delivery of instruction is a term that can certainly overlap with methodology and content adaptations. Major adaptations in the delivery of content can include language mode (e.g., sign language, total communication, Braille, large print) or technology (e.g., augmentative communication, single switch software), assistance (e.g., using a scribe, recorder, or reader), and general instructional adaptations.

The list of possible instructional adaptations is extensive and can range from special seating, to a simple low technology device such as a slant board writing accommodation or special scissors. The following are several examples of possible classroom adaptations:

- **A scribe to write responses**
- **Adapting assignments**
- **Computer text**
- **Encouraging classroom participation**
- **Extended time to respond**
- **Frequent and immediate feedback**
- **Individual attention**
- **Large print**
- **Outlining tasks**
- **Peer tutoring**
- **Positive feedback and encouragement**
- **Preferential seating**
- **Study carrel**
- **Study guides**
- **Text readers**
- **Using assignment notebooks**
- **Using visual and auditory**[118]

Many of the above instructional adaptations are simply good teaching strategies, while others might warrant inclusion in a child's IEP. For the consultant teacher, ideas and suggestions regarding effective teaching strategies are an important part of "consulting," while IEP-mandated services and activities require careful implementation and monitoring.

Should all adaptations be included in a child's IEP? Not all. Checking a study carrel or the need to outline tasks might suggest that a study carrel must be used or that all tasks must be outlined. Adaptations that are absolutely necessary for classroom participation (e.g., a child with an orthopedic impairment might *absolutely* need a scribe) should be included in the IEP, but many adaptations are simply good ideas that would apply to all children (e.g., encouraging classroom participation).

TRADING

If the solution to a child's needs is the assignment of an aide, and training and supervision have are not provided, the child is not receiving an appropriate education, a reasonably calculated education, or an education in the least restrictive environment.

Enabling a child to participate in regular classes is immeasurably easier when regular teachers, administrators, paraprofessionals and other service providers have a clear understanding of the role of special education, the IEP process, and a child's right to be educated with nondisabled children to the maximum extent appropriate.

1. **The consultant teacher must play an active role in the provision of in-service training for school personnel and paraprofessional training.**

2. **Training should not be haphazard but should address specific needs and be provided on a scheduled basis.**

3. **Training should be an integral part of the consultant teacher's responsibilities.**

Special education services will not be effective if the consultant teacher is unable to delegate authority and to use the considerable expertise of others. A consultant teacher who believes they must do everything, will probably accomplish little. But a consultant teacher who enlists teachers and personnel to provide direct and indirect services, to assume many of the responsibilities of the consultant teacher, will establish an infrastructure for the inclusion of all children with disabilities.

Parent Training

Although not frequently treated as such parent training can be a related service in that this "term also includes school health services, social work services in schools, and parent counseling and training."[119] For assistive technology services training or technical assistance are required, "if appropriate, for a child with a disability or the child's family.[120] Also, parents might need training relating to adaptations and communication. For example, "the IEP team

172

may also wish to consider whether there is a need for members of the child's family to receive training in sign language in order for the child to receive FAPE."[121] Make parents an integral part of special education. Provide time for parents to become aware of their role in the IEP process, procedural safeguards and how they can generalize skills learned in school to home and vice versa.

IEP Team Training

Most IEP team members will have little knowledge about regulations, the role of teachers or parents, how to write measurable annual goals, the least restrictive environment, etc. To this end the consultant teacher might provide a brief in-service session for IEP team members. This need not be formal presentation, and certainly should not result in a reading of the law and regulations, but a discussion or key IEP team issues should be undertaken before the team considers a single child's case.

Key concepts to discuss with the IEP team include what is needed to receive services under IDEA, present levels of performance, measurable annual goals, special education, related services, supplementary aids and services, test accommodations, LRE considerations, the continuum of services, and placement. Most importantly the IEP team should be aware that the presumed placement is the regular classroom with supplementary aids and services. With the parents in attendance, this is also an excellent time to provide "a full explanation of all of the procedural safeguards available,"[122] to parents. The IEP team should also be aware of Section 504 for children who are not disabled under IDEA but eligible for services under this provision. The consultant teacher's effectiveness is enhanced if the IEP team makes a decision in concert with both the letter and spirit of idea. Before the first meeting suggest an in-service training for team members to the chairperson of special education, the chairperson of the IEP team, or whoever is responsible.

IDEA Training Resources

The *National Dissemination Center for Children with Disabilities or NDCCD* (formerly the National Information Center for Children and Youth with Disabilities or NICHCY) *is an excellent source for IDEA*, No Child Left Behind Act resources, and resources relating to research-based information on educational practices which are important for the most recent revision of IDEA. NDCCD receives funding through the Office of Special Education Programs (OSEP), U.S. Department of Education, and is operated by the Academy for Educational Development (AED). The following are several useful NDCCD websites:

NDCCD website: **http://www.nichcy.org/index.html**

Training materials: **http://www.nichcy.org/ideatrai.htm**

Overheads: **http://www.nichcy.org/regohs/regohtoc.htm**

In-service Training: Absolutely provide in-service training for regular class-room teachers as part of a Superintendent's day, on a voluntary basis, after school, in the teacher's lounge, wherever. The school administration can certainly hire an outside consultant to provide in-service training but this is not the most effective strategy. The consultant teacher will know many of the regular classroom teachers, know their concerns, and will be able to provide a presentation to address issues relating to the school and district. An in-service presentation need not be as in-depth as that provided for IEP team members, but regular classroom teachers should be aware of what is necessary before a child receives services under IDEA, the assessment and IEP process (and the availability of the IEP to all teachers involved in the implementation of the IEP), LRE and placement (viz., the regular classroom is the presumed placement), and supplementary aids and services to enable regular classroom participation.

Paraprofessional Training: Paraprofessionals (viz., aides, assistant teachers) provide an important source of classroom support. However, paraprofessionals must be "appropriately trained and supervised, in accordance with state law, regulations, or written policy"[123] The key to this provision is *appropriately trained and supervised.* Far too often aides are not trained, are not supervised, yet are responsible for important, and sometimes all, instructional decisions, curriculum content. This is unfair to the aide and certainly unfair to the child receiving the services of the aide. If an aide is assigned to a child, especially on a one-on-one basis, the school, not the aide, is responsible for including the child in the classroom. An aide is not intended to be a means to consolidate all necessary supplementary aides and services, but to support (and not supplant) special education services and regular classroom participation.

SUPPORT, SUPPORT, SUPPORT

The regular classroom teacher has the potential to provide the most important support service that a child with a disability can receive in the classroom.

Support for whom? The student, the regular classroom teacher, the consultant teacher? Under IDEA children with disabilities are provided with "appropriate supports in order to successfully progress in the general curriculum"[124] and "support services includes implementing the comprehensive system of personnel development . . . recruitment and training of mediators, hearing officers, and surrogate parents, and public information and parent training activities relating to FAPE for children with disabilities."[125]

The IEP must include "a statement of the program modifications or supports for school personnel" but the one consistent complaint from many teachers is a lack of support. To create an atmosphere of inclusion rather than resentment, the consultant teacher must ensure that the classroom teacher recognizes that each child with a disability will have direct and indirect support from a qualified special education consultant teacher. As with all services, the IEP provides the basis for classroom support. When considering the "modifications and supports for school personnel"[126] the IEP team should consider teaching support, related service support, paraprofessional support, supplemental support (i.e., resource room), planning support, and remedial support.

How to Support the Classroom Teacher

- **Consider how the classroom teacher will be supported at the IEP team meeting.**

- **Specify the specific regular classroom accommodations, modifications, and supports that must be provided for the child in the IEP.[127]**

- **Be sure that the regular classroom teacher understands his or her IEP-related responsibilities, and what supports will enable the classroom teacher to meet these responsibilities.**

- Meet with the regular classroom teacher on a scheduled basis to ensure that the supports have been implemented and that the supports are effective.

- If an aide is assigned to the regular classroom, the regular classroom teacher should be absolutely clear as to the role and responsibilities of the aide.

- Provide opportunities for the regular classroom teacher to develop specific skills (e.g., survival sign language skill), working with an AT device or service) under the guidance and training of qualified personnel.

- Evaluate the need and effectiveness of classroom supports at least annually.

Program modifications or supports for school personnel are critical elements of every child's IEP.[128] The consultant teacher is a primary source for support, but other support services might include staff development, consultation, direct classroom services, indirect services, paraprofessionals training and supervision, related services, coordinated supplementary services (viz., resource room services), related service providers, remedial specialists, the use of volunteers, and planning time.

Every IEP should have a section that clearly designates classroom support. The Arkansas IEP devotes a section to Supports for Preschool/School Personnel. The support services cited include consultant services, staff development, specialized materials, and professional literature. The South Dakota IEP also has a section entitled Supports for School Personnel which includes consultant services and specialized materials. Rhode Island identifies Supplementary Aides and Services to Support Child (e.g., assistive technology), Modifications and Accommodations to Support Child and Support to School Personnel to Assist Child. Massachusetts differentiates between consultation (or **indirect services** to school personnel and parents) and special education and related services (**direct services**) in "general education" or in other settings. More often than not, support for school personnel might be mentioned in the IEP because the regulations state that the classroom teacher must be informed of "the specific accommodations, modifications and supports." However, an IEP might simply include a section to detail these "modifications and supports" without explaining what supports are effective, available, or feasible. Well, one support we all know that is effective, available, and feasible is consultant teacher services.

☛ **Begin designating supports for the classroom teacher by outlining the direct and indirect consultant teacher services needed for a child to participate in the classroom.**

One of the reasons why the regular classroom teacher attends the IEP meeting is to assist in determining needed classroom supports, program modifications, and supplementary aids and services. The consultant teacher establishes a foundation for successful classroom participation at the IEP meeting by encouraging regular classroom teacher input. At the IEP team meeting, when the regular classroom teacher is a contributing member of the team, planned support and program modifications help ensure successful classroom participation.

> *Congress did not leave school administrators powerless to deal with dangerous students; it did, however, deny school officials their former right self-help, and directed . . . that in the future the removal of disabled students could be accomplished only with the permission of the parents or, as a last resort, the courts.*
>
> -U.S. Supreme Court
> HONIG v. DOE, 484 U.S. 305 (1988)

After an IEP has been developed, the classroom teacher must be informed of "his or her specific responsibilities related to implementing the child's IEP, and the specific accommodations, modifications, and supports that must be provided for the child in accordance with the IEP."[129] The consultant teacher is often best qualified to discuss each child's IEP with the classroom teacher, what is expected of the classroom teacher in order to implement the IEP, and what supports will be provided so that the classroom teacher is not overwhelmed by the time or skill required to enable a child with a disability to participate in the classroom. One very just criticism by classroom teachers is the **dumping** of children in the regular classroom without adequate support. Placing a child in a regular classroom without supporting the classroom teacher is a recipe for failure. Special education services and program modifications cannot occur independent of the classroom teacher with a realistic expectation that the services will nurture independent classroom functioning. The goal of special education is participation in the regular classroom with the least restrictions required, and this can only be achieved if the regular classroom teacher is a meaningful member of the team and a supported member of the team.

Part V
The Regular Classroom and the Consultant Teacher

"The new focus is intended to produce attention to the accommodations and adjustments necessary for disabled children to access the general education curriculum and the special services which may be necessary for appropriate participation in particular areas of the curriculum due to the nature of the disability."

-Senate Report 105-17

CLASSROOM BEHAVIOR

In the case of a child whose behavior impedes his or her learning or that of others, consider, if appropriate, strategies, including positive behavioral interventions, strategies, and supports to address that behavior.[130]

If there is one area that can limit or prevent regular classroom participation, it is inappropriate behavior or misconduct. Behavior is an area which demands support for the regular classroom teacher. Without indirect consultation, direct classroom services, and concrete support in terms of strategies and personnel, the classroom teacher will be resentful, angry, and feel abandoned. And good for the classroom teacher. These feelings are a logical consequence of not providing specific supports, a specific plan, and adequate personnel to address classroom behavioral needs. The following are several areas to consider when addressing the critical issue of classroom behavioral needs:

❑ Using Aides
❑ Applied behavior analysis
❑ Assertive discipline
❑ Behavioral Intervention Plan
❑ Classroom seating
❑ Collaborative behavior strategies
❑ Strategies for acting out behavior
❑ Decreasing off-task behavior
❑ Delineating classroom rules
❑ Delineating consequences
❑ Develop school/parent partnerships
❑ Develop specific measurable goals
❑ Functional Behavioral Assessment
❑ Generalizing appropriate behavior
❑ Identifying specific behaviors
❑ Life space interviewing
❑ Modeling behavior
❑ Ignoring inappropriate behavior
❑ One-to-one services

❑ Parent support
❑ Peer tutor/role model
❑ Practicing appropriate behavior
❑ Provide positive social interactions
❑ Recording classroom behavior
❑ Rewarding on-task behavior
❑ Resource room support
❑ Establishing classroom routines
❑ Small group activities
❑ Social skills training
❑ Structure the classroom
❑ Structure the curriculum
❑ Study carrel
❑ Increasing supervision
❑ Teacher proximity
❑ Team teaching
❑ Time management
❑ Time out
❑ Understanding student perceptions

SUCCESSFUL CLASSROOM PARTICIPATION

To improve academic performance, the consultant teacher should focus on classroom data: quizzes, grades, teacher evaluations, work samples, homework, test scores, curriculum-based assessments, and observational data.

Successful classroom participation begins by identifying the specific classroom behaviors or academic skills that prevents a child from participating in the classroom or participating in the general curriculum.

> **Present Levels of Educational Performance**
> **34 CFR 300, Appendix A**
>
> The IEP team's determination of how each child's disability affects the child's involvement and progress in the general curriculum is a primary consideration in the development of the child's IEP. In assessing children with disabilities, school districts may use a variety of assessment techniques to determine the extent to which these children can be involved and progress in the general curriculum, such as criterion referenced tests, standard achievement tests, diagnostic tests, other tests, or any combination of the above.

If a child is not able to participate in the regular classroom because of the child's behavior, common sense indicates that the only way to enable participation is to address the child's behavioral needs. If there is one area that will provide the basis for success, it is the determination of specific needs that should be addressed. To this end the consultant teacher can assist in determining specific classroom needs that a child has that might interfere with classroom success, and then providing opportunities in the regular classroom to determine whether interventions and/or accommodations have been successful for enabling a child to participate in the classroom. If a child interrupts lessons and other children on the average of fifty times a day, this information becomes essential for addressing classroom needs. In other words, something must be done to reduce the number of interruptions from fifty to ten, five or even zero interruptions. If this need is addressed with supplementary aids and services (e.g., an aide, direct consultant teacher services, a behavioral intervention plan), the identification of the specific need is the basis for classroom success. If this specific behavior is not addressed and the child's behavioral need is ignored or tolerated in a restricted setting, special education is not a vehicle for meeting the child's needs to enable classroom participation but rather a place to segregate the child from classroom participation.

As is the case with behavior, the consultant teacher can assist in determining specific academic needs. The key to understanding specific academic needs is an understanding of the difference between general and specific levels of performance. Standardized tests such as IQ assessments (e.g., Wechsler Intelligence Scale for Children-III) and achievement tests (e.g., Stanford Achievement Test) provide information concerning the general direction of a child's needs. To say that a child needs help in reading, or even help in reading comprehension because of a below average grade equivalent or standard score provides no clear-cut benchmark for determining what should be done to address the child's needs or how the child's performance can be improved. Be specific; be behavioral. Identify, as best as possible, what exactly is needed to successfully participate in the classroom and the curriculum.

RELATED SERVICES AND
THE REGULAR CLASSROOM

*As used in this part, the term related services means transportation
and such developmental, corrective, and other supportive services as
are required to assist a child with a disability to benefit from
special education.*[131]

The consultant teacher must not only collaborate with regular classroom teachers but with all related service providers to enable children to participate in the regular classroom. Related services are not independent of IDEA special education services; related services are provided to assist a child to benefit from special education. Because specially designed instruction is intended to adapt content, methodology or the delivery of instruction to meet a child's unique needs and to ensure access to the general curriculum, related services are intended to help a child to achieve these goals.

Special education should enable, to the maximum extent appropriate, regular classroom and curriculum participation. Related services should support this endeavor. If a child has a disability under IDEA, and needs-related services to benefit from special education, a variety of services are available to meet these needs including:

- **Audiology services**

- **Counseling services**

- **Diagnosis/speech or language impairments**

- **Early identification**

- **Employment preparation**

- **Evaluating effectiveness of amplification**

- **Group and individual counseling**

- **Leisure education**

- **Medical services**

- Occupational therapy

- Occupational therapy services

- Orientation and mobility services

- Parent counseling and training

- Physical therapy

- Psychological services

- Recreation programs

- Rehabilitation counseling services

- School health services

- Social work services

- Speech-language pathology services

- Therapeutic recreation services

- Transportation services

- Travel in and around school buildings

- Vocational rehabilitation services

Related services providers such as social workers, school psychologists, or occupational therapists often might provide direct and indirect services to enable regular classroom participation. If the speech-language specialist collaborates with the regular classroom teacher to develop skills to enable regular classroom participation and/or provides services in the classroom, these would be consultant teacher services. Of course, the degree to which a related service enables classroom participation depends on how the related service generalizes to regular classroom performance. The importance of consultation and collaboration is of the reason for a change in credential standards in California because of a "shift in service delivery systems, including the increasing emphasis upon collaboration and consultation between speech-language specialists and audiologists and other educational professionals. Speech-language specialists are presenting language lessons in the classroom with greater frequency and/or carrying over classroom content in their small group and individual treatment."[132]

Assistive technology is often provided by a special education teacher, a related service provider (e.g., occupational therapist, speech-language specialist), or a paraprofessional with expertise in assistive and computer technology. Although a related service provider often is a source of invaluable direct and indirect services, a special education consultant teacher is necessary to provide and supervise specially designed instruction.

The presumed location for related services, if appropriate, is the regular classroom. Certain related services might require privacy (e.g., counseling) or a special location/equipment (e.g., physical therapy), and when classes are tied to content areas special education and related service might require a different location.

A related service provider might work directly with a child in the regular classroom or other settings, but the related service will require coordination with the regular classroom so that skills are generalized to the regular classroom and to enable classroom participation. Related services are not intended to be provided completely apart from the regular classroom although this is what frequently occurs when the service is offered on a pull-out basis and the service provider has no idea how the service impacts regular classroom performance. A related services might require a separate location (e.g., speech therapy, counseling, or services requiring special equipment), but the goal of all services is to enable regular classroom participation.

Although related services frequently involve consultant teacher services (i.e., direct and indirect services), whether these services meet the "special education" requirement depends on whether the services provided by a speech pathologist, physical or occupational therapist, etc., consists of specially designed instruction and is therefore considered special education.[133] For example, speech and language can be either a related service or special education depending on the disability and the affect on educational performance.[134]

For many related service providers working cooperatively with staff, families and agencies is essential. One of the core values for occupational therapists is collaboration and teamwork and "cooperation with the client, family members, significant others, team, and community resources and individuals, when appropriate."[135] The related services cited in the regulations for IDEA emphasize the importance of collaboration and consulting so that a child can benefit from special education and includes consulting with staff members, counseling and guidance of parents and teachers, working in partnerships with parents and others, and the integration in the workplace and community of a student with a disability. The consultant teacher is often required to collaborate with a variety of related service providers to facilitate special education and regular classroom participation. The consultant teacher must strive to generalize the related services provided to the regular classroom, and to work in cooperation with related service providers to identify classroom needs, evaluate the effectiveness of services in the regular classroom, and to plan with the related service provider to use strategies and techniques in the regular classroom which reinforce the related services provided.

Related Services and the Regular Classroom

- Encourage related service providers to attend IEP meetings (which many do) when "consultation" might be necessary (e.g., addressing a child's AT needs).

- Remember: "Individuals who have knowledge or special expertise regarding the child, including related services personnel" can be members of the IEP team "at the discretion of the parents or agency."[136]

- Plan with related service providers to identify classroom needs.

- Plan with related service providers to generalize skills to the regular classroom.

- If possible, make arrangements for the related service to be provided in the regular classroom.

- Welcome every related service provider as part of the team to maximize regular classroom participation.

THE REGULAR CLASSROOM

What constitutes a *regular classroom* is an important factor when including children with disabilities to participate in the regular classroom. Assigning a large number of children to a teacher who is especially effective or accepting of children with disabilities can result in a de facto self-contained or remedial classroom. In Illinois a regular classroom is one in which the classroom "is composed of students of whom at least seventy percent are without identified special education eligibility, that utilizes the general curriculum, that is taught by an instructor certified for regular education, and that is not designated as a general remedial classroom."[137] This is in contrast to a resource room placement where a student "receives special education instruction for less than fifty percent of the school day."

Lawton suggests a classroom comprised of ten percent of children with disabilities is manageable,[138] while another rule of thumb is that the number of children with disabilities in a regular classroom should approximate the number of children with disabilities in the district (Burns, 2003, p. 149). How a regular classroom is defined will vary but, at the very least, a common sense approach should be used when meeting the needs of a child with disability in regular classrooms so that there are actually opportunities for the child to participate with nondisabled children (which might not occur if the majority of the children in the regular classroom have disabilities).

Although the number of children assigned to a regular classroom will vary, the criteria for a *regular classroom placement* is more rigorous. The Office of Special Education Programs (OSEP) defines a regular classroom placement where a child spends less than twenty-one percent of the school day outside of the regular classroom; a resource room placement entails between twenty-one percent and sixty percent of the school day outside of the regular classroom; and a separate placement is more than sixty percent of the school day outside of the regular classroom. South Dakota uses a variation of the OSEP guideline for determining a regular classroom placement: eighty to one hundred percent of the day n the regular classroom entails a regular classroom placement (with modifications), forty to seventy-nine percent in the regular classroom is a resource room placement, and between zero to thirty-nine percent is a self-contained classroom placement.[139]

OSEP Guidelines for Defining Placements

- Regular Classroom placement: <21% of the time outside of the regular classroom.

- Resource Room placement: between 21% and 60% of the time outside of the regular classroom.

- Separate placement: More than 60% of the time outside of the regular classroom.

For a five-hour or 300 minute school day, a regular classroom placement means that no more than sixty-three minutes is spent outside of the regular classroom and at least 237 minutes of the day are spent in the regular classroom.

THE REGULAR CLASSROOM TEACHER

The first member of the IEP team listed in the regulations are the parents, followed by "at least one regular education teacher of the child (if the child is, or may be, participating in the regular education environment)."[140] When the regulations for special education were first published, the only teacher required to serve on the IEP team was "the child's teacher" (121a.344)[141] and this often meant a special education teacher providing self-contained services. The current law and IDEA emphasize the importance of the regular classroom teacher in the identification of needs, planning and enabling regular classroom participation.

> **Regular Classroom Teacher Requirement**
> **34 CFR 300.346(d)**
>
> The regular educaton teacher of a child with a disability, as a member of the IEP team, must, to the extent appropriate, participate in the development, review, and revision of the child's IEP, including assisting in the determination of:
>
> (1) Appropriate positive behavioral interventions and strategies for the child; and
> (2) Supplementary aids and services, program modifications or supports for school personnel that will be provided for the dhild

The regular classroom teacher is absolutely essential for not only determining regular classroom needs, but in developing an IEP to address those needs. If the regular classroom teacher does not attend the IEP meeting, there is little likelihood that the classroom participation will be successful. If the regular classroom teacher attends the IEP meeting but does not contribute to the planning, this is an indication that what is needed for classroom success has not been considered. If success in the regular classroom is a primary concern, the undisputed expert for classroom success is the regular classroom teacher. The input of the regular classroom teacher is especially important when considering the supplementary aids and services that a child might need to be successful in the classroom and behavior needs.

How to Include the Regular Classroom Teacher

As is the case with parents of children with disabilities, the consultant teacher must actively seek the involvement of classroom teachers. Several guidelines for the consultant teacher to follow include:

1. **Regard the regular classroom teacher as the key to success in the regular classroom.**

2. **Listen to the classroom teacher.**

3. **Remember that the classroom teacher is the "expert."**

4. **Plan with the classroom teacher.**

5. **Make the classroom teacher an integral part of the IEP team.**

6. **Attempt to accommodate the teacher's concerns.**

7. **Acknowledge the importance of the teacher's expertise.**

8. **The classroom teacher is instrumental in the development of all Functional Behavioral Assessments.**

9. **Make the classroom teacher a part of all behavioral intervention plans.**

10. **Realize that teacher input is the key to the regular classroom success.**

CLASSROOM PARTICIPATION DATA

Educational benefits are not mainstreaming's only virtue. Rather mainstreaming may have benefits in and of itself. For example, the language and behavior models available from nonhandicapped children may be essential or helpful to the handicapped' child's development.
-**Daniel v. State Board of Education**

Of all the data that the special education consultant teacher must carefully monitor, none is more important than the amount of time a child participates in the regular classroom. Carefully track the amount of time a child spends in the regular classroom, outside of the regular classroom and all services provided.

Every school receiving IDEA funding is required to report to the Office of Special Education and Rehabilitative Services (OSERS), Office of Special Education Programs (OSEP) data relating to child count and FAPE. The following is the type of data required by OSERS/OSEP:

STATE: _____

SECTION C: EDUCATIONAL ENVIRONMENT OF CHILDREN WITH DISABILITIES AGES 6-21

Educational Environment:	(A) Children who received special education outside the regular class less than 21 percent of day by age category			(B) Children who received special education outside the regular class at least 21 percent of day but no more than 60 percent of day by age category		
Disability	(1) 6-11	(2) 12-17	(3) 18-21	(4) 6-11	(5) 12-17	(6) 18-21
Mental Retardation						
Hearing Impairments						
Speech or Language Impairments						
Visual Impairments						
Emotional Disturbance						

Educational Environment:	(A) Children who received special education outside the regular class less than 21 percent of day by age category			(B) Children who received special education outside the regular class at least 21 percent of day but no more than 60 percent of day by age category		
Disability	(1) 6-11	(2) 12-17	(3) 18-21	(4) 6-11	(5) 12-17	(6) 18-21
Orthopedic Impairments						
Other Health Impairments						
Specific Learning Disabilities						
Deaf-Blindness						
Multiple Disabilities						
Autism						
Traumatic Brain Injury						
Developmental Delay*						
Total:						

An excellent source of IDEA data and forms (such as the above form) from the Office of Special Education Programs:

http://www.ideadata.org/documents.asp#fact

The special education consultant teacher should be aware of the exact percentage of time each child with a disability is in the regular classroom. How to do this? Because a child's schedule might vary from day to day, this is best done on a weekly basis (or whatever cycle the school uses). Determine the length of the school day for "which has the same for all children in school, including children with and without disabilities."[142] Generally the length of the school day will vary between four (more so for first and second grade) and six (e.g., high school) hours or between 240 and 360 minutes per day and between 1200 and 1800 minutes per week (depending on the state, school, level, and whether lunch and recesses are included or excluded...and the length of the day seems like such a simple matter!). If your school uses periods, calculate the percentage in minutes rather than periods. Removing a child for less than a period can be disruptive but there might be occasions when only a part of a period is needed for a pull-out service. If a child has not been included in a classroom because of the length of the period, a partial period might be the only way to accommodate the child (or the child's behavior). The maximum extent appropriate is not restricted by the length of a school period and could mean thirty minutes, twenty minutes or even five minutes. The consultant teacher should always attempt some level of regular classroom participation and then build from there.

When calculating the extent of participation, don't mislead. If there are eight periods in the school day, and forty periods in a school week, eight (actually 8.4) or less periods a week outside of the regular classroom would be a regular classroom placement. However, this does not take into account partial time spent in the regular classroom, related services, transportation, so that eight periods per week could actually be much more (or less) than twenty-one percent in minutes. Use minutes to calculate regular classroom participation...a bit more work but much more accurate.

Let's say that the school day is six hours or 360 minutes, and the day is broken down into eight forty-five minute periods. There will be a variety of other factors to consider such as the length of periods, the number of periods, and the time between periods or whether there even are periods (not to mention of possibility of extended periods or abbreviated periods). In the below table special education requires a total of fifteen periods out of the forty weekly periods available. Of these fifteen periods, nine periods entail pull-out servcies and six involve consultant teacher services in the regular classroom (CT). Speech requires three pull-out periods (SP-P), physical therapy one pull-out period (PT-P), and five periods are provided for resource room support (RR).

Period	Mon.	Tues.	Wed.	Thur.	Fri.
1. 9:00 - 9:44		SP-P			SP-P
2. 9:45 - 10:29	CT		CT		CT
3. 10:30 - 11:14			SP-P		
4. 11:15 - 11:59		PT-P			
5. 12:00 - 12:44	CT		CT		CT
6. 12:45 - 1:29	RR	RR	RR	RR	RR

Period	Mon.	Tues.	Wed.	Thur.	Fri.
7. 1:30 - 2:14					
8. 2:15 - 3:00					
SP = Speech (I) PT = Physical Therapy (O) RR = Resource Room CTS = Consultant Teacher					

For each child with a disability data should be available to indicate the percent of time in the regular classroom, the percent of total special education and related services, the percent of pull-out services, and the percent of consultant teacher services (or special education and related services provided in the regular classroom). This data should be considered each time an IEP is reviewed or at least annually.

Date: September 1, 2004

	Periods	Minutes	Percent
Total	40	1800	100
Regular Classroom	31	1395	77.5
Total Special Education	15	675	37.5
Total Pull Out Special Ed.	9	405	22.5
Consultant Teacher Services	6	270	15

The above percentages are not meant to be static or engraved in stone; for each child and for each year the goal should be to increase regular classroom participation and reduce services if appropriate. If placement data never changes for a school or district, special education is a place and not a service. Every time an IEP is developed or reevaluated, or when needed, consideration should be given to:

- **Increasing regular classroom time.**

- **Increasing regular classroom support.**

- **Increasing regular classroom-related services.**

- **Increasing consultant teacher services.**

- **Increasing special education classroom services.**

- **Increasing indirect teacher support and services.**

- **Increasing the amount of nonacademic participation.**

- **Decreasing total special education time.**

- **Decreasing total pull-out special education.**

The task is not only to increase the amount of time in the regular classroom, but to provide an appropriate education while the child is in the regular classroom. If a child is placed in the regular classroom with a full-time aide but is given no specially-designed instruction, and the regular classroom teacher is given no support, this is hardly an appropriate education . . . and this is not the intention of IDEA. If a child is in the regular classroom, the goal is not to simply "be" in the classroom but to be successful in the classroom. Systematically increase the amount of time a child can be educated with nondisabled children successfully, and you will have done a good thing as a consultant teacher. If you have achieved this to the maximum extent appropriate, you will have done a very good thing.

CLASSROOM PARTICIPATION BY STATE

The classification rate for mental retardation per 1000 is 21.987 among blacks but 7.74 among white children.

The degree of participation outside of the regular classroom will obviously depend, among other factors, on the type and severity of disabilities within each state and within each school district. Compare your school, district or state to data from the 24th Annual Report to Congress for all children with disabilities participating in different educational environments in Table 3[143]

Table 3: Placement Data for All Children with Disabilities

State	ALL DISABILITIES							
	Outside Regular Class			Public Separ Facil	Private Separ Facil	Public Resid Facil	Private Resid Facil	Home Hosp Envir
	<21%	21-60%	>60%					
Alabama	52.23	36.45	8.57	1.02	0.18	0.95	0.33	0.28
Alaska	58.84	28.33	10.8	1.66	0.08	0.01	0.15	0.13
Arizona	48.09	31.62	17.3	0.91	1	0.69	0.14	0.26
Arkansas	38.4	44.52	14.48	0.24	0.88	0.49	0.61	0.39
California	49.44	20.19	26.84	0.82	1.78	0.16	0.31	0.46
Colorado	71.21	15.81	8.94	1.23	0.42	0.53	1.27	0.59
Connecticut	56.43	21.52	16.2	1.63	2.74	0.14	1.18	0.17
Delaware	29.76	52.18	13.12	3.58	0.07	0.16	0.61	0.53
Dist Colum	22.89	44.72			0.43	11.44	19.93	0.6
Florida	49.79	26.25	21.99	0.93	0.31	0.41	0.04	0.29
Georgia	35.09	35.44	27.47	0.95	0.02	0.89	0.03	0.11
Hawaii	18.82	59.03	19.86	0.72	0.24	0	0.47	0.87

ALL DISABILITIES							
State	Outside Regular Class			Public Separ Facil	Private Separ Facil	Public Resid Facil	Private Resid Facil	Home Hosp Envir
	<21%	21-60%	>60%					
Idaho	65.8	25.56	7.03	0.64	0.24	0.37	0.09	0.27
Illinois	37.34	28.03	28.41	3.61	1.97	0.25	0.24	0.14
Indiana	57.37	15.77	24.8	0.47	0.01	0.87	0.3	0.41
Iowa	46.29	34.83	15.21	2.34		0.75	0.41	0.17
Kansas	59.68	25.05	12.17	1.94	0.34	0.32	0.29	0.21
Kentucky	49.91	31.88	15.68	0.71	0.1	0.76	0.29	0.68
Louisiana	39.96	25.4	31.63	0.61	0.15	1.51	0	0.75
Maine	51.3	32.45	13.22	0.59	1.04	0.07	0.92	0.42
Maryland	46.51	21.96	23.96	3.19	3.06	0.57	0.46	0.28
Massachusetts	63.85	14.6	14.72	1.98	3.36	0.2	0.84	0.45
Michigan	45.25	27.07	20.47	6.65		0.27	0.13	0.15
Minnesota	64.13	22.09	8.14	4.01	0.27	0.68	0.49	0.2
Mississippi	47.92	28.49	20.96	0.46	0.42	0.73	0.4	0.63
Missouri	51.93	31.62	13.14	2.35	0.44	0.08	0.04	0.4
Montana	54.85	31.93	10.93	0.51	0.88	0.41	0.32	0.17
Nebraska	55.86	25.32	16.74	0.97	0.22	0.21	0.23	0.46
Nevada	49.9	32.8	14.65	2.31	0	0	0.05	0.3
New Hampshire	74.49	16.46	4.4	0.09	2.26	0.24	1.82	0.24
New Jersey	45.26	25.8	19.25	3.44	5.45	0.12	0.06	0.62
New Mexico	28.69	31.82	37.42	0.53	0	0.8	0.07	0.67
New York	47.62	13.16	30.73	4.42	2.15	0.47	0.79	0.65
North Carolina	58.25	22	17.32	1.26	0.26	0.45	0.04	0.42

State	ALL DISABILITIES							
	Outside Regular Class			Public Separ Facil	Private Separ Facil	Public Resid Facil	Private Resid Facil	Home Hosp Envir
	<21%	21-60%	>60%					
North Dakota	79.7	14.71	3.84	0.32	0.18	0.49	0.6	0.15
Ohio	64.84	24.94	5.23	3.64	0	0.38	0	0.97
Oklahoma	47.41	39.02	12.07	0.49	0.06	0.45	0.08	0.43
Oregon	73.55	15	7.74	1.44	1.13	0.51	0.27	0.35
Pennsylvania	35.78	32.81	27.71	1.73	1.21	0.38	0.22	0.16
Puerto Rico	58.07	15.68	19.87	3.26	1.49	0.08	0.05	1.49
Rhode Island	47.58	19.37	27.23	0.71	2.46	0.37	1.42	0.86
South Carolina	32.19	40.46	25.53	0.89	0.06	0.36	0.04	0.47
South Dakota	66.26	24.1	6.26	0.83	0.61	0.75	0.99	0.19
Tennessee	44.97	34.1	18.39	0.73	0.48	0.14	0.03	1.15
Texas	28.24	52.04	17.95	0.69	0.02	0.07	0.01	0.98
Utah	44.27	31.09	21.22	2.99	0.01	0.05	0	0.36
Vermont	78.27	10.15	5.52	1.7	2.16	0.06	1.43	0.72
Virginia	37.53	33.93	25.44	1.16	0.66	0.61	0.28	0.4
Washington	51.25	33	14.44	0.53	0.24	0.28	0.04	0.22
West Virginia	48.54	37.31	13.13	0.2	0.01	0.29	0.02	0.5
Wisconsin	41.5	41.14	15.59	1.07	0.1	0.32	0.05	0.23
Wyoming	51.39	32.05	11.91	2.7	0.23	0.76	0.71	0.25

IEPs AND THE REGULAR CLASSROOM TEACHER

One of the more important activities that the consultant teacher can perform is to make the IEP a meaningful part of the regular classroom. All too frequently the regular classroom teacher is completely unaware of the IEP, his or her role in the implementation of the IEP, and the fact that the classroom teacher is a vital part of the IEP process.

The regular classroom teacher should

- Be a contributing member of the IEP team,

- Suggest IEP interventions for including children in the classroom,

- Suggest IEP strategies for including children in the regular curriculum,

- Discuss with the IEP team classroom supports that will enable participation,

- Discuss with the IEP team specific needs that might be addressed by measurable annual goals,

- Discuss with the IEP team modifications that might be specified in the IEP,

- Have a copy of each child's IEP,

- Read each child's IEP.

IEP RESPONSIBILITIES FOR THE REGULAR CLASSROOM TEACHER

1. At least one regular education teacher of the child is a member of the IEP team.

2. The regular education discusses with the IEP team relevant behaviors and skills that either do or do not enable classroom participation.

3. The regular classroom teacher should feel that he or she is the "expert" regarding regular classroom performance.

4. The IEP specifies classroom supports for the child and for the regular classroom teacher.

5. The regular classroom teacher is a part of all planning involving direct consultant teacher services provided in the regular classroom.

6. The classroom teacher is clear about his or her IEP responsibilities, especially supplementary aids and services that will enable regular classroom and curriculum participation.

7. The IEP be accessible to each regular education teacher involved in its implementation.[144]

IEP/REGULAR CLASSROOM CHECKLIST

For the consultant teacher the IEP provides the foundation for regular classroom participation and is essential for regular classroom success. Two factors are especially important for the consultant teacher: 1) the participation of the regular classroom teacher in the IEP process, and 2) an IEP which promotes regular classroom participation.

The regular classroom teacher:

• Participates in the IEP process

• Helps determine necessary services for classroom participation

• Helps determine necessary behavioral interventions

• Reviews the IEP

• Knows her or her role to enable classroom participation

The IEP describes:

• Levels of performance to relating to classroom needs

• Participation in the general curriculum

• All of the child's needs

• Services to achieve goals

• Regular classroom support (e.g., aides)

• Direct and Indirect consultant teacher services

• Services to participate in the general curriculum

• All necessary curriculum accommodations and modifications

- Why a child will not participate in the regular classroom

- The exact extent of classroom participation

CONSULTANT TEACHER CASELOAD

The number of students receiving consultant teacher services will have an impact on the quality of those direct and indirect services. If the caseload for the consultant teacher is not a fair caseload, the children with disabilities being served will not receive an appropriate education. If a child receives services in excess of those needed, or the IEP specifies excessive services, the services provided will be unduly restrictive. Providing a child with daily direct services, when several hours a week would suffice might detract from the development of independent classroom performance and detract from services for other children. This is why a fixed number of consultant teacher hours for all children is inappropriate, and why the assignment of a consultant teacher to provide a fixed amount of direct services is inappropriate. The intent of IDEA if to provide the least restrictive services, and the first step for achieving this goal is a fair consultant teacher caseload.

Of course, providing too few services can also undermine the appropriateness of a child's individualized education program. This frequently occurs when the consultant teacher's caseload is so large that the provision of necessary direct services and the many indirect services required for children to successfully participate in the regular classroom simply cannot be provided.

Using a single formula when considering a fair caseload for the consultant teacher is difficult, but factors to consider include:

- **The extent of direct services required by IEPs,**

- **The extent of indirect services required by IEPs,**

- **The number of classrooms and/or schools visited,**

- **Travel time,**

- **Planning time,**

- **Paraprofessional training and supervision,**

- **Section 504 services being provided,**

- **Pre-referral and pre-intervention responsibilities,**

• **The number of students receiving services,**

• **The number of students requiring extensive services.**

Although there is certainly a need to provide caseload guidelines for the consultant teacher, the task is not easy. A high school consultant teacher might provide primarily indirect consultant services while a primary consultant teacher might spend a considerable amount of time in the regular classroom collaborating with the regular classroom teacher and working with children with and without disabilities. For a child with cerebral palsy who is able to participate in the regular classroom and regular curriculum with extensive supplementary aids and services, ten or more hours of direct instruction might be required to provide direct services and preparing assistive technology materials.

What is a fair caseload for a consultant teacher? Restricting the number of children assigned to a consultant teacher to twenty or twenty-five may or may not be a fair caseload, depending on the services being provided. The caseload for the Texas School for the Blind and Visually Impaired is twenty-five but consideration is given for instructional services, evaluation, consultation with special and regular education personnel, report writing and travel.[145] In Pennsylvania the caseload can vary between fifteen and fifty.[146] Of course, whether the maximum is ten, twenty or thirty, providing an appropriate education for children with disabilities must take into consideration the amount of time that a teacher has available to provide direct and indirect services.

The problem with determining caseload is further exacerbated by such factors as travel, the number of students being served in specific classrooms, and the extent of indirect services which, in certain circumstances, might be more extensive than direct services. Obviously, every special education teacher providing consultant teacher services must follow state guidelines concerning the number of students being served. Nonetheless, IEP teams should be aware of the services being provided for each child and that the consultant teacher has the necessary time to provide the service specified.

One approach for a reasonably accurate method for quantifying needed services is to use what is referred to as FTE or Full-time Equivalent. For itinerant teachers of students with visual impairments the maximum caseload in Iowa is ten full-time equivalents with consideration given to time spent traveling. Each student receiving direct services is counted as one FTE "regardless of the amount of contact time," five students receiving consultative services is counted as one FTE, and one hour of daily average time spent traveling is counted as one FTE.[147]

Teachers for students with visual impairments are well aware of the importance between caseload and the types of services being provided. The

Atlantic Provinces Special Education Authority (APSEA) has subdivided services into direct services, consultation, adapting materials, and preparation. Hours are assigned to each student receiving services based on these four categories with the goal that a teacher is able to provide between thirty-five and forty-five hours of services. For students who are classified as blind, between five and eight hours of service are recommended, while for students with a vision of 20/200 direct services are between one to five hours and for students with vision between 20/70 and 20/200, zero to three hours are recommended.[148]

For the special education consultant teacher the determination of caseload is very similar to that of itinerant teachers in that certain students might require intensive services, some direct and indirect services, and others indirect support for the classroom teacher. In order to reflect these different needs in a fair caseload, consideration must be given to the intensity of the services required by each child.

Caseload is also related to the age of students receiving services, the severity of disability and, of course, individual need. For children with more severe disabilities, the consultant teacher might work with a variety of disabilities in a variety of settings. For children in early grades the consultant teacher might provide the majority of services in the regular classroom. For children with more severe disabilities, the caseload might be quite different than for a teacher working primarily with high incidence disabilities such as specific learning disabilities. As is often the case with speech and language specialists, caseload for high-incidence disabilities might be as high as thirty or more, but five children with severe learning in the regular classroom might be a full load. For older students with severe disabilities the special education teacher might provide services in the self-contained classroom and consultant teacher services when mainstreaming or pushing-in students.

As services are designated in each child's IEP, a corresponding tally should be recorded for each consultant teacher providing services. The IEP team must be aware of the amount of direct services required and the variety of indirect services (e.g., planning/consultation, curriculum modifications, assistive technology, etc.) provided by each consultant teacher. The purpose of the following table is to track the nature and scope of services provided. No attempt is made to determine exactly the most appropriate teaching load but to give the IEP team some idea as to each consultant teacher's activities and responsibilities.

Unlike the teacher for students with visual impairments where the disability and curriculum (e.g., Braille) is relatively specific and the number of children within regular classes small, the consultant teacher must deal with a wide range of disabilities and classrooms in which there are often several

Student	IEP Services	
	Direct	Indirect
Mark K.	1	1
Leonard L.	1	1
Martin A.	5	3
Fran W.	3	2
Robert Y.	5	2
Herman D.	2	1
Roger E.	2	1
Philip W.	0	2
Martha S.	0	2
Total	**19**	**15**

children receiving services. As a result, for the consultant teacher caseload cannot be determined by simply adding the direct and indirect services specified in the IEPs of children receiving services. A teacher providing indirect services to five classes would be different than a teacher providing direct and indirect services to two or three classes, and certainly different than a consultant teacher who provides direct and indirect services to two or three schools.

With all these provisos, reservations, and the downright difficult task of determining a fair special education caseload, the following is offered as a general guideline for a special education consultant teacher's caseload. But, as already discussed, common sense must prevail in the determination of a child's caseload. If the consultant teacher is responsible for providing direct instruction for as few as three children with severe disabilities in the regular classroom, this might be a full caseload if the direct services are extremely intensive and each child requires extensive curriculum modifications. Likewise, if the consultant teacher provides only indirect services (e.g., is responsible for declassified students or students needing minimal support), a caseload of thirty or thirty-five, although high, might be manageable. Finally, the following table does not take into consideration travel, the number of classrooms, schools or even districts being served. So with these cautionary remarks, the following guideline is a "something-to-think-about" guideline and absolutely not the last word concerning the special education consultant teacher's caseload.

Direct Services	Indirect Services		
	High	Medium	Low
High	6	9	12
Medium	11	15	19
Low	16	21	26

FREQUENCY, LOCATION AND DURATION

A child's IEP must contain "the projected data for the beginning of services . . . and the anticipated frequency, location, duration of these services and modifications."[149]

Must the IEP indicate the frequency, location, and duration of direct **and** indirect services? This is might seem a difficult task because of the variability of indirect services and changing needs of direct services within the regular classroom, but IDEA does require the specification of the frequency, duration, and location of services. This means that the amount of direct and indirect services should be indicated in the IEP.[150] As noted in the Senate Report for IDEA "the location where special education and related services will be provided to a child influences decisions about the nature and amount of these services and when they should be provided to a child. For example, the appropriate place for the related service may be the regular classroom, so that the child does not have to choose between a needed service and the regular educational program."[151]

The consultant teacher must not leave scheduling to a school-wide computer program. Each child's schedule must be carefully crafted so each child is able to receive maximum benefit from regular classroom instruction, to participate in the regular classroom to the maximum extent appropriate, and to participate in the regular classroom without frequent and disruptive pull-out services.

Specifying the frequency, location, and duration of the regular classroom, direct services provides a clear indication of the consultant teacher's primary responsibilities and the extent of services each child needs. The child, the regular classroom teacher, and the consultant teacher will all benefit from knowing when, where, and the extent of direct services being provided in the classroom, and the frequency of indirect services. Indicating the duration

> Read all about State reviews of special education hearings at:
>
> **http://www.sro.nysed.gov/**

and frequency of indirect services is often a **guestimate**, but doing so will provide an expectation for classroom supports, planning, supervision and training, and curriculum modifications. When indirect services entail a weekly meeting, the IEP might simply indicate thirty minutes of indirect weekly services a week. However, if the consultant teacher must modify classroom text, make extensive curriculum accommodations, or manage a child's augmentative communication device, the service and required time to provide the service should be clearly recorded in the IEP.

The need to specify the extent of direct and indirect services was considered by a New York State review of a hearing in which the hearing officer found the IEP for a child inappropriate because the CSE had failed to describe the student's consultant teacher services with sufficient specificity on his IEP. The Board of Education challenged the finding because state regulations do "not require an IEP team (CSE) to indicate whether the consultant teacher services which it recommends shall be direct or indirect." This is sort of correct. The regulations for New York specify "direct and/or indirect services" but the regulations also require that the IEP indicate "the classes in which the child will receive consultant teacher services."[152] If direct services are specified, and the total service must be specified (direct and/or indirect services), the IEP should indicate the extent of indirect services. In any case, the State Review officer disagreed based on the rationale that a CSE should "specify the special education services which it is recommending in a student's IEP."

New York's requirement specifying a minimum of two hours of indirect/direct services a week,[153] is probably not an uncalled-for bureaucratic threshold for providing services in that some children might receive no services under the guise of consultant teacher services. But is two hours of consultant teacher services restrictive if only one hour is required? First, consider that minimal indirect services might be appropriate during declassification or to test the need for services under IDEA as part of an interim placement with parent consent and specific timelines (e.g., 60 days) for reconvening the IEP team to consider the placement.[154] For children who do need special edu-

---

New York City Request for Review of a Hearing Officer Decision
00-032, May 21, 2001[155]

"The supervisor of education evaluators for Community School District 3, (supervisor) testified that the consultant teacher model would benefit respondents' son because the consultant would work with him in his classroom to apply his skills. She described the ways in which a consultant teacher could assist the student to take notes, create an outline, and become a better writer (Transcript pp.82-83). In addition to such direct service (see 8 NYCRR 200.1[1][l][1]), the consultant teacher would provide indirect service by working with the child's teacher to adapt the curriculum to the child's needs. As an example, she explained that the consultant teacher would work with the child's regular education teacher to make sure the latter used techniques to ensure that the student understood oral directions. The supervisor testified that the CSE had not specified on the student's IEP the amounts of time to be devoted to direct and indirect consultant teacher services in order to give the classroom teachers and the consultant teacher flexibility during the school year to adjust to the student's changing needs. "

But . . . the appeals officer agreed with an earlier state appeal (97-5, August 14, 1997) that "although State regulation may not explicitly require the CSE to indicate on a child's IEP whether the consultant teacher services will be direct or indirect, I must note that it does provide that each child requiring consultant teacher services " . . . shall receive direct and/or indirect services consistent with the student's IEP . . . " (8 NYCRR 200.6 [d][2]). I know of no way in which this requirement could be meaningfully enforced unless the child's IEP indicated whether the child's consultant teacher services were to be direct, indirect, or a combination of both. I concur with the hearing officer's determination that the CSE should have specified the nature of the child's consultant teacher services."

cation, some level of services is obviously necessary. The test should not be a minimum level of services, but services that meet each child's needs. This, for the most part, will be reflected by IEPs which have varying levels of direct and indirect services that correspond to the varying needs of each child. However, if all children receive the same level of services, there is a strong possibility that services are being provided based on disability and not individual need.

THE ARGUMENT FOR NOT SPECIFYING FREQUENCY, LOCATION, AND DURATION

A UNIQUE GOAL: NOT TO BE NEEDED

Over 20 years of research and experience has demonstrated that the education of children with disabilities can be made more effective by— (A) having high expectations for such children and ensuring their access in the general curriculum to the maximum extent possible.[156]

The consultant teacher provides support and services so that children with disabilities can participate in the regular classroom as independently as possible. For the consultant teacher, the ultimate goal is not to be needed, for a child to be successful with no special help or support, and for the classroom teacher to meet the needs of all children in the classroom.

In many ways the consultant teacher has a unique responsibility to decrease the need for services. Possibly the highest accolade that can be given a consultant teacher is that his or her services are no longer needed because the child can function independently in the classroom and in the curriculum with only the resources that are available to all nondisabled children. For someone who has a need to be needed, who does not like to delegate responsibility, who has difficulty letting go, this ultimate responsibility might be difficult to achieve.

Independence in the classroom brings risk; independence in the classroom is not always achieved. However, providing the opportunity for independent classroom behavior is the litmus test for the actual success of the direct and indirect service provided by the consultant teacher.

NEW YORK CONSULTANT TEACHER SERVICES

Even though IDEA does not mandate regular class placement for every disabled student, IDEA presumes that the first placement option considered for each disabled student by the student's placement team, which must include the parent, is the school the child would attend if not disabled, with appropriate supplementary aids and services to facilitate such placement.[157]

Most states reiterate IDEA and the regulations when citing the continuum of services available to a child with a disability. New York State has been uncharacteristically creative by expanding the continuum of services to include consultant teacher services. Very nice, New York State!

However, if the schools must provide Supplementary Aids and Services to enable a child to participate in regular classrooms, what is the purpose of including consultant teacher services as part of the continuum of services? After all, the regulations clearly identify "instruction in regular classes"[158] as one of the placements listed in the continuum? All true, but by identifying a consultant teacher option, the regular classroom is clearly identified as the place where services are provided via direct and indirect consultant teacher services. The reason for the extensive use of consultant teacher services in New York is because direct and indirect consultant teacher services were added to the continuum of services in the New York State Section (200.6[d]) Code (Part 200[159]).

By specifying consultant teacher services in a child's IEP, there is a legal expectation that the services will be provided in the regular classroom as stated in the IEP. Interestingly, when the consultant teacher component was first added to the continuum of services in New York State, the requirement was that one hundred percent of the services were to be provided in the regular classroom. Apparently, in order to accommodate for necessary pull-out services such as related services and resource room support, this was changed to "a student with a disability who attends regular education classes and/or to such student's regular education teachers."

In New York State, consultant teacher services are defined as services "provided to a student with a disability who attends regular education classes and/or to such student's regular education teachers." Direct and indirect consultant teacher services are further defined as:

> **Direct consultant teacher services means specially designed individualized or group instruction provided by a certified special education teacher . . . to a student with a disability to aid such student to benefit from the student's regular education classes.**

and

> **Indirect consultant teacher services means consultation provided by a certified special education teacher . . . to regular education teachers to assist them in adjusting the learning environment and/or modifying their instructional methods to meet the individual needs of a student with a disability who attends their classes.**[160]

New York State Part 200.6 Continuum of Services

(d) Consultant teacher services. Consultant teacher services shall be for the purpose of providing direct and/or indirect services to students with disabilities enrolled in regular education classes, including career and technical education. Such services shall be recommended by the committee on special education to meet specific needs of such students and shall be included in the student's individualized education program (IEP). Consultant teacher services shall be provided in accordance with the following provisions

(1) The total number of students with disabilities assigned to a consultant teacher shall not exceed 20

(2) Each student wiht a disability requiring consultant teacher services shall receive direct and/or indirect services consistent with the student's IEP for a minimum of two hours each week.

(3) Upon application and documented educational justification to the commissioner, approval may be granted for a variance for the number of students with disabilities assigned to a consultant teacher as specified in paragraph (1) of this subdivision.

After a child's IEP has been prepared, and thus based on the child's IEP, placement and services must be identified in the least restrictive environment. Because the presumed placement is always the regular classroom, the first consideration when considering where services should be provided is the regular classroom. For a child receiving services under IDEA, if services are provided in the regular classroom, the services must be provided under the direction of a special education teacher. The special education teacher could be certified in generic special education, a consultant teacher specialist, resource room specialist, learning specialist, or have expertise in a specific disability such as a teacher of the visually impaired or teacher of the deaf. The only criteria for providing consultant teacher services, regardless of what the person providing these services is called, is that the teacher is **qualified** and **certified** or **licensed** to provide the service.

SUPPLEMENTARY AIDS AND SERVICES

Supplementary Aids and Services provide the framework for consultant teacher services.

Supplementary aids and services are provided by special education teachers and, when appropriate, other professionals "in regular education classes and other education-related settings to enable children with disabilities to be educated with nondisabled children to the maximum extent appropriate."[162] The consultant teacher identifies, implements, and supervises supplementary aids and services to enable regular classroom participation.

Supplementary aids and services, or "the full range of services,"[163] provides the basic test for determining the least restrictive placement for a child after a child has been determined to have a disability, and an IEP is developed. If supplementary aids and services, which include all "aids, services, and supports" needed to participate in the regular classroom, cannot be achieved satisfactorily, then and only then, can an alternative placement or more restrictive setting be considered.

Supplementary aids and services enable regular classroom participation; the consultant teacher or qualified special education teacher is responsible for the, implementation of supplementary aids and services. The mandate is "to enable students with disabilities to be educated with nondisabled students to the maximum extent appropriate."[164] For a child with a disability this is accomplished by providing special education in the regular classroom or, if this is not possible with supplementary aids and services, in the least restrictive setting by providing a continuum of services.

Before a child is placed in an alternative setting the *full range of supplementary aids and services* must be provided. When these supplementary aids and services are not successful, only then can a child be removed from the regular education class and placed in an alternative classroom or setting.

Many of the responsibilities of the consultant teacher involve supplementary aids and services, but the consultant teacher is not limited to the regular classroom. The consultant teacher might also be responsible for ensuring that children in more restrictive settings are able to participate in the regular curriculum to the maximum extent appropriate, and able to participate in the regular classroom to the maximum extent appropriate. The primary supplementary aids and services responsibilities for the consultant teacher include:

Supplementary Aids and Services
34 CFR 300.28

As used in this part, the term supplementary aids and services means, aids, services, and other supports that are provided in regular education classes or other eduction-related settings to enable children with disabilities to be educated with nondisabled children to the maximum extent appropriate.
(Authority: 20 U.S.C. 1401(29))

First, ensuring children with disabilities are provided with all necessary supplementary aids and services so that each child can be educated with nondisabled children satisfactorily,

Second, ensuring that children in more restrictive settings are educated with nondisabled children satisfactorily,

Third, ensuring that children with disabilities in more restrictive settings are able to participate in the regular curriculum to the maximum extent appropriate.

As stated in the regulations, supplementary aids and services include "aids services, and other supports" that are provided in regular education classes or other settings to enable children with disabilities to be educated with nondisabled children. The "other settings" include all the various nonacademic and extracurricular activities and settings,[165] and can mean pull-out services that supplement the regular classroom. In this context pull-out services also enable regular classroom or regular curriculum participation.

In order to provide special education in the regular classroom or in the regular classroom to the maximum extent appropriate, each school district must have personnel who can provide supplementary aids and services to enable regular classroom participation. Supplementary aids and services are not restricted to either regular classroom program modifications or resource room services but include all modifications, accommodations and services that are provided to ensure regular classroom participation. The regulations refer to the resource room as a *supplementary service* so that the continuum of alternative placements (i.e., continuum of services) must "make provision for supplementary services (such as resource room or itinerant instruction) to be provided in conjunction with the regular classroom."[166] The 1990 regulations refer to "modifications" as supplementary aids and services that are modifications to the regular education program that are necessary to ensure participation.[167]

Depending on the area of expertise, the consultant teacher might focus on very specific or even the whole range of supplementary aids and services. The types of services provided by the consultant teacher will depend on the teacher's area of expertise (general special education, hearing or visual impairments, reading, a related service, etc.) and the teacher's contractual responsibilities. An itinerant teacher for children with visual impairments might provide extensive indirect services in the form of curriculum modifications (e.g., Braille or large print), while a consultant teacher in special education at the elementary level might spend considerable time providing direct services in the regular classroom.

Supplementary aids and services "includes special education, related services, support and supplementary services (e.g., consultant teacher, itinerant teacher, remedial specialist, aides), resource room support, test accommodations and modifications, curriculum adaptations, classroom aids and modifications, positive behavioral supports and indirect services (e.g., text adaptations or modifications, teacher consultation), assistive technology and all academic and nonacademic program options available to nondisabled children."[168]

IDENTIFYING SUPPLEMENTARY AIDS
AND SERVICES

. . . before the school district may conclude that a handicapped child
should be educated outside the regular classroom . . . the school district
must consider the whole range of supplemental aids and services,
including resource rooms and itinerant instruction . . .[169]

Supplementary aids and services are the basis for ensuring the least restrictive environment. Supplementary aids and services provide the key test for determining whether the regular classroom is appropriate. In many ways supplementary aids and services provide the foundation for consultant teacher services. An important role of the consultant teacher is to help plan a sequence of supplementary aids and services that will enable a child to be successful in the regular classroom. The seven areas to consider when providing supplementary aids and services include:[170]

Special Education: First, determine what special education is needed to be successful in the regular education classroom. If a child has a disability and needs special education, the child must receive special education services. If a child has a disability, but does not need special education, accommodations should be provided under Section 504, the Rehabilitation Act of 1973.

Support Services: Support services go hand-in-hand with special education. Special education can entail direct services with a child in the regular classroom (e.g., one-to-one, small group), or indirect services in which the consultant teacher assists a child indirectly in participating in the regular classroom or curriculum.

Full Program Options: To be "educated with children who are not disabled" means not just the regular education classroom but art, physical education, labs, music, shop, health, school clubs, choir, cheerleading, sports, intramural sports, plays. These activities enrich the lives of children who are not disabled and will enrich the lives of children who are disabled if services are provided that allow regular classroom participation.

Accommodations and Modifications: For the regular classroom and nonacademic and extracurricular activities consider modifications and accommodations to scheduling, classroom environment, method of instruction, curriculum that will enable regular classroom participation.

Related Services: There can be considerable overlap between special education, related services and supplementary aids and services. Every service or support offered "to enable children with disabilities to be educated with nondisabled children to the maximum extent appropriate" is a supplementary aid or service. What related services all have in common is that each helps a child with a disability to benefit from special education.[171] For the consultant teacher related services are important to ensure that each service is provided to enable a child with a disability to participate in the regular classroom and regular curriculum to the maximum extent appropriate. This does not mean that the consultant teacher must participate in providing related services, but must plan with and, when appropriate, work with related service providers to ensure that children with disabilities can benefit from special education provided in regular classroom and other educational settings.

Test Accommodations: The consultant teacher will participate in the determination of need classroom, district, and statewide test modifications. Accommodations and modifications for these tests are not necessarily identical. The first level of accommodations and modifications are those needed in the classroom to participate in the curriculum. To a large degree these accommodations should guide the initial determination for needed test modifications. If a child is able to participate in the curriculum without time accommodations, providing extended time could be an overly restrictive modification. The purpose of accommodations is not to give a child with a disability an advantage but to allow the child to participate on an equal basis with nondisabled children. As with all services and modifications, the least restrictive test modifications should be used that will allow participation with nondisabled children. Test accommodations for district-wide tests (e.g., Stanford Achievement Test, Terra Nova, California Achievement Test) should be based on the accommodations needed to participate in the regular curriculum, accommodations and modifications provided for classroom test and quizzes, and the guidelines provided by the test publisher.

Assistive Technology: There are three elements to consider with respect to assistive technology needs. First, assistive technology is one of the special factors that must be considered by the IEP team for every child with a disability.[172] Second, an assistive technology device is "any item" that improves "the functional capabilities of a child with a disability." An assistive technology device can range from a pair of left-handed scissors or bookstand (low-technology devices) to synthesized speech or a computerized text reader (high-technology devices). Third, the consultant teacher might not have expertise in many AT but these services must be identified, implemented, and supervised to enable regular classroom participation. For the consultant teacher the key for the effective use of assistive technology is not the availability of technology or the implementation in isolated training activities, but the use of AT devices and services to enable participation in the regular classroom and regular curriculum.

"THE FULL-RANGE OF SERVICES" CHECKLIST

The key phrase for supplementary aids and services is "the full range of services" necessary to enable regular classroom participation. To this end every checklist will be incomplete in that each child's unique needs will dictate the appropriate service or accommodation . . . which might well be unique and not necessarily include in a checklist of services or accommodations. Nonetheless, the following represent a large segment of the "full range" of supplementary aids and services:

- Special education: classroom support

- Collaborative instruction

- One-to-one instruction

- Resource room support

- Support services: consultation

- Curriculum adaptations

- Remedial support

- Aides

- Paraprofessionals

- Translators/ESL accommodations

- Full program options: consider "all" academic options

- Extracurricular activities

- Physical education

- Nonacademic services (e.g., transportation, counseling athletics)

- Accommodations and modifications: classroom environment

- Curriculum accommodations

- Format accommodations (e.g., Large print, Braille, ASL, Scribe)

- Related services (e.g., speech, physical therapy)

- Test accommodations: time (e.g., breaks, extended)

- Response accommodations

- Test aids (e.g., calculator, magnification aids, examiner aid)

- Assistive technology: low technology

- High technology (e.g., computers, synthesized speech)

- Services, training and support

- Aide supervision

- Classroom observation

- Indirect consultant teacher support

THE SUPREME COURT, CONSULTANT
TEACHER SERVICES, AND PRIVATE SCHOOLS

This case began with parents (Patricia and Paul Russman) requesting services in a parochial school and eventually landed in the Supreme Court. The case involved a child with an IQW in the 50 range who was classified as mentally retarded. The IEP team decided to place the child in a parochial school setting with a part-time consultant teacher and a full-time aide. The school board rejected this decision on the constitutional ground that services could not be provided because the First Amendment's Establishment Clause prohibited it from doing so. A hearing officer agreed with the parents by the Board of Education. Upon appeal to the State (92-14, April, 1992) the appeal officer dodged the constitutional question because (among other reasons) the IEP did not specify whether consultant teacher services were direct or indirect, because the areas in which the child was to receive consultant teacher services were not specified, and because the responsibilities of the consultant teacher were not specified.

The persistent parents took the matter to district court (945 F.Supp. 37 [N.D.N.Y., 1995]) who agreed with the Board of Education, and then to the court of appeals for the second circuit (150 F.3d 219 (2nd Circuit, 1998) who also agreed with the Board.

Well, in 1997 the Supreme Court (521 U.S. 1114 [1997] decided that schools "may" provide on-site services to children in a parochial school setting. In other words, the decision to provide services is permissive in that a school is not prevented by First Amendment's Establishment Clause from doing so. Indeed, when IDEA was revised in 1997 the law was changed to include the following provision: "Such services may be provided to children with disabilities on the premises of private, including parochial, schools, to the extent consistent with law" (20 U.S.C. 1412[a][10][B][i][II])

The questions raised by the state appeals officer were somewhat lost in argument over the constitutionality of services, but several guidelines do emerge from important case:
- Consultant teacher services should be specified in the IEP.
- The responsibilities of the consultant teacher should be articulated in terms of direct and indirect services.
- The regular education classes where consultant teacher services are provided should be described.
- Consultant teacher services *may* be provided in private schools.

Part VI
The Least Restrictive
Consultant Teacher

"Moreover, children placed in segregated or partially segregated settings must be simultaneously included in mainstream components 'to the maximum extent appropriate.'"
-Oberti v. Board of Education

THE LEAST RESTRICTIVE CONSULTANT TEACHER

This might be a bit of a stretch in terms of philosophy (Sartre is not necessarily must-reading for the consultant teacher), but existentialism is founded in the belief that we are responsible for what we do and that responsibility is not always easy to do or accept (and thus a cause of more than a bit of anguish). In any case, with apologies to Sartre for this interpretation of existentialism, the consultant teacher should focus on developing regular classroom success and independence by:

1. **Planning for independent behavior.**

2. **Providing the classroom teacher with opportunities to offer direct services.**

3. **Using school-wide resources to enable classroom success.**

4. **Providing opportunities for independent behavior.**

5. **Using the regular classroom to "test" independent behavior.**

6. **Focusing on skills that will result in successful classroom participation.**

7. **Nurturing responsibility.**

8. **Decreasing services when appropriate.**

9. **Supervising paraprofessionals to achieve classroom independence.**

10. **Being "less needed" without sacrificing success.**

11. **Becoming a "least restrictive" consultant teacher by providing: the least restrictive curriculum, the least restrictive environment, the least restrictive accommodations, the least restrictive services.**

THE LEAST RESTRICTIVE ENVIRONMENT

The regular classroom is "the" least restrictive environment.

The least restrictive environment should not be conceptualized as a means to remove a child from the regular classroom, but as the maximum extent a child can participate in a placement before a more restrictive placement is needed. This can only be achieved if each child's placement is truly the least restrictive placement. If a child can function in the regular classroom fifty percent of the day but is not afforded this opportunity, the placement is not the least restrictive; if a child can function in the regular classroom twenty percent (or 10%, or 5%, or even 1%) of the day but does not, the placement is not the least restrictive.

The least restrictive placement can be one placement (e.g., the regular classroom), but is more often a mix of placements. A child might be placed in the regular classroom, or in a special class or special school. The test for the restrictiveness of a placement is whether the child is able to participate in a less restrictive setting. If a child is in a restrictive setting, and is able to participate in a less restrictive setting *to some extent*, then the restrictive setting is not the least restrictive placement.

What is the least restrictive environment? We know that *the* (the italic is intentional) least restrictive environment is satisfactory performance in the regular classroom involving the regular curriculum with minimal services and accommodations. The key words here are *satisfactory, regular classroom, regular curriculum,* and *minimal services.* Supplementary aids and services are provided so that a child can be educated in regular classes "satisfactorily."[173] If a child is in the regular classroom and involved in the general curriculum, but the child's education is far from satisfactory, this environment can be very restrictive in that the placement prevents meaningful participation in the classroom or the curriculum.

Placement: What the Consultant Teacher Should Believe

• **The regular classroom is the presumed placement for every child.**

• **Services are provided in the regular classroom to the maximum extent appropriate so that a child with a disability can be educated with nondisabled children.**

228

• Special education is about "service" and not a "place" for services.

• Special education is about being educated with nondisabled children to the maximum extent appropriate.

• An alternative placement might be necessary, but an alternative placement is not the presumed placement and not the goal of special education.

The consultant teacher should provide services and accommodations necessary for successful classroom participation. In special education, more is not always better. More direct teaching by the consultant teacher is not better if more is not necessary; more classroom accommodations are not better because a child has a disability if the accommodations are not necessary; more services are not necessary if the child can participate successfully without the services.

The regular curriculum in a restrictive setting might be less restrictive, from a curriculum standpoint, than a specialized curriculum in a regular classroom. For that matter, a child who receives all services in a regular classroom, but does not participate in other activities or in the general curriculum, might actually have a more restrictive placement than a child in an alternative placement who is provided with opportunities to participate in the regular curriculum and regular classroom. Restrictiveness is partly defined by the location of the placement, but the context of the restrictiveness is defined by the extent a child is able to participate with nondisabled children and in the regular curriculum to the maximum extent appropriate.

There is **the** least restrictive environment which is **the regular classroom**, and then there is **the least restrictive environment** for each child. The presumed placement is always the regular classroom, and the least restrictive environment for each child is selected from a continuum of services (or environments). There are many variations to this continuum which imposes varying degrees of restrictions. Providing indirect support for the regular classroom teacher might be a very unimposing service, while the restrictiveness of direct services and resource room support is a function of the extent of the services and the impact on regular classroom and regular curriculum participation.

Least Restrictive	*No Services*
	Declassified Services **Indirect Services** **Direct Services**

Least Restrictive	***No Services***
▼	**Resource**
▼	**Special classes**
▼	**Special schools**
▼	**Home**
Most Restrictive	**Hospitals and institutions**

The above "continuum" does not tell the entire story. The task is not to find the specific environment from a series of discrete placements in which a child can function successfully, but to enable "to the maximum extent appropriate" a child with a disability to be educated with nondisabled children. The choice is not a regular classroom or a special classroom, but to

> **Continuum of Alternative Placements.**
> **34 CFR 300.551**
>
> (a) Each public agency shall ensure that a continuum of alternative placements is available to meet that needs of children with disabilities for special education and related services.
> (b) The continuum required in paragraph (a) of this section must--
>   (1) Include the alternative placements listed in the definition of special education classes, special schools, home instruction, and instruction in hospitals and institutions); and
>   (2) Make provision for supplementary services (such as resource room or itinerant instruction) to be provided in conjunction with regular class placement.

maximize the amount of time that a child can be educated with nondisabled children. If an alternative placement is required, the task is to provide the least restrictive placement. The continuum of services cited in the regulations is often incorrectly interpreted as distinct and mutually exclusive program options ranging from least to most restrictive. If a child is identified as having a specific learning disability, resource room services are automatically provided. This, however, is contrary to the "maximum extent appropriate provision." For some children with specific learning disabilities, all services might be provided in the regular classroom and for other children the resource room services required might range from one hour to ten hours per week.

The continuum of services is not a discrete series of placements so that if a child cannot participate in the regular classroom one hundred percent, the next consideration is a one hundred percent placement in a self-contained setting, or a one hundred percent placement in a residential setting. "The school must take intermediate steps where appropriate, such as placing the child in regular education for some academic classes and in special education for others, mainstreaming the child for nonacademic classes only, or providing interaction with nonhandicapped children during lunch and recess. The appropriate mix will vary from child to child and . . . from school year to school year as the child develops. If the school officials have provided the maximum appropriate exposure to nonhandicapped students, they have fulfilled their obligation under the EHA."[174]

Although not explicitly stated in the regulations, consultant teacher services are a part of the continuum of services to enable children with disabilities to participate with nondisabled children to the maximum extent appropriate. In order to enable classroom participation, the IEP team might determine that a child can spend one hundred percent of the school day in the regular classroom, with supplementary aids and services, and no time in a restrictive setting. There is no requirement for a special education placement; nor is there a requirement that a special education teacher must work individually in a separate location. If a child receives services under IDEA, the following must be provided:

First, specially-designed instruction which "means adapting, as appropriate to the needs of an eligible child under this part, the content, methodology, or delivery of instruction."[175]

Second, specially designed instruction in the least restrictive environment.

Third, an opportunity to participate in the regular classroom and the regular curriculum.

Of course, there is no one model for all possible consultant teacher services. Several children might need primarily direct services to participate in a regular classroom, another school or grade might emphasize indirect consultant teacher services, and a district with several schools might provide consultant teacher services on an itinerant basis for children in public and private schools.[176]

If services cannot be provided satisfactorily in the regular classroom with supplementary aids and services, the child must participate with nondisabled children to the maximum extent appropriate; that is, the regular classroom is not an all-or-nothing placement but every child with a disability should participate in the regular classroom and in the general curriculum to the maximum extent appropriate. New York State has expanded the recommended continuum of placements to include transitional support services and consultant teacher services.[177] These placement options are not mutually exclusive so that "the percent of each instructional school day during which a student is provided any one or combination of the special education programs and services shall be in keeping with the unique needs of the student."[178] Arkansas has extended the sensitivity of the continuum of services by differentiating between indirect and direct teacher services. The least restrictive environment is one in which a child receives indirect services (e.g., a consultant teacher assists in planning, modifications, etc.), while the next placement on the continuum is one in which some direct instruction is involved (e.g., by a special education teacher or consultant teacher) but less than twenty-one percent of the time is spent outside of the regular classroom.

Consultant teacher services play an important role in the continuum of services. When considering the least restrictive environment from the continuum of services, the regular classroom with only indirect services provides a minimally restrictive access to the regular classroom and regular curriculum. Arkansas and Massachusetts both include a regular classroom placement option with only indirect services as part of the continuum of services. Massachusetts refers to this as a *consultation* (indirect services to school personnel and parents) service deliver option, followed by special education and related services in the general education classroom (a direct service option), and special education and related services in other settings (also a direct service option). This is similar to Arkansas which has an indirect service option, followed by some direct instruction, up to fifty percent of the instructional day in resource room services, a minimum of fifty percent of the instructional day in special classes, school-based day treatment, special day school facility, residential school, hospital program, and homebound instruction.

A school district need not have a position called consultant teacher, or that there is an option in the state code called direct or indirect services, or consultant teacher services. The least restrictive environment mandate requires a continuum of services and this begins with indirect services, followed by direct/indirect services, resource room support, special classes, etc.

Can consultant teacher services be restrictive? Absolutely! If accommodations are made to the general curriculum that are in excess of what a student needs, or hinders access to the regular curriculum (no matter how altruistic the motive), the services are too restrictive. The purpose for consultant teaching direct services is not simply to provide direct instruction in the regular classroom, but to enable regular classroom participation, and these services should be focused and as least restrictive as possible.

COMPARING IDEA, SECTION 504 AND DSM-IV DISABILITIES

This might seem confusing that a child could have a disability under Section 504 but not IDEA but it does make sense . . . sort of. To be disabled under IDEA you must meet two conditions: First, you must have one of the **disabilities listed in the regulations**;[179] second, you **must need specially designed instruction**.

The criteria for a disability under Section 504 is different than IDEA because the purpose of IDEA is to ensure an appropriate education, while the purpose of Section 504 is prevent a child with a disability from being "excluded from the participation in, be denied benefits of, or be subjected to discrimination under any program or activity receiving Federal financial assistance."[180] Under IDEA a disability must be one of those listed in the regulations and there must be a need for special education; under Section 504 a disability means "any person who:

a. has a physical or mental impairment which substantially limits one or more major life activities,

b. has a record of such an impairment, or

c. is regarded as having such an impairment.[181]

Students who have been misclassified under IDEA as disabled would be covered by Section 504, as well as students with a record of heart disease, cancer, etc. Likewise, Section 504 "includes some persons who might not ordinarily be considered handicapped, such as persons with disfiguring scars, as well as persons who have no physical or mental impairment but are treated by a recipient as if they were handicapped."[182]

For all professionals interested in inclusion, an essential mandate is not to classify children who are not disabled simply because they have learning problems. An IEP team might be all too willing to say that a child has a disability and then fret about including the child in regular classes. If a child does not have a disability, inclusion in regular classes should be automatic. By not classifying a child as having an IDEA-based disability when they do, or classifying a child as having an IDEA disabilities when they do not have a disability under IDEA or do not need special education, resources will be

233

siphoned from children who are eligible for IDEA services. Furthermore, children who are misclassified are often segregated from the regular classroom and from the general curriculum, or at least not educated the way chil-

---

Section 504 Impairments
34 CFR 104.3(j)(iv)

Is regarded as having an impairment means (A) has a physical or mental impairment that does not substantially limit major life activities but that is treated by a recipient as constituting such a limitation; (B) has a physical or mental impairment that substantially limits major life activities only as a result of the attitudes of others toward such impairment; or (C) has none of the impairments defined in paragraph (j)(2)(i) of this section but is treated by a recipient as having such an impairment.

---

dren without disabilities are educated (especially when access to the regular classroom or general curriculum is restricted). Rather than being a license to exclude children from regular classes, the IDEA criteria for services should be viewed as the first line of defense for ensuring that children are not needlessly removed from the regular classroom or deprived of regular classroom services.

When IDEA first appeared in 1975 (P.L. 94-142) the impetus for the law was the realization that many children with disabilities were not being served, and many who were receiving special education were receiving a less than appropriate education. In some cases, a self-contained classroom is tantamount to *de jure* segregation or segregation that is sanctioned by law. If children who are not disabled are incorrectly identified, not only will resources that would otherwise be directed toward children with real disabilities be misused, but the reason for the identification might be because of lack of instruction or because of a segregative intent.

Lack of instruction is not a disability, and neither is poverty or environmental disadvantage, and these factors should not be used to correct deficiencies in an educational system under the guise of special education.

Just as a correct classification can ensure an appropriate allocation of resources and prevent unwarranted or discriminatory services (e.g., segregating black children in self-contained classes), an appropriate IDEA identification can ensure that children with real disabilities receive services. A child with traumatic brain injury might need extensive services, even though these services are quite costly to the school district; a child with a visual or hearing impairment might need specialized curriculum accommodations, and a child with autism or emotional disturbance might require an array of school and special education resources. For the most part, with the exception of the much tainted mental retardation category, the classification process provides direction for a child's needs and a threshold test that the child does require special education.

For the very large specific learning disabilities category, the definition of a specific learning disability excludes problems caused by "environmental, cultural, or economic disadvantage,"[183] and for all disabilities a child cannot receive services under IDEA because of "lack of instruction in reading or math" or because of limited English proficiency.[184] In Wisconsin, identifying a child as learning disabled cannot be the result of "learning problems result-ing from extended absence, continuous inadequate instruction, curriculum planning, or instructional strategies. Discrepancies between ability and school achievement due to motivation. Functioning at grade level but with potential for greater achievement."[185]

Even if a child has a disability under IDEA, the IEP team might decide that the child does not need special education. In this case, the child is not eligible for IDEA services, but the child is eligible for any and all services, devices and accommodations under Section 504 (because the child does have a disability).

DSM-IV! This stands for the Diagnostic Statistical Manual of Mental Disorders, fourth edition, which is often used by psychologists (and lawyers) to interpret the meaning of behaviors (or the lack thereof). The DSM-IV is useful for determining emotional disturbance, autism, attention-deficit/hyperactivity disorder, etc. A DSM-IV classification can be used in conjunction with either IDEA or Section 504 to establish the existence of a disability. Although the DSM-IV often provides more explicit guidelines, as is the case with attention-deficit/hyperactivity disorder, which can be used in conjunction with Section 504 or IDEA, DSM-IV criteria do not override IDEA and must be consistent with IDEA and/or Section 504 disability cri-teria. For example, the only guideline under IDEA for hyperactivity is that the disability category Other Health Impairment can include "a heightened alertness to environmental stimuli that results in limited alertness with respect to the educational environment"[186] while for *inattention* the DSM-IV requires six or more of the following symptoms to have existed for at least six months: careless mistakes, sustained attention, not listening, failure to fin-ish tasks, organizational difficulties, avoids tasks requiring "sustained mental effort," loses things required for tasks, easily distracted by stimuli, and often forgetful.

As can be seen DSM-IV for certain disabilities can be more explicit than IDEA and far more explicit than the very general definition for disabilities given under Section 504. For example, the determination of an Other Health Impairment (OHI) might be very clear when the disability is a specific life-threatening or debilitating disease (e.g., heart condition, leukemia, diabetes, asthma), but very murky when the problem is ADD/ADHD which is defined under OHI as "a heightened alertness to environmental stimuli that results in limited alertness with respect to the educational environment."[187]

SECTION 504 MADE EASY
(OR SECTION 504 IS YOUR FRIEND!)

Disability classification ensures that children who need services receive services, and children who do not need services are not misclassified.

Section 504 is a friend of the consultant teacher. Section 504 ensures that a child who has a disability, who has had a disability, or who is perceived of as having a disability is provided with all necessary special education, related services, and accommodations and modifications to receive an appropriate education. If a child has a disability but does not need special education, or if a child no longer has a disability, schools are required to accommodate each child's needs resulting from the disability. Traditionally, Section 504 is used when a child needs specific accommodations such as an air purifier or special desk, or a specific service such as an aide or interpreter, but Section 504 can also be used to provide any and all services when a child has a disability under the Section 504 definition of a disability and when IDEA does not apply. Although Section 504 services or accommodations can be documented by a Section 504 plan, a simple written statement, or an IEP can be used to specify services.

THE ESSENTIAL CONSULTANT TEACHER
SECTION 504 GUIDE

1. The law refers to the Rehabilitation Act of 1973 (P.L. 93-112, and P.L. 102-569) and, specifically, to the Rights and Advocacy section of this law.

2. Section 504 is simple and concise and states that you cannot discriminate against a child (or anyone else for that matter) because of a disability.

3. Section 504 is not intended to provide financial support for services (like IDEA) but to prevent discrimination.

4. Section 504 has a very broad definition of a disability (unlike the very specific IDEA disability categories).

5. Under Section 504 all necessary services must be provided for a child who has a disability but does not need special education (e.g., a child with an Other Health Impairment who needs an accommodation but not "special education"), no longer has a disability (e.g., has been declassified), or is treated as having a disability.

6. A Section 504 plan means that a child does not have a disability under IDEA, or does not need specially designed instruction, but has a disability under the broad Section 504 definition.

7. The school district (or local educational agency) has the ultimate responsibility for providing Section 504 Services. This could be done under the auspices of the IEP team (good choice) or Section 504 team, or a group designated by the school district.

8. The law does not use the words "Section 504 plan" although a school can use an IEP, a plan or Section 504 services document or whatever to specify services.

9. If a child is not eligible for IDEA services, the child is not eligible under IDEA to receive related services such as speech or occupa-

tional rehabilitation. However, a student who has a disability under Section 504 would be eligible to receive these and all other necessary services.

10. A student can receive special education under Section 504 if necessary. For example, a student who was declassified might need special education services, consultant teacher services, or resource room services.

11. Section 504 is frequently used to provide accommodations for children with disabilities who do not need special education (e.g., large print materials, an air purifier for a child with asthma, wheelchair accommodations, extended time for students with special test needs).

12. The special education consultant teacher is often in the best position to monitor and, if necessary, provide Section 504 services.

13. Section 504 is frequently used for children who need specific accommodations (e.g., extra time, computer, large print) but who do not need special education. A child requires an accommodation to mitigate the effects of a disability, but does not require special education to adapt "the content, methodology, or delivery of instruction" as with IDEA.[188]

14. Section 504 can be use to provide services and accommodations for students who have been declassified, or who are not disabled under IDEA.

The mandate to require services via Section 504, when IDEA does not apply, should be clear to schools and IEP teams. The school district has the ultimate responsibility to ensure that children with disabilities are not discriminated against because of their disability. Unlike IDEA which has guidelines for providing an appropriate education (the "regulations"), the regulations for Section 504 are sketchy. However, the mandate is certainly clear enough for all concerned: Don't discriminate by not providing appropriate services and accommodations.

SECTION 504 CONSULTANT TEACHER SERVICES

In all likelihood the consultant teacher will be employed to provide direct and indirect services for children identified under IDEA who need specially designed instruction. Nonetheless, children with disabilities who do not need specially designed instruction or who are otherwise not eligible for services under IDEA will need supervision and/or services to ensure that each child receives all accommodations and services as per Section 504. Every child receiving a Section 504 accommodation or service should have a qualified service provider, and when the service or accommodation involves special education, this should be the consultant teacher.

Consultant Teacher Section 504 Responsibilities

- Provide information concerning the difference between IDEA and Section 504.

- Ensure that children not disabled under IDEA, but are under Section 504, receive appropriate services.

- Present Section 504 as an option, when appropriate, at IEP team meetings.

- Ensure that Section 504 services are provided and supervised by qualified personnel.

- Evaluate the effectiveness of Section 504 services.

- Consider Section 504 services during the declassification process.

OBERTI v. BOARD OF EDUCATION
995 F.2D 1204 (3RD CIR. 1993)[189]

Oberti v. Board of Education emphasizes that school districts must consider the "whole range of supplemental aids and services," and provides a cogent rationale for *inclusion* by quoting an earlier hearing decision that the parents "have left no stone unturned in seeking to have their child educated in a fashion which will prepare him for inclusion as an adult in the community at large" (p. 1324).

Rafael Oberti was classified as having a developmental disability including mental retardation resulting from Down's Syndrome. The school wanted to place Rafael in an out-of-district while the parents objected and requested a regular kindergarten placement. After unsuccessful mediation an administrative hearing affirmed the school's request for a segregated placement. The District Court of New Jersey opined that "the parties presented contrasting and self-serving characterizations of Rafael's experiences." The parents emphasized Rafael's progress in school, while the school focused on behavioral and communication difficulties.

The district court reasoned that if behavior was such a problem then the "the School District's remedial responses to these problems appear to have been woefully inadequate." The school district's approach was "informal" and "reactive," and that no plan was no written plan or real consideration given to the development and implementation of "an individualized educational or management plan." After hearing additional testimony the court decided in 801 F.Supp. 1392 (D.N.J. 1992) that the school district had not established that Rafael could not be educated in the regular classroom with supplementary aids and services.

The court of appeals affirmed this decision in 995 F.2d 1204 (3rd Cir. 1993) by stating that "the record reflects that the School District had access to information and expertise about specific methods and services to enable children with disabilities like Rafael to be included in a regular classroom, *see supra* at 1211, but that the School District did not provide such supplementary aids and services for Rafael in the kindergarten class" and that "the School District develop a more inclusive program for Rafael in compliance with IDEA for the upcoming school year."

PLACEMENT GUIDELINES FOR THE CONSULTANT TEACHER

Today, the growing problem is over identifying children as disabled when they might not be truly disabled.

-Senate Report 105-17

1. Regular classroom teacher input is important before, during and after placing a child.

2. Parents must participate in the placement process.

3. Indicate the type of special education needed in the regular classroom.

4. Indicate needed supplementary (e.g., resource room) services.

5. Determine needed classroom accommodations before placement.

6. Consider academic and nonacademic participation.

7. Determine needed support services for the placement.

8. Consider needed supplementary services (e.g., resource room services).

9. Develop goals to increase the amount of regular classroom placement.

10. The placement must be based on the child's IEP.

11. The placement "is as close as possible to the child's home."

12. "Unless the IEP of a child with a disability requires some other arrangement, the child is educated in the school that he or she would attend if nondisabled."

13. "In selecting the LRE, consideration is given to any potential harmful effect on the child or on the quality of services that he or she needs."

14. "A child with a disability is not removed from education in age-appropriate regular classrooms solely because of needed modifications in the general curriculum".

15. If an alternate setting is required, the setting should be directed toward regular classroom placement which is the purpose of developing independence.

16. The placement should be reviewed at least annually.[190]

PULL-OUT SERVICES

In a case where the segregated facility is considered superior, the court should determine whether the services which make that placement superior could be feasibly provided in a non-segregated setting. If they can, the placement in the segregated school would be inappropriate under the Act.[191]

A pull-out service might be a necessary supplement to the regular classroom (e.g., resource room or itinerant services), or to develop a skill, ability, or behavior necessary to participate in the classroom or curriculum. This is the reason why the continuum of services required by every school district requires "supplementary services (such as resource room or itinerant instruction) to be provided in conjunction with regular class placement."[192]

The goal of "full-inclusion" is certainly noteworthy, but the obligation is to provide appropriate services and there are occasions when pull-out services are necessary and appropriate. For example, pull-out services might be necessary for resource room services, itinerant services, related services (e.g., counseling, psychological services, speech and language services), testing when specialized accommodations are required (e.g., reading a test to a child), specialized remediation, and remediation and activities involving specialized equipment.

Although a pull-out service might be appropriate, these services can be disruptive and ineffective unless the consultant teacher carefully orchestrates each pull-out service with overall classroom participation by collaborating with the regular classroom teacher and related service provider, ensuring only **needed** pull-out services are provided, and using pull-out services to promote (and not limit) regular classroom participation.

244

PULL-OUT SERVICE TIPS FOR THE CONSULTANT TEACHER

Collaborate with the regular classroom teacher in the identification and implementation of pull-out services. If the regular classroom teacher is unaware of a service, the pull-out service has been poorly planned.

Consider whether the pull-out service can be provided in the regular classroom.

Plan with the pull-out service provider how the service can be generalized to the regular classroom, and what the regular classroom teacher and consultant teacher can do to facilitate this generalization.

Identify classroom skills which might be improved by the pull-out service.

Ensure that a pull-out service does not conflict with important classroom activities.

Coordinate and schedule each pull-out activity with regular classroom participation and all other services.

Evaluate the regular classroom effectiveness of each pull-out service.

Remember that pull-out services should be as least restrictive and disruptive as possible.

DECLASSIFICATION

The 24th Annual Report to Congress indicated that 162,580 students between the ages of 14 and 21+ graduated with a high school diploma.

Declassification should be considered on an annual basis. Special education or remediation might be effective so the disability is minimized (e.g., a child with a specific learning disability in basic reading now reads at grade level) or the need for specially designed instruction no longer exists.

Often the task of the consultant teacher is to increase regular classroom and regular curriculum participation while decreasing the need for his or her services. In many cases a child's disability is not eliminated, but the need for special education is. A child with an orthopedic impairment is able to fully participate in the regular classroom and speech services are no longer needed, or classroom behavior is entirely consistent with regular classroom expectations.

The goal, over a period of time, should be to develop independent classroom participation to the maximum extent appropriate and that, under ideal circumstances, the role of the special education consultant teacher should decrease rather than increase. Certainly there are situations when a child will need a constant level of services, or possibly even an increase in the level of extent of direct and indirect services, but this should not deter the special education consultant teacher from the goal of independent classroom participation to the maximum extent appropriate. Table 4 provides data relating to the exit pattern from IDEA services for children with various types of disabilities.[193] These data are based on reports from schools for children who no longer receive special education but "who were served in special education during the previous reporting year but at some point during that twelve-month period, returned to regular education as a result of having met the objectives of their IEP. These are students who no longer have an IEP and are receiving all of their educational services from a general education program."[194]

As shown in Table 4 the percentage of children who no longer receive services is inversely related to age for all disabilities, but this inverse relationship is most prominent for speech and language impairments.

As part of the annual review[195] the IEP team must determine whether the child continues to have a disability[196] or "whether the child continues to need special education and related services."[197] If there is some concern as to whether a child is ready to be declassified, indirect services consisting of

246

Table 4: Number of Students With Disabilities Exiting Special Education

Age	All Dis.		SLD		Speech&L	
	N	%	N	%	N	%
14	15587	23.16	8395	21.41	4178	41.08
15	15358	22.82	9070	23.13	2539	24.96
16	13974	20.76	8445	21.54	1572	15.45
17	11975	17.79	7142	18.21	1101	10.82
18	7236	10.75	4356	11.11	580	5.70
19	2198	3.26	1314	3.35	157	1.54
20	553	0.82	299	0.76	32	0.31
21+	405	0.60	181	0.46	11	0.10
Total	67286	100	39202	100	10170	100

observation and planning with regular education teachers might be an appropriate step in the declassification process. If a child is declassified, and no longer has a disability under IDEA or no longer needs special education, declassification support services and/or any modifications that a child might need would still be required under Section 504. For a child who is declassified, and no longer receives services under IDEA, an IEP might be used to designate necessary support services and modifications.[198] After a student has been declassified the consultant teacher (under the auspices of the IEP team responsible for the declassification should:

- Monitor the student's progress at least quarterly.

- Meet with the regular classroom teacher at least quarterly.

- Evaluate the student's overall classroom progress (e.g., tests, final grades, state and district-wide test participation) annually.

- Discuss with the student's parents school progress and needs.

- Don't abandon a student who has been declassified.

- Ensure that post-classification accommodations are being provided.

- Declassified students are eligible for all needed services and accommodations under Section 504 (because they have "a record of such an impairment").

MAINSTREAMING

... the mainstreaming issue imposes a difficult burden.
-Roncker v. Walter

The term **mainstreaming** is often used to refer to children who are placed in special education classes and who are subsequently mainstreamed into regular education classes. This use of the term is not entirely correct because it suggests that a child with a disability is first placed in a special education setting and then mainstreamed to the maximum extent appropriate. The IDEA actually presumes "mainstreaming" and a child is only removed from regular classes if participation in the classroom or curriculum have not been satisfactory with supplementary aids and services.

Essential Mainstreaming for the Consultant Teacher

- **Mainstreaming is a presumption and not an earned right. The first placement for every child is always the "mainstream."**

- **There is a "mainstream" classroom (The Regular Classroom) and a "mainstream" curriculum (The General Curriculum).**

- **Supplementary aids and services are the key to mainstreaming.**

- **The goal is to enable a child to participate "satisfactorily."**

- **Support for the regular classroom teacher is essential for effective mainstreaming.**

- **Mainstream to the maximum extent possible.**

- **The consultant teacher should strive to increase participation in the regular classroom.**

- **Regardless of a child's placement, the consultant teacher should promote participation in the general curriculum to the maximum extent appropriate.**

Mainstreaming is not mentioned in the law or regulations, and what is regarded as "mainstreaming" is really the Least Restrictive Environment provision of IDEA "for with this provision Congress created a strong preference for mainstreaming."[199] The term predates the first comprehensive special education law (P.L. 94-142) and refers to the placement in the educational mainstream unless "the nature or severity of the disability of a child is such that education in regular classes with the use of supplementary aids and services cannot be achieved satisfactorily."

There are actually two "mainstreams" which are of concern to the consultant teacher: The **regular classroom mainstream** and the **general curriculum mainstream**. There are certainly benefits from being educated with nondisabled children besides academic growth, but the phrase "educated with children who are nondisabled" obviously places a strong emphasis on the benefits of the general curriculum in the regular classroom. If a child is not able to participate in the general curriculum in the regular classroom, the consultant teacher should ensure that the child is able to participate in the general curriculum in whatever alternative setting is provided.

"THE MAINSTREAMING PROVISION"[200]

The Act does not require mainstreaming in every case but its requirement that mainstreaming be provided to the maximum extent appropriate indicates a very strong congressional preference.
-Roncker v. Walter, p. 1063

The following is the "mainstreaming" provision . . . and the "inclusion" provision and the basic requirement underlying all special education laws and regulations:

(A) IN GENERAL- To the maximum extent appropriate, children with disabilities, including children in public or private institutions or other care facilities, are educated with children who are not disabled, and special classes, separate schooling, or other removal of children with disabilities from the regular educational environment occurs only when the nature or severity of the disability of a child is such that education in regular classes with the use of supplementary aids and services cannot be achieved satisfactorily.

(B) ADDITIONAL REQUIREMENT-
(i) IN GENERAL-[201] If the State uses a funding mechanism by which the State distributes State funds on the basis of the type of setting in which a child is served, the funding mechanism does not result in placements that violate the requirements of subparagraph (A).

(ii) ASSURANCE- If the State does not have policies and procedures to ensure compliance with clause (i), the State shall provide the Secretary an assurance that it will revise the funding mechanism as soon as feasible to ensure that such mechanism does not result in such placements.

INCLUSION

Must a child's IEP address his or her involvement in the general curriculum, regardless of the nature and severity of the child's disability and the setting in which the child is educated? Yes.[202]

Like mainstreaming, "inclusion" is not mentioned in either the law or regulations. How does mainstreaming differ from inclusion? Some regard the two concepts as essentially the same, others treat inclusion as both a philosophy and a legal mandate, while others consider inclusion the right for all children. As of late the term inclusion has gained in popularity because *inclusion* refers to a far-reaching inclusion and acceptance of individuals with disabilities, while mainstreaming has been associated (especially by the courts) with the educational mainstream.

Many schools adopt an inclusion or mainstreaming philosophy that dictates the type of direct service a child receives. As is the case with placements, services are selected based on need rather than on what is available, what is convenient, or what seems to be the most cost-effective approach. Consultant teacher services should not be married to one methodology or philosophy, but should draw upon a variety of strategies, resources and methodologies to achieve the ultimate goal for all children with disabilities: the ability to function independently in the regular classroom to the maximum extent appropriate.

Inclusion is not mentioned in IDEA but the term is cited in Title II of the amended Rehabilitation Act of 1973 (P.L. 102-569) when describing activities "to maximize the full inclusion and integration into society, employment, independent living, family support, and economic and social self-sufficiency of individuals with disabilities of all ages, with particular emphasis on improving the effectiveness of services authorized under this Act." When used in schools the term inclusion certainly "includes" mainstreaming but also emphasizes the broader and post-school need to prepare students for inclusion in the work force, for independent living, and in society in general. The term *inclusion* goes beyond the judicial interpretation of the LRE provision as a preference for mainstreaming and concerns our core attitudes and practices for a truly inclusive society, but as is the case for mainstreaming, there is a decided preference for inclusion in IDEA.

For the consultant teacher **mainstreaming** and the requirements for the Least restrictive Environment represent the bottom line in terms of what a child is entitled to under IDEA; inclusion is an environment in which all school personnel are dedicated to including children with disabilities in all school academic and nonacademic activities.

IDEA-based Inclusion for the Consultant Teacher

1. Inclusion is based on the premise that all children will be included in regular education classes; IDEA mandates that children with disabilities will be included in regular education classes to the maximum extent appropriate.

2. A successful inclusive environment is predicated on a school-wide belief that children with disabilities should be included in regular education classes. Requiring participation with nondisabled children is one thing; believing that nondisabled children should participate with nondisabled children is quite another.

3. Inclusion requires collaboration between the regular class-room teacher, the consultant teacher, related service providers and the school administration.

4. Children are included in special education classes by providing the full range of supplementary aides and services.

5. If supplementary aids and service are not successful for including a child in a regular classroom, the child must be included to the maximum extent appropriate.

6. Inclusion applies to all children with disabilities, regardless of the severity of the disability.

7. A child should not be included in regular classes if the placement is not satisfactory and the child's needs are not met.

8. Full inclusion which negates the concept of a continuum of alternate placements is inconsistent with the law.

Inclusion on the Web: The Special Education Service Agency (Anchorage, Alaska) has an excellent site for inclusion "tips" for various disabilities:
http://www.sesa.org/sesa/agency/docs/incltips.html

TOP STATES FOR INCLUSION

What is it about Vermont, North Dakota, and New Hampshire that results in more than seventy-nine percent of children with disabilities to be served in the regular classroom? These states have a commitment to the regular classroom and the inclusion of children in the educational mainstream. These states don't just talk about inclusion and mainstreaming, these states do it, and do it well. And the "it" is educating children with disabilities with nondisabled children to the maximum extent appropriate. Based on OSEP data from the 24th Annual Report to Congress our top ten blue-ribbon states for inclusion are:

1. **North Dakota**
2. **Vermont**
3. **New Hampshire**
4. **Oregon**
5. **Colorado**
6. **South Dakota**
7. **Idaho**
8. **Ohio**
9. **Minnesota**
10. **Massachusetts**

How does your state measure up to including children with disabilities in regular classes? Table 5 shows the percentage of children with disabilities in each state ranked by the percent of time in the regular classroom.[203]

Table 5: Regular Classroom Placements by State

STATE	PERCENTAGE OUTSIDE REGULAR CLASS		
	< 21%	21-60%	> 60%
North Dakota	79.7	14.71	3.84
Vermont	78.27	10.15	5.52
New Hampshire	74.49	16.46	4.4

STATE	PERCENTAGE OUTSIDE REGULAR CLASS		
	< 21%	21-60%	> 60%
Oregon	73.55	15	7.74
Colorado	71.21	15.81	8.94
South Dakota	66.26	24.1	6.26
Idaho	65.8	25.56	7.03
Ohio	64.84	24.94	5.23
Minnesota	64.13	22.09	8.14
Massachusetts	63.85	14.6	14.72
Kansas	59.68	25.05	12.17
Alaska	58.84	28.33	10.8
North Carolina	58.25	22	17.32
Puerto Rico	58.07	15.68	19.87
Indiana	57.37	15.77	24.8
Connecticut	56.43	21.52	16.2
Nebraska	55.86	25.32	16.74
Montana	54.85	31.93	10.93
Alabama	52.23	36.45	8.57
Missouri	51.93	31.62	13.14
Wyoming	51.39	32.05	11.91
Maine	51.3	32.45	13.22
Washington	51.25	33	14.44
Kentucky	49.91	31.88	15.68
Nevada	49.9	32.8	14.65
Florida	49.79	26.25	21.99

STATE	PERCENTAGE OUTSIDE REGULAR CLASS		
	< 21%	21-60%	> 60%
California	49.44	20.19	26.84
West Virginia	48.54	37.31	13.13
Arizona	48.09	31.62	17.3
Mississippi	47.92	28.49	20.96
New York	47.62	13.16	30.73
Rhode Island	47.58	19.37	27.23
Oklahoma	47.41	39.02	12.07
Maryland	46.51	21.96	23.96
Iowa	46.29	34.83	15.21
New Jersey	45.26	25.8	19.25
Michigan	45.25	27.07	20.47
Tennessee	44.97	34.1	18.39
Utah	44.27	31.09	21.22
Wisconsin	41.5	41.14	15.59
Louisiana	39.96	25.4	31.63
Arkansas	38.4	44.52	14.48
Virginia	37.53	33.93	25.44
Illinois	37.34	28.03	28.41
Pennsylvania	35.78	32.81	27.71
Georgia	35.09	35.44	27.47
South Carolina	32.19	40.46	25.53
Delaware	29.76	52.18	13.12

STATE	PERCENTAGE OUTSIDE REGULAR CLASS		
	< 21%	21-60%	> 60%
New Mexico	28.69	31.82	37.42
Texas	28.24	52.04	17.95
Dist. Columbia	22.89	44.72	
Hawaii	18.82	59.03	19.86

Use the above table to determine how your school or district compare to state percentages and then give your school, district or state a grade: A (>80%), B+ (>70%), B (>60%), C+(>50%), C (>40%), D+ (>30%), D (>20).

If a state is low in terms of regular classroom placements (e.g., Hawaii and the District of Columbia), there is usually a corresponding increase in resource room placements (see Table 5 and the Resource Room Top Ten shown below).

☛ Resource room services are appropriate when the service supplements the regular classroom and promotes regular classroom participation; resource room services are not appropriate when a child can be educated in the regular classroom with supplementary aids and services.

The Resource Room Top Ten

STATE	< 21%	21-60%	> 60%
HAWAII	18.82	59.03	19.86
DELAWARE	29.76	52.18	13.12
TEXAS	28.24	52.04	17.95
DIST. OF COLUMBIA	22.89	44.72	
ARKANSAS	38.4	44.52	14.48
WISCONSIN	41.5	41.14	15.59

STATE	< 21%	21-60%	> 60%
SOUTH CAROLINA	32.19	40.46	25.53
OKLAHOMA	47.41	39.02	12.07
WEST VIRGINIA	48.54	37.31	13.13
ALABAMA	52.23	36.45	8.57

Five states have regular classroom placements for children with disabilities in excess of 70%, and five states have inclusion rates less than 30%. The following table compares the number of children with various disabilities served in high and low-inclusion states.

NORTH DAKOTA	79.7
VERMONT	78.27
NEW HAMPSHIRE	74.49
OREGON	73.55
COLORADO	71.21
DELAWARE	29.76
NEW MEXICO	28.69
TEXAS	28.24
DIST. COL.	22.89
HAWAII	18.82

Increasing the amount of time children with disabilities spend in the regular classroom has been steadily on the rise. As shown in Table 6 the percentage of regular classroom placements has increased from 1990-1991 to 1999-2000 from 32.83 percent to 49.9 percent. This has resulted in a corresponding decrease in resource room placements from 36.46 percent in 1990 to 29.87 percent in 2000.[204] The number of self-contained classroom placements (>60% of the time outside of the regular classroom) decreased, but at a slower rate, from 25.09 percent in 1990 to 21.38 percent in 2000. The trend for regular classroom participation will continue, and to this end all special education consultant teachers and the ever increasing number of special education teachers providing consultant teacher services must focus on enabling children with disabilities to participate in the regular classroom and regular curriculum.

Table 6: Special Education Placements from 1990 to 2000

Year	Time Outside of Regular Classroom			
	< 21%	21-60%	> 60%	Other
1990-91	32.83	36.46	25.09	5.62
1991-92	34.91	36.30	23.52	5.27
1992-93	39.82	31.67	23.45	5.06
1993-94	43.38	29.46	22.73	4.43
1994-95	44.48	28.75	22.44	4.33
1995-96	45.35	28.68	21.60	4.38
1996-97	45.80	28.52	21.41	4.26
1997-98	46.42	29.04	20.41	4.13
1998-99	48.92	29.33	20.69	4.06
1999-00	49.90	29.87	21.38	4.07

THE DO'S AND DON'TS OF INCLUSION

DO'S

• Do encourage the regular classroom teacher to include the child in classroom activities.

• Do encourage group activities and peer-assisted help.

• Do prepare the child for the regular classroom curriculum.

• Do have high expectations.

• Do provide structure when appropriate.

• Do have classroom rules for all children.

• Do use the IEP as a road map for providing classroom accommodations and modifications.

• Do allow the child to function as independently as possible.

DON'TS

• Don't place a child in a regular classroom without planning with the regular classroom teacher.

• Don't provide a separate curriculum.

• Don't minimize or prevent opportunities to participate in the regular classroom.

• Don't entrust a child's regular classroom participation to an aide.

• Don't ignore instructional needs in the regular classroom: The regular classroom setting is half the battle but the test is whether education in regular classes with the use of supplementary aids and services can be achieved satisfactorily.[205]

• Don't treat the regular classroom as a privilege.

• Don't dump a child with a disability in a regular classroom without adequate support.

• Don't focus solely on one-to-one instruction either by an aide or special education teacher.

• Don't ignore the regular classroom teacher's expertise.

• Don't exempt a child from activities in which the child is able to participate with modifications: Remember that a child cannot be "removed from education in age-appropriate regular classrooms solely because of needed modifications in the general curriculum."[206]

Part VII
Consultant Teacher Essentials

"The appropriate placement for a particular child with a disability cannot be determined until after decisions have been made about the child's needs and the services that the public agency will provide to meet those needs. These decisions must be made at the IEP meeting, and it would not be permissible first to place the child and then develop the IEP. Therefore, the IEP must be developed before placement. (Further, the child's placement must be based, among other factors, on the child's IEP.)"[207]

PARENTS AND SERVICES

Related services are not just for children with disabilities but can also be provided for parents. The purpose of a related service is to help a child to benefit from special education and parents play an integral role in whether or not a child will benefit from special education. Psychological services can involve "consulting with other staff members in planning school programs to meet the special needs of children as indicated by psychological tests, interviews, and behavioral evaluations" and "planning and managing a program of psychological services, **including psychological counseling for children and parents.**"[208] Social work services can entail "**Working in partnership with parents** and others on those problems in a child's living situation (home, school, and community) that affect the child's adjustment in school" and "mobilizing school and community resources to enable the child to learn as effectively as possible in his or her educational program.[209] Speech-language pathology can involve "**Counseling and guidance of parents**, children, and teachers regarding speech and language impairments."[210]

CLASSROOM AIDES

Every aide for a child with a disability should be trained and supervised on a daily basis by a qualified special education teacher.

For many children an aide is essential for inclusion in the regular classroom and/or curriculum. A classroom aide can provide individual instruction, make curriculum modifications, and provide invaluable assistance for dealing with behavior management issues. The reason why aides for children with disabilities are often misused in the classroom is the result of insufficient training and supervision.

> Personnel Standards
> 34 CFR 300.136(f)
>
> Use of paraprofessionals and assistants. A State may allow paraprofessionals and assistants who are appropriately trained and supervised, in accordance with State law, **regulations**, or written policy, in meeting the requirements of this part to be used to assist in the provision of special education and related services to children with disabilities under Part B of the Act.

The most inappropriate use of a classroom aide is assign the aide responsibility for a child's education. When this occurs, the intent is not to include the children in the classroom, nor to provide special education, but to create a fiction that an unsupervised and untrained aide, albeit provided on a full-time basis, somehow will provide a child an "appropriate" education. This is the criticism *Oberti v. Board of Education* that if the child in this case "was as difficult as the defendants claim he was, provision of a personnel aide in March (instigated by a request from the parents), without any definite plan with respect to her functions, and irregular, *ad hoc*, assistance from another teacher and the school psychologist, were wholly insufficient efforts" (p. 1332) to meet this child's needs.

Classroom aides can be invaluable for making classroom and curriculum accommodations, and providing the daily assistance necessary for a child to successfully participate in the classroom. However, an aide, assistant teacher, or paraprofessional is never the teacher of record for a child with a disability and should never have sole responsibility for the implementation of services and program modifications.

So that children with disabilities do "participate" and are "successful" in regular classrooms, classroom aides, and paraprofessionals must be included in classroom planning, must be an integral part of the "mainstreaming" or "inclusion" plan to enable classroom participation, and must be adequately trained and supervised. Hints that the use of an aide or paraprofessional is inappropriate:

"The aide does everything for the child."

"The aide does all the special education."

"Ask the aide what to do."

"The aide doesn't like the IEP."

"The aide does the child's work."

"The aide runs the classroom."

"The aide supervises the teacher."

"The aide does not like to be told what to do."

"The aide is the boss."

"The aide knows best."

"The aide has her own program."

In reality, aides and all paraprofessionals should be part of the team, and if not part of the team, either by choice or inclination, they should not be on the team. The following are several basic considerations which apply to all aides and paraprofessionals.

Aides must be trained: Yes, you have read this before, but it deserves repeating, and being repeated many times over! Aides must be trained. Provide training for aides relating to all instructional activities, testing, and curriculum accommodations. Do not assume that an aide or paraprofessional will know what to do, or how or when to do it.

A basic provision of IDEA is that states "may allow paraprofessionals and assistants who are appropriately trained and supervised, in accordance with State law, **regulations**, or written policy, in meeting the requirements of this part to be used to assist in the provision of special education and related services to children with disabilities "[211] Also see the No Child Left Behind Act of 2002 for guidelines concerning the duties and responsibilities of paraprofessionals.[212]

Aides must be supervised: As noted by the district court in *Oberti v. Board of Education*[213] when discussing the use of an aide to manage a child's behavior, the use of an aide without a real plan and with only token assistance from another teacher is "wholly insufficient." An aid, whether working with a child with a disability in the regular classroom or in a more restrictive setting, must be supervised by a teacher qualified in special education and, to some degree, by the regular education teacher. This "irregular, ad hoc assistance" from a regular classroom teacher is exactly what is wrong with the use of aides in the regular classroom. No wonder that aides assume authority and responsibility for which they are often dedicated but ill-equipped. Aides must be supervised and this supervision should be provided by a qualified special education teacher and in collaboration with the classroom teacher.

Aides are not special education teachers: State guidelines for permissible aides responsibilities must be followed. If the purpose of a classroom aide is to provide added instructional time for the classroom teacher (e.g., making curriculum modifications, materials), this role does not change when a child with a disability is in the classroom. If an aide is assigned to work with a child with a disability, so that the aide is the *de facto* special education teacher, the purpose of the aide and the purpose of special education is compromised. In *Girty v. Valley Grove School District*, classroom teachers were given, at the very best, token support (e.g., voluntary in-service training) and the education of the child identified as being mentally retarded was entrusted to that of an aide with little training or supervision.[214] In this situation the use of an aide, and therefore special education, seems be a step back from an appropriate education. If a child needs special education and specially designed instruction, that instruction must be provided by qualified personnel. Although paraprofessionals and assistants can "be used to assist in the provision of special education,"[215] "suitable qualifications for personnel providing special education"[216] must be established by states.

The general rule of thumb is that an aide should not be assigned to a child as the sole provider of services. An appropriate education means services professionals trained to provide specially designed instruction. Doing otherwise (assigning an aide as the primary and often only service provider) is the most inappropriate service an IEP team can provide. This is not what parents should expect, this is not what children deserve, and this is not what the IEP team should do. This is professionally unethical, contrary to IDEA and the regulations, and discriminatory.

Aides must have a clear idea of responsibilities: The task is not for the aide to create activities for a child. The aide assists in the implementation of activities, strategies, interventions, modifications stated in the IEP that enable participation in the classroom. Decisions relating to specially designed instruction are not made by the aide, but by qualified special education personnel (the consultant teacher). The task of the aide is not to "occupy" a child while the class engages in academic or other classroom activities, but to facilitate the child's participation in the curriculum. To achieve this goal the aide must be given clearly defined tasks concerning how the child can and should participate in the curriculum.

The services provided by a classroom aide must be planned: What is most unfair is to expect an aide to function effectively if different school personnel are assigning different and even conflicting responsibilities. This is the result of poor planning and poor management among teachers and staff. If an aide is assigned to a regular education classroom, the regular education teacher and the consultant teacher should plan and discuss the role and responsibilities of the aide. The regular classroom teacher should be involved as much as possible in helping the aide meet his or her responsibilities. The successful use of an aide in the regular classroom is always the result of collaboration between the regular classroom teacher, the special education/consultant teacher and the aide.

Aides must be aware of required IEP services and modifications: One school would not allow aides to see the IEP because of confidentiality. This is ridiculous. The IEP must be accessible to all service providers who are responsible for the implementation of the IEP.[217]

Aides must develop independent behavior: Every aide must understand that their role is not to function on behalf of the child but to develop independent classroom behavior. An aide might feel that he or she is helping a child by doing what the child could do, albeit with some difficulty. Depriving a child the opportunity to develop independent skills is a very restrictive learning environment and is contradictory to every aspect of a free appropriate public education.

Aides must understand permissible test and curriculum modifications: This is easily resolved by discussing IEP accommodations with the aide, and providing an explanation why certain accommodations are or are not permissible.

Aides must be able to understand a Behavioral Intervention Plan (BIP): Often inappropriate behavior is the reason why a child is not able to participate in the classroom. If a BIP is developed for a child to address classroom behavior, the classroom aide must be aware of his or her responsibilities.

Aides must have high expectations: Aides, and classroom and consultant teachers, should always focus on what a child can rather than cannot do. We have or should have high expectations for nondisabled children, and children with disabilities should be afforded no less.

Aides must not exceed their job parameters: In some states an aide might be able to participate in only noninstructional activities which allows the teacher to focus on instruction. If this is the case, an aide should not be assigned instructional activities.

Specific aide responsibilities for the consultant teacher include:

- **Identifying skills needed by aides,**

- **Providing pre-service and in-service training,**

- **Providing daily supervision,**

- **Supervising classroom accommodations,**

- **Providing daily planning,**

- **Providing feedback concerning job performance,**

- **Developing teacher-aide collaboration,**

- **Working with aides and specialists (e.g., itinerant teachers).**

PARAPROFESSIONAL SUPERVISION

Every paraprofessional assigned to a child with a disability must be supervised and trained by a qualified special education teacher. Nothing is more remiss than a paraprofessional assigned to a child with a disability with no guidance concerning the curriculum, classroom participation, or appropriate strategies and interventions. Although a child with a disability is assigned a full-time paraprofessional in the regular classroom, lack of training and supervision can be extremely restrictive, especially if the lack of supervision and training prevents participation tin the classroom and curriculum.

> As part of much needed general planning, the NEA has outlined several supervisory and management tasks and competencies performed by teachers "to effectively integrate paraprofessionals into the instructional team."
>
> NEA Paraeducator Handbook:
> **http://www.nea.org/esphome/documents/paraeducator-handbook.doc**

Is *paraprofessional* a synonym for *aide*? Paraeducator or paraprofessional is a very inclusive teacher and includes a variety of roles and job descriptions ranging from teacher aides, to job coaching, to technology specialist. The NEA Paraeducator Handbook lists a variety of paraeducator roles including behavior interventionist, classroom assistant, early childhood education assistance program (ECEAP), educational assistant, educational paraprofessional, educational technician, English as a second language (ESL)/bilingual assistant, guidance specialist, home liaison instructional aide, instructional assistant, interpreter, job coach learning assistance program (LAP), special education assistant, teacher assistant, teacher aide, technology assistant, transition specialist, and tutor.

In addition to the excellent NEA handbook for paraeducators,[218] Washington State has an excellent resource relating to core competencies for paraprofessionals.[219]

http://www.wa.nea.org/Prf_Dv/PARA_ED/RCMDTNS.HTM

Duties of Paraprofessionals-
No Child Left Behind Act of 2001
P.L. 107-110, Section 1119(g)(1)

A paraprofessional described in paragraph may be assigned–
- to provide one-on-one tutoring for eligible students, if the tutoring is scheduled at a time when a student would not otherwise receive instruction from a teacher;
- to assist with classroom management, such as organizing instructional and other materials;
- to provide assistance in a computer laboratory;
- to conduct parental involvement activities;
- to provide support in a library or media center;
- to act as a translator; or
- to provide instructional services to students in accordance with paragraph.

GUIDELINES FOR THE TRAINING AND SUPERVISION OF PARAPROFESSIONALS

1. Involve paraprofessionals in the planning process.

2. Assign duties consistent with the paraprofessionals training and experience.

3. Provide training for the paraprofessional in the form of observation, "internships," training-specific sessions, in-service, team meetings, etc.

4. Provide paraprofessionals with training and direction relating to the implementation of "specific, accommodations, modifications and supports."[220]

5. For paraprofessionals with no background in special education, but who are assigned to work with children with disabilities, a qualified special education teacher should provide training.

6. Each child's IEP is accessible to "other service providers" (including paraprofessionals) who are responsible for its implementation.[221]

7. Provide daily supervision for all the paraprofessionals.

8. Provide support so that the paraprofessional becomes an integral part of the classroom.

9. Provide "constructive" feedback about the paraprofessional's performance.

10. Consider the "ability to practice ethical and professional standards of conduct, including the requirements of confidentiality."[222]

11. Ensure that professionals have "knowledge of effective instruction to assist teaching and learning as developed by the certificated/licensed staff in a variety of settings."[223]

PARAPROFESSIONALS:
NO CHILD LEFT BEHIND ACT P.L. 107-110
(SECTION 1119)

(c) NEW PARAPROFESSIONALS-

(1) IN GENERAL- Each local educational agency receiving assistance under this part shall ensure that all paraprofessionals hired after the date of enactment of the No Child Left Behind Act of 2001 and working in a program supported with funds under this part shall have –
    (A) completed at least 2 years of study at an institution of higher education;
    (B) obtained an associate's (or higher) degree; or
    (C) met a rigorous standard of quality and can demonstrate, through a formal State or local academic assessment –
        (i) knowledge of, and the ability to assist in instructing, reading, writing, and mathematics; or
        (ii) knowledge of, and the ability to assist in instructing, reading readiness, writing readiness, and mathematics readiness, as appropriate.

(2) CLARIFICATION- The receipt of a secondary school diploma (or its recognized equivalent) shall be necessary but not sufficient to satisfy the requirements of paragraph (1)(C).

(d) EXISTING PARAPROFESSIONALS- Each local educational agency receiving assistance under this part shall ensure that all paraprofessionals hired before the date of enactment of the No Child Left Behind Act of 2001, and working in a program supported with funds under this part shall, not later than 4 years after the date of enactment satisfy the requirements of subsection (c).

No Child Left Behind Internet Resources

http://www.ed.gov/policy/elsec/leg/esea02/index.html

http://thomas.loc.gov/bss/d107/d107laws.html

http://thomas.loc.gov/cgi-bin/query/z?c107:H.R.1:

http://www.ed.gov/nclb/landing.jhtml

SPECIFIC LEARNING DISABILITIES AND THE CONSULTANT TEACHER

Because over fifty percent of the children receiving IDEA services are identified as having specific learning disabilities, many of the children served by the consultant teacher will have specific learning disabilities. The difficulty with the specific learning disability category is a failure by the IEP team to consider what is and what is not a specific learning disability, how a specific learning disability must be assessed and documented, and the purpose of services for children with specific learning disabilities.

The consultant teacher can help misidentification by collaborating with the regular classroom teacher and IEP team to ensure that:

I. **A specific learning disability involves one of the following:**
   - **Oral expression.**
   - **Listening comprehension.**
   - **Written expression.**
   - **Basic reading skill.**
   - **Reading comprehension.**
   - **Mathematics calculation.**
   - **Mathematics reasoning.**

II. **A specific learning disability under IDEA is not the result of**
   - **a visual, hearing, or motor impairment,**
   - **mental retardation,**
   - **emotional disturbance**
   - **environmental, cultural, or economic disadvantage.**

III. **The child must be observed in the regular classroom.**

IV. **The IEP team must include a written report documenting the disability.**

V. **A resource room is not an automatic option for all children who have specific learning disabilities.**

VI. **A child may not be determined to be eligible for special education if the determinant factor for eligibility:**
   - **Lack of instruction in reading or math; or**
   - **Limited English proficiency.**[224]

Children who are identified as having a specific learning disability should not automatically receive resource room services, and specific learning disabilities is not synonymous with a resource room placement. Under IDEA the presumed placement for every child with a disability is the regular classroom. To achieve this goal the IEP team must consider ways in which the needs of a child with a specific learning disability can be met in the regular classroom with supplementary aids and services. If these needs cannot be met in the regular classroom, supplemental resource room help can be considered.

Before assigning a child to a resource room, the ability to meet a child's needs in the regular classroom with supplementary aids and services should be considered. Automatically assigning a child to a resource room based on the child's disability is contrary to the mandate that a child's placement is based on the child's IEP.

GRADE LEVEL AND SERVICES

Exempting a student from an academic or nonacademic activity based on the child's disability and not based on need is discriminatory.

As a child proceeds through school, indirect services play an increasingly important role. This is so for two reasons: First, there should be a transition from direct to indirect services to reflect the growing independence of the student to function in a mainstreamed environment. Second, the ability to provide direct services in the regular classroom becomes increasingly more difficult as grade level increases.

Generally speaking, there are more opportunities to provide direct services at the elementary level than at middle or secondary levels. A child in the second grade might require one hour of direct services a day, a child in the fifth grade one-half hour, but a student in the twelfth grade receives no direct services. There are simply more opportunities to provide direct instruction and to co-teach in the elementary grades as opposed to high school. One of the challenges for the high school consultant teacher is to become knowledgeable about many different academic disciplines (and probably a master of none!).

The consultant teacher will need to be aware of a student's academic needs in order to prepare appropriate remedial activities and materials, but as the sophistication of the academic discipline increase, the ability of the consultant teacher to provide direct instruction in the classroom and to co-teach decreases. The consultant teacher might have little difficulty providing direct help in an elementary grade with basic reading or math skills, but in upper grades graphing equations and multistep inequalities may be a problem for both student and consultant teacher. And in high school calculus or French might be more than a challenge! Calculus and French for students with disabilities? Absolutely! If these are appropriate curriculum choices, and a student is able to participate in these courses with supplementary aids and services, this is exactly what the law means by an "appropriate public education" and "high expectations."

Direct consultant teacher services are most appropriate and most often used in the early grades, but this does not mean that inclusion at the secondary level is precluded by the severity of the disability. A student with limited mobility and communication skills might have the cognitive ability to participate in classes, and classroom support would be required in the classroom, to move from class-to-class, for taking notes, testing and modifying the curriculum (e.g., taped lessons, taped textbooks, computer-scanned access).

For the majority of children with disabilities, especially high-incidence disabilities such as specific learning disabilities and speech or language impairment, the ratio between direct and indirect services will decrease with increasing grade level, and the overall need for consultant teacher services will also decrease with increasing age. Ideally, well before the student graduates, the student will not need services.

Two factors can influence the direct/indirect service ratio and the overall need for consultant teacher services as a function of grade level. First, for children requiring specific instructional methodologies (e.g., Braille, sign language, assistive technology), a certain level of direct services might be required at each grade level. Second, if a student requires a relatively constant level of indirect services, especially in the form of curriculum accommodations, the overall need for consultant teacher services might exist through high school. Of course, if a student requires indirect services but no longer needs specially designed instruction, the student should be declassified and the indirect services offered under Section 504.

SO YOU HEARD ABOUT THIS JOB . . .

Is there anything that should be asked when interviewing for a job as a consultant teacher? Yes, indeed! One thing is certain: no two special education consultant teacher positions will be the same.

When interviewing for a job as a consultant teacher there are many factors that must be considered when making job-related inquiries. An uppermost consideration might be to understand each and every responsibility (which is not likely), or a less lofty interview goal might be something as simple as gainful employment. The interview is not the time to be demanding or abrasive, but there are certain questions that should be asked. The purpose of asking these questions is not to disagree, or to quote legal guidelines but to have a clear understanding of what the job entails. The list below is not exhaustive and there are many other questions that probably should be asked. Too many questions? Maybe, if directed at one individual in a barrage of information gathering. A better approach might be to seek information from a variety of sources such as a regular education teacher, an itinerant teacher, or a consultant teacher. Of course, there are many other interview questions relating to salary, travel reimbursement, benefits, schedules, contractual responsibilities, retirement (. . . it will happen!) that makes interviewing such a fun-filled experience. In any case, questions relating to specific consultant teacher responsibilities include the following:

What-to-Ask-About-the-Job Checklist

- **How many students will be served by the consultant teacher?**

- **What disabilities are being served?**

- **Is travel involved? Is there a travel budget?**

- **Is there a budget for materials and supplies?**

- **What is the severity of the disabilities?**

- **How many different grades, classrooms or schools are involved?**

- **Are consultant teacher services documented in IEPs?**

- What types of consultant teacher services are currently being provided?

- Are regular classroom teachers provided with planning time?

- Are consultant teachers involved or expected to be involved in co-teaching and collaboration?

- Are pull-out services provided by the consultant teacher?

- Is there a room/office for the consultant teacher?

- How does the consultant teacher participate in the IEP team process?

- How does the consultant teacher report progress to parents?

Philosophy? Travel? Caseload? Visit with a special education teacher who is a consultant teacher, or who provides consultant teacher services. This will be time well spent. Meet with the itinerant consultant teacher. Visit the inclusion teacher or someone responsible for mainstreaming. No inclusion, no mainstreaming—you have your work cut out!

ALTERNATE PLACEMENT CONSULTANT TEACHER SERVICES

A primary focus of the consultant teacher is the provision of supplementary aids and services in the regular classroom. However, the consultant teacher might also provide direct and indirect services in alternative placements. In this capacity the consultant teacher provides services that enable participation in the regular curriculum by **preparing** children to participate, and to provide special expertise that a child will need in a restrictive setting in order to receive a free and appropriate public education.

For children in self-contained settings because of behavior problems, the primary reason why such settings often fail to provide an appropriate education is because of haphazard curriculum standards. If a child is removed from the regular curriculum because of behavior, and not because of an inability to master the curriculum, providing a curriculum different than what is used in the classroom is inappropriate.

A child cannot be removed from the regular classroom "solely because of needed modifications in the general curriculum."[225] Likewise, a child should not be deprived of the regular curriculum because of an alternative placement. When this occurs, when the alternative placement defines the curriculum and thus limits participation in the regular classroom curriculum, the placement is no longer IEP-based. This, of course, is contrary to the very foundation of the IEP which is to meet a child's needs "that result from the child's disability to enable the child to be involved in and progress in the general curriculum."[226] The importance or regular curriculum participation is also clearly stated when a child is removed from the regular classroom to an interim alternative educational setting from not more than 45 days because there is a substantial likelihood of injury to the child or to others.[227] In this circumstance, when the need for the alternative setting is school conduct, the interim alternative setting must be selected "to enable the child to continue to progress in the general curriculum."[228]

For children in interim alternative settings the consultant teacher is often a vital link between the regular classroom, the regular curriculum, and the alternative setting. The consultant might provide curriculum materials from the regular classroom to ensure that the child is involved in general curriculum and not curriculum activities created to accommodate the needs of personnel in the restricted setting.

The blatant disregard for the general curriculum and the mandate to provide an appropriate education as defined by each child's IEP is never more obvious than in self-contained, separate school and residential school placements. If children are drawn from a variety of educational districts or schools, different grade levels, the regular classroom curriculum needs of each child might be very unique. Nonetheless, a bureaucratic strategy is often to address alternative setting needs rather than individual learning needs based on each child's IEP. The preclusion of regular classroom participation is often the result of the location of the restrictive setting; that is, a child in a restricted setting might be able to participate in the regular classroom to some degree but the opportunity is never provided because of transportation, the time involved, possibly insurance and liability concerns the general inconvenience of providing such participation. The consultant teacher has a responsibility to ensure the participation of all children with disabilities in the regular classroom, and "all" means all.

RESOURCE ROOM SUPPORT

Evaluating resource room services: The purpose for evaluating resource room services is not to criticize the resource room teacher or to offer nitpicking advice, but to determine how resource room services can impact regular classroom performance.

Of all the supplementary aids and services that can be provided a child, resource room services can be the most restrictive. Resource room and other pull-out models can be highly effective if the focus is to enable a child to successfully participate in the regular classroom or regular curriculum. What should not be done is to automatically assign a child to a resource room setting based on the child's disability.

As with all other services resource room support should be as least restrictive as possible. Time in the resource room should be based on need and not an immutable time slot; resource room support is intended to supplement and not conflict with regular classroom participation; and the purpose of the resource room is not to create a new curriculum. In the New Hampshire continuum of services, resource room includes children with disabilities who attend regular classes and receive "assistance at or through the resource room program." However, resource room services are preceded by (a) Regular classroom placements (with supports and services required in the IEP); (b) Regular classroom with consultative assistance; and (c) Regular classroom with assistance by specialists.

Resource room support can be provided to develop content-area reading skill, improve specific classroom behavior, or to develop study skills, but the duration and frequency of this support cannot be constant for all children. Assigning a child to a resource room for a minimum of one hour per day because the child has been identified as having a specific learning disability would be inappropriate for the simple reason that the placement is not based on need. Resource room support must be based on need, must provide a level of services to meet this need, and must be coordinated with the regular classroom and with the regular classroom teacher. To this end, the consultant teacher, or the resource room teacher providing consultant teacher services should consider the following:

Consultant Teacher/Resource Room Support Guidelines

1. Resource room support should not be based on a student's disability.

2. Resource room support should supplement the regular classroom.

3. Resource room support should not create a new curriculum.

4. Resource room support should be as least restrictive as possible.

5. The effectiveness of resource room support to enable regular classroom participation should be reviewed quarterly.

6. The resource room teacher should work closely with the regular classroom teacher to identify regular classroom and curriculum needs.

7. Resource room skills should generalize to the regular classroom.

8. **The effectiveness of the resource room should be based on regular classroom performance.**

As previously mentioned, resource room support is a supplementary service if the support is directed toward enabling the child to participate in the regular classroom.[229] If the resource room support provides services unrelated to the general curriculum, or the resource room teacher provided services completely apart from the regular classroom, the resource room service is more a *de facto* self-contained classroom than a resource to supplement the regular classroom.

Many resource room teachers have the difficult task of balancing multiple responsibilities entailing providing resource room services, mainstreaming children into regular classrooms, and providing direct and indirect consultant teacher services. When a teacher is both a consultant teacher and a resource room teacher, ample time must be provided to provide the necessary direct, indirect, and resource room services, and a suitable amount of time to conduct the necessary planning.

RESOURCE ROOM QUESTIONS

What is the difference between a resource room teacher and a special education consultant teacher? Location and where services are provided. The consultant teacher is concerned with participation in the regular classroom, while the resource room teacher provides pull-out services to enable regular classroom participation. The distinction between the two can be very minimal as is the case in Portland, Oregon where a resource Teacher/consultant is described as "an educational program for students with mild disabilities who need assistance in basic skills such as reading, mathematics, and written language. One of the most important roles of the Resource Teacher/Consultant is to collaborate with the general classroom teacher in areas such as teaching strategy, curriculum material, modified instruction, and learning environment."[230] Vermont makes a distinction between "learning specialist services" which are "provided by a learning specialist or by a consulting teacher and include direct instruction or direct supervision of services provided by an aide, and "resource room services" which are "provided by a Resource Room Teacher of the Handicapped."[231]

Can the resource room teacher also serve as a consultant teacher? Yes, but this must be reflected in the consultant teacher's caseload. If children receiving consultant teacher services in the regular classroom require twenty hours of direct and indirect services, a teacher might not be able to manage more than two or three hours a day in a resource room. The consultant teacher model is not a way to save money or to double a teacher's caseload.

What is the purpose of the resource room? Simple: to supplement the regular classroom. Thus, the resource room teacher must collaborate with the regular classroom teacher to accomplish this end by pre-teaching, re-teaching, remedial teaching.

Must the resource room teacher use a special curriculum? Absolutely not. The purpose of the resource room, of special education, is to enable a child to participate in the regular curriculum to the maximum extent appropriate.

How much time should be spent in the resource room? As little as possible. One child might do with one hour of support a week or even less which might be in keeping with meeting a need in a specific deficit area[232] or requiring only "a small amount of extra assistance."[233] Another child might require ten hours of support a week to meet several more intensive academic needs. A requirement (or mistaken belief) that all children receive a certain level of support is clearly inappropriate in that the support is based on something other than the IEP; the service itself could be inappropriate if a student does not need resource room support, or the support could be provided in the regular classroom with supplementary aids and services. Three hours of resource room services might be mandated by state code, but a child might need only one hour. If an amount of resource room support is in excess of what is need, the support is restrictive. When this occurs, the disability and not the child's IEP is the basis for the placement. If all services were viewed as a continuum designed to provide the least restrictive service, independence in the regular classroom would be enhanced and special education would truly be a service and not a place.

Is the resource room an alternative placement? Again, the purpose of the resource room is to support the regular classroom and not to provide an alternative placement. The regulations do not list resource room services as an alternative placement but as a supplementary service "provided in conjunction with regular class placement."[234] Although the intent of the resource room is to supplement the regular classroom, many schools, IEP teams, and state regulations treat the resource room as a separate placement. In Massachusetts, the code requires that "the Team shall first consider in-district settings such as a general education classroom, a resource setting, a separate classroom, a work setting, a vocational school program, and/or another type of setting identified by the Team as appropriate and able to provide the services on the IEP in a natural or less restrictive environment."[235] Last, the Office of Special Education Programs defines a regular classroom placement as one in which a child spends between twenty-one percent and sixty percent of the school day. If a child spent forty minutes a day in the resource room, this would be a regular classroom placement. However, a resource room placement (between 21% and 60%) could result in daily resource room services between one and three hours. One hour a day in a resource room might supplement the regular classroom, but three hours a day would certainly seem to indicate a resource room being used as an alternative setting rather than a supplementary service to the regular classroom.

THE BIG MISTAKE

The services and placement needed by each child with a disability to receive FAPE must be based on the child's unique needs and not on the child's disability.[236]

The need for an alternative placement does negate the need to educate a child with nondisabled children to the maximum extent appropriate. If the placement is based on a child's disability and not individual needs, the placement becomes more important than being educated with nondisabled childre. The most common example of this occurring (38% of states) is when placement decisions are almost entirely disability based.[237] In some instances local educational agencies (who are responsible for each child's IEP belonging to that system) inappropriately absolve themselves of IDEA requirements such as goals, least restrictive environment and continuum of services by using a restrictive environment in a separate school or location or outside of the district (e.g., residential settings). When this occurs, usually because of a child's disability, inclusion with nondisabled children is virtually denied regardless of the extent of participation that is possible.

REASONS FOR NOT BECOMING A
CONSULTANT TEACHER

Being a special education consultant teacher is not for everyone.

For many special education teachers enabling a child with a disability to function independently in the regular classroom is a source of considerable satisfaction. But when you have a job in which the goal is to reduce the need for your services, job satisfaction can be an issue. Listed below are a few reasons for not becoming a consultant teacher, or, if you are a consultant teacher, reasons why you might be doing a great job (but no one seems to notice . . . and this is good!).

A need for approval: As a consultant teacher your success is measured by the extent to which children with disabilities are able to participate in the regular classroom and regular curriculum. An effective consultant teacher has the unusual goal of not being needed; an effective consultant teacher should strive to be needed less and thus allow children to become increasingly independent in the classroom. This role does not encourage praise, and the efforts of the consultant teacher often go unnoticed. Ah, but to see a child succeed in the regular classroom . . .

A need for a classroom: There are many special education positions which center about a classroom in which services are contained (thus *self-contained*). However, a consultant teacher is not about self-contained settings, but about the participation of children with disabilities in the regular classroom. If a self-contained special education teacher provides skills that might eventually result in inclusion, isn't this teacher also providing consultant teacher services? Not if there is no interaction between the regular classroom teacher and the special education teacher, and not if the skills acquired in the restrictive setting do not generalize to the regular classroom.

A low tolerance for criticism: The consultant teacher should expect criticism. Some of the criticism will be on the mark, other criticisms will be based on misinformation (e.g., special education is a place and not a service), and much criticism will be the result of venting. In addition, IEP team members might be critical because of your instance on the law and regular classroom participation; parents might be critical for a variety of reasons, and the administration might be critical because of your focus on children with disabilities participating in regular education classes and not on budgets and school-wide needs. Lots of criticism in the consultant teacher business!

An aversion for risk: Risk is not easy; risk leaves you vulnerable; risk often results in failure. Without a willingness to risk regular classroom participation the consultant teacher is doomed to failure. Consultant teaching requires the ability to take risks, and the primary risk is providing a child with a disability an opportunity to participate in the regular classroom as independently as possible. Determining the level of independent classroom functioning requires risk. Only by knowing what a child can and cannot do can we determine each child's individual needs. For the consultant teacher, for the regular classroom teacher and for the child, the risk is the eventuality that a child will not always be one hundred percent successful and that classroom participation will not be without problems. But no risk, no gains. There is decidedly less risk if failure in the regular classroom is simply avoided. The illusion of control, and thus the self-contained classroom, is that success can be ensured by carefully controlling the difficulty of curriculum and avoiding the interaction between disabled and nondisabled children as much as possible. When there is no risk, there is no failure; when there is no risk, growth is limited, regular classroom participation avoided, and the development of independent living skills stymied.

A lack of focus: Consultant teaching requires focus on the task of enabling children to participate in the regular classroom, focus on services and accommodations that will achieve this, and focus on independent and intentional behavior that will promote regular classroom participation. If a consultant teacher expects to be told what to do, and is satisfied with simply keeping students busy, albeit happy and actively engaged, the teacher might be satisfied and the children happy as larks, but this undermines the purpose of consultant teaching. The successful consultant teacher must keep focus on the primary task to enable classroom participation to the maximum extent appropriate, and this requires focus.

Problems! Consultant teacher services are about problems. If you don't like problem solving, you will not like the job of consultant teacher. Problems relating to regular participation, the regular curriculum, concerns of regular classroom teachers learning problems, motivation problems, accommodation problems and of course, for the consultant teacher there is one major problem: to enable children to be educated with nondisabled children to the maximum extent appropriate. This is what the consultant teacher wants; this is the purpose of consultant teacher services. Although a constant flow of problems can be disquieting for some, this does provide for a less than humdrum school day. For the consultant teacher every day is different, every day is interesting every day is a problem to confront, a problem to solve, or maybe not to. Lots of problems; interesting job.

RONCKER v. WALTER 700 F.2D 1058 (1983)

This case involved a nine year-old who was classified as trainable mentally retarded and who had an IQ less than 50. The parents recognized the need for special education but wanted a placement in a special class in a public school to allow contact with nondisabled children. The school district believed that the child "could not benefit significantly from mainstreaming and that any minimal benefits would be greatly outweighed by the educational benefits" (p. 1061) of a separate special education school placement. The district court agreed with the school district, but this appellate court for the sixth district ruled that the school district did fully consider the mainstreaming mandate; that is, the school district did not consider supplementary aids and services that would enable a child to be educated with nondisabled children.

The preference for mainstreaming is strong and a child should not be placed in a segregated facility solely for educational reasons. Indeed, "in a case where the segregated facility is considered superior, the court should determine whether the services which make that placement superior could be feasibly provided in a non-segregated setting. If they can, the placement in the segregated setting would be inappropriate under the Act" (p. 1063).

THE SEARCH FOR "APPROPRIATE"

Prior to the enactment of P.L. 94-142 in 1975, the opportunity and inclination to educate children with disabilities was often in separate programs and schools away from children without disabilities. The law and this bill contain a presumption that children with disabilities are to be educated in regular classes.

-Senate Report 105-17

Special education has grown considerably since the enactment of Public Law 94-142, the Education of All Handicapped Children Act (EAHCA), in 1975. Of the many amendments to the law and corresponding regulations none is more noteworthy than the emphasis on regular classroom participation. The concept of "full educational opportunity," 'free appropriate public education," "all children can learn," "no child left behind" all begin with a mandate for an appropriate education. Special education exists to provide this appropriate education. If the special education is not appropriate, the result is a failure to meet a child's individual needs. If the special education is inappropriate, the result is an exacerbation of a child's disability and woeful neglect on the part of those providing special education services.

> **Maximum Extent Appropriate**
>
> is not full inclusion
> is not mainstreaming
> is not a resource room
> is not a self-contained classroom
>
> The key word is "appropriate," and the "maximum extent appropriate" occurs when supplementary aids and services are no longer successful for educating a child with nondisabiled children.

As noted by Congress in its findings to IDEA-1997, "improving educational results for children with disabilities is an essential element of our national policy of ensuring equality of opportunity, full participation, independent living, and economic self-sufficiency for individuals with disabilities."[238] Providing full participation in the regular classroom and general curriculum means providing opportunities to participate to the maximum extent appropriate. Not every child with a disability will be able to participate on a full-time basis in the regular classroom, and many children with disabilities will require extensive curriculum adaptations or a curriculum that emphasizes very basic communication, daily living, social, and motor skills. Nonetheless, the first consideration for every child with a disability is to ensure that each child participate in the regular classroom and curriculum. This is the fundamental goal for the special education consultant teacher, and is a philosophy consistent with the findings by Congress that special education can be more effective by having high expectations, providing regular classroom participation when appropriate, and reducing the need to label children as disabled.

What Congress has Found
20 U.S.C. 1400(c)(5)

"over 20 years of research and experience has demonstrated that the education of children with disabilities can be made more effective by—

(A) having high expectations for such children and ensuring their access in the general curriculum to the maximum extent possible;

(B) strengthening the role of parents and ensuring that families . . . have meaningful opportunities to participate in the education of their children at school and at home;

(C) . . . and that special education can become a service for such children rather than a place where they are sent;

(D) providing appropriate special education and related services and aids and supports in the regular classroom to such children, whenever appropriate;

(E) supporting high-quality, intensive professional development for all personnel . . . (i) to meet developmental goals and, to the maximum extent possible, those challenging expectations that have been established for all children; and (ii) to be prepared to lead productive, independent, adult lives, to the maximum extent possible;

(F) providing incentives for whole-school approaches and pre-referral intervention to reduce the need to label children as disabled in order to address their learning needs; and

(G) focusing resources on teaching and learning while reducing paperwork and requirements that do not assist in improving educational results."

For the consultant teacher an "appropriate education" is predicated on several basic beliefs which include:

- **Special education as a service and not a place,**

- **Participation in the regular classroom to the maximum extent appropriate,**

- **Participation in the regular curriculum to the maximum extent appropriate,**

- **Participation in nonacademic activities to the maximum extent appropriate,**

- **Providing children with disabilities the least restrictive environment,**

- **Providing children with disabilities the least restrictive accommodations,**

- **High expectations for children with disabilities,**

- **Increasing the role of parents,**

- **Increasing the role of the regular education teacher.**

MEASURING AND REPORTING PROGRESS

Progress for achieving the annual goals must be reported to parents at least as often as progress is reported to parents of children who are not disabled. These goals center about meeting the child's needs "to enable the child to be involved in the general curriculum" and meeting other educational needs.

> **Measuring and Reporting Progress**
> **34 CFR 300.347(a)(7)**
>
> A statement of
> (i) how the child's progress toward the annual goals described in paragraph (a)(2) of this section will be measured; and
> (ii) How the child's parents will be regularly informed (through such means as periodic report cards), at least as often as parents are informed of their nondisabled children's progress, of–
> (A) Their child's progress toward the annual goals; and
> (B) The extent to which that progress is sufficient to enable the child to achieve the goals by the end of the year.

What to measure? Focus on measuring progress of specific skills, behaviors, or levels of performance which enable participation in the classroom (e.g., a specific behavior) or curriculum (e.g., reading comprehension). As is the case for much of what the consultant teacher does, there are indirect and direct measures of student progress:

Indirect measures of progress include ratings and observational data. For example, the Senate report IDEA suggests a report card for goals in which each goal is evaluated by the following scale: No progress; some progress; good progress; almost complete; completed.

Direct measures of progress include specific levels of performance. For example, the number of sight words known, the number of mathematics problems correctly answered, the frequency of classroom disruptions. Most important, don't neglect existing measures of progress used by the regular classroom teacher such as daily classroom assignments, homework, quizzes, tests, papers, projects, student reports, report cards, attendance, etc. There is often a wealth of information relating to a child's classroom performance that is often ignored at the expense of standardized test scores which often have a shaky connection to actual classroom needs.

In addition to measuring progress toward achieving measurable annual goals, the consultant teacher should plan with the classroom teacher to measure the overall "satisfaction" of classroom and curriculum participation. "Satisfaction" is the word of choice for the Least Restrictive Environment provision ". . . such that education in regular classes with the use of supplementary aids and services cannot be achieved satisfactorily."

Regular Classroom Teacher Participation Rating Scale							
Student:	Degree of Satisfaction						
	Very		Somewhat			Not	
1. How satisfied are you with the amount of time in the classroom?	1	2	3	4	5	6	7
2. How satisfied are you with the extent of participation in the regular curriculum?	1	2	3	4	5	6	7
3. How satisfied are you with the ability to master the regular classroom curriculum?	1	2	3	4	5	6	7
4. How satisfied are you with the extent the curriculum must be modified?	1	2	3	4	5	6	7
5. How satisfied are you with the educational benefit that results from participation in the regular classroom?	1	2	3	4	5	6	7
6. How satisfied are you with behavior in the classroom?	1	2	3	4	5	6	7
7. How satisfied are you with the nonacademic benefits of regular classroom participation?	1	2	3	4	5	6	7
8. How satisfied are you with your ability to meet this student's needs in the classroom?	1	2	3	4	5	6	7
9. How satisfied are you with the services that are provided in the classroom?	1	2	3	4	5	6	7
10. How satisfied are you with the motivation to participate in the classroom?	1	2	3	4	5	6	7

TRANSITION SERVICES

Transition services means a coordinated set of activities for a student with a disability that is designed within an outcome-oriented process, that promotes movement from school to post-school activities . . .[240]

Planning is never more important than when addressing an important educational transition. When a child is eligible for services under Part B of IDEA, and will no longer be eligible for Infants and Toddlers with Disabilities services, a transition plan is required from Part C to preschool programs.[241] For older students post-school transition planning is a vital component of every IEP.[242] The transition of students with disabilities to post-school settings, planning has taken an added importance so that "the IDEA Amendments of 1997 also contain provisions that greatly strengthen the involvement of students with disabilities in decisions regarding their own futures, to facilitate movement from school to post-school activities."[243]

The purpose for transition services is to prepare every student for post-school employment, post-school opportunities and post-school outcomes. To achieve this goal, the consultant teacher must absolutely work with school personnel, nonschool personnel and agencies. The special education teacher who oversees transition services is serving as a consultant teacher. In this capacity the special education consultant teacher must collaborate and plan with school personnel, nonschool personnel and agencies, and the student to best meet post-school needs. For the consultant teacher transition services place a great emphasis on indirect services. For students beginning at age fourteen, the emphasis is on school-related courses and programs, while for students beginning at age sixteen (or younger if necessary) the emphasis is on school-to-work transition services and establishing all necessary "interagency responsibilities or any needed linkages."[244] The following lists various transition activities in which the consultant teacher might help plan, coordinate, or manage:

- **Adult education**

- **Advanced-placement courses**

- **Community experiences**

- **Community participation**

- Continuing education

- Daily living skills

- Employment objectives

- Functional vocational evaluation

- GED preparation

- Independent living

- Integrated employment

- Interagency responsibilities

- Job coaching

- Occupational counseling

- Placement examinations

- Post-school adult living objectives

- Postsecondary education

- Related services

- Special education

- Supported employment

- Vocational education program

- Vocational training

BEHAVIORAL INTERVENTION PLAN

A point of controversy for IDEA is the matter of discipline for children with disabilities. The provisions regarding discipline in the law and regulations can be confusing but the consultant teacher can play a pivotal role in clarifying questions relating to discipline and developing plans to address discipline problems.

If a child with a disability is disciplined for a violation of a school rule, within 10 days from the disciplinary action the school must conduct a functional behavioral assessment and implement a behavioral intervention plan. If a plan already exists, the IEP team must review and modify the plan as necessary. If the disciplinary action involves a change in placement (e.g., the placement is no longer the regular classroom), the school must conduct a manifestation determination review to determine whether the disability caused the misconduct. If the misconduct was the result of the student's disability, the school must remediate deficiencies in the student's IEP. If the disability was not the cause of the misconduct, the school disciplinary procedures may be applied as they would be applied to children without disabilities.

What does this very abbreviated interpretation of the regulations mean for the consultant teacher? First, the consultant teacher should participate in the development of a Functional Behavioral Assessment (FBA) and Behavioral Intervention Plan (BIP), especially in relation to behaviors that prevent or restrict regular classroom participation. The consultant teacher can accomplish this by planning with the regular classroom teacher to:

1. **Identify settings, events, or conditions that make the problem behavior worse (e.g., diet, medical conditions/illness, sleep, fatigue, social conflicts).**

2. **Identify events that predictably trigger problem behavior (e.g., teacher instruction).**

3. **Identify problem behaviors that are maintained by a common function (e.g., attention, escape/avoidance).**

4. **Discuss with the classroom teacher events that predictably follow and maintain problem behavior (positive or negative reinforcement).**

5. Identify reasons (hypotheses) why the behavior occurs.

6. Plan with the classroom teacher strategies for desired and acceptable alternative behaviors.

7. Identify specific actions concerning what will be done, and specific responsibilities by the consultant teacher, the classroom teacher and others (viz., aides).

8. Evaluate the effectiveness of the behavior support plan and make necessary modifications.[245]

AND . . . ONE-MINUTE CONSULTANT TEACHING

No time for five-minute consultant teaching? No problem. Kenneth Blanchard and Spencer Johnson (1983) wrote a best selling book entitled The *One Minute Manager* (Berkley Books) which extols the virtues of one-minute activities such as one-minute goal development and one-minute feedback. The book is short, exceedingly simple, and widely read because the advice is focused and effective. The essence of the book centers about three basic principles: One-Minute Goal Setting, One-Minute Praising, and One-Minute Reprimands.

Certainly a child's IEP will require more than one minute of consideration, feedback might be quite extensive, and for the consultant teacher "reprimand" is something to be avoided. Nonetheless, the whole point of one-minute attention to real goals does not require a vast amount of time. And a word or two of praise or positive feedback is easy to do and the benefits can be extensive.

Why these three principles are important in the business world is that too often there is no goal setting, there is no positive feedback to reinforce behavior, and no corrective feedback when things go awry. For the consultant teacher these principles are extremely important although the last (the idea of a *reprimand*) requires some reinterpretation. One minute for real goal setting is far more effective than an endless stream of busy work. An appropriate education has purpose and goals; an inappropriate education is characterized by unrelated activities and activities without purpose, and a disregard for real needs. One-minute praise is often sufficient to indicate that a child is on track or that a teacher is doing a great job helping a child participate with nondisabled children.

But what about reprimands? What to do if a child is not on track or a teacher prevents a child from participating with nondisabled children? For the consultant teacher constructive feedback is necessary, reprimanding is not. This is not to say that certain behaviors should not be identified to a student as unacceptable but that the purpose of the feedback is not simply to reprimand but to provide direction that will result in acceptable behavior and thereby enable classroom participation.

The situation regarding feedback is even more challenging when working with colleagues. A consultant teacher would be naïve to think that an endless stream of criticism direct toward a colleague will enable classroom or curriculum participation. If anything, reprimanding a colleague will result in animosity and a lack of support for including children with disabilities. More importantly, unless your role as a consultant teacher is also an administrative position, a reprimand leans more toward unpleasant collegiality than administrative directive. With colleagues (and certainly with children) the consultant teacher should attempt to show what should be and not dwell on what hasn't been; the consultant teacher should provide direction, and not focus on what has not been accomplished.

One-Minute One-to-One: The consultant teacher is right on task if encouragement or opportunities are provided **for the regular classroom teacher** to help a child with a problem, to assist the child in some small way will make the child feel part of the classroom, and empower the teacher to enable participation in the classroom. Note that a minute devoted to helping a child is not one-to-one instruction, five hours a day, five days a week. The one minute is to clarify, encourage, evaluate, guide—a small investment of time but potentially huge rewards.

One-Minute Student Praise: Or even 5 seconds! So little energy for so much return (i.e., reinforcing positive student behavior). If the consultant teacher and regular classroom teacher plan and focus on specific behaviors to reinforce, not only will the probability for classroom success increase but the classroom teacher will become an important part of classroom inclusion.

One-Minute Teacher Praise: The classroom teacher should know, and should be told, that he or she is indispensable for including children with a disabilities in the classroom.

One-Minute Parent Praise: Parents have a tough go. They receive a letter that their child might have a disability, they are told how educational performance has been impacted, and correspondence from the school is usually about meetings, progress (or lack thereof), and procedural gobbledygook that requires a lawyer to interpret. A periodic call to inform Herbert's parents that he is doing great, what really nice thing he did today, and to keep up the great work at home!

One-Minute IEP Check: One or two questions, one or two problems, having a child read a sentence, asking the regular classroom teacher about specific behaviors will help the consultant teacher focus on relevant behaviors and skills and develop a better sense of what needs must be addressed to enable classroom participation.

One-Minute Feedback: Easy to do, effective and requires little time: say something nice, provide positive feedback, encourage positive behavior. Sometimes you will have to dig deep to find something positive to say, but there is always a level of behavior or level of skill that provides the basis for the next level and that is what should be reinforced.

NOTES

1. *Oberti v. Board of Education*, 789 F. Supp. 1322 9(D.N.J. 1992), p. 1335
2. 20 U.S.C. 1400(c)(5)(F)
3. *Roncker v. Walter* 700 F.2d 1058 (1983), p. 1062
4. *Ibid.*, p. 1063
5. 34 CFR 300.347(a)(2)
6. For a copy of the *Hudson v. Rowley* decision see
   http://caselaw.lp.findlaw.com/scripts/getcase.pl?navby=search&linkurl=&gra-phurl=&court=US&case=/us/458/176.html
7. *Oberti v. Board of Education*, 789 F.Supp. 1322 (D.N.J.) 1992), p. 1326,ee 34 CFR
   300.130(b) which prohibits funding settings which violate the least restrictive
   environment mandate.
8. (see 34 CFR 300.121, and especially note 34 CFR 300.121(d) *FAPE for children
   suspended or expelled from school.*
9. National Council on Disability. (2000). Back to School on Civil Rights:
   Advancing the Federal Commitment to Leave No Child Behind. Washington,
   D.C.
10. 34 CFR 300.342(b)(3)
11. *Davis v. District of Columbia Board. of Ed.*, 530 F.Supp. 1209,1211 (D.D.C. 1982)
12. 334 F. Supp. 1257 (ED Pa. 1971) and 343 F. Supp. 279 (ED Pa. 1972)
13. 348 F. Supp. 866 (DC 1972)
14. Vermont Department of Education, State Board of Education Manual of Rules
    and Practices, 5440-85 Consulting Teacher,
    http://www.state.vt.us/educ/new/pdfdoc/board/rules/5440.pdf#sped_consulting
15. *Hudson v. Rowley,* 458 U.S. 176 (1982)
16. TITLE 23: EDUCATION AND CULTURAL RESOURCES SUBTITLE A:
    EDUCATION CHAPTER I: STATE BOARD OF EDUCATION SUBCHAP-
    TER b: PERSONNEL PART 28, STANDARDS FOR CERTIFICATION IN
    SPECIAL EDUCATION SUBPART A: GENERAL, Section 28.360
    Standards for the LBS II/Curriculum Adaptation Specialist
17. 34 CFR 300.26(a) and 34 CFR 300.26(b)(3)
18. see Sec. 300.136 Personnel standards. (a) Definitions. As used in this part--(1)
    Appropriate professional requirements in the State means entry level require-
    ments that--(i) Are based on the highest requirements in the State applicable to
    the profession or discipline in which a person is providing special education or
    related services; and (ii) Establish suitable qualifications for personnel providing
    special education and related services under Part B of the Act to children with
    disabilities who are served by State, local, and private agencies (see Sec. 300.2);
19. http://www.ed.state.nh.us/Certification/rules507-01to612-05.htm#Ed 506.02
    Assistant Superintendent and Teacher Consultant.
20. Licensing Endorsements, A-88, http://www.state.vt.us/educ/new/pdfdoc/
    board/rules/5440.pdf#sped_consulting

21. Standards of Quality and Effectiveness for Education Specialist Credential Programs (Including University Internship Options) and Clinical Rehabilitative Services Credential Programs Handbook for Postsecondary Institutions and Accreditation Reviewers, California Commission on Teacher Credentialing, State of California, December 1996: http://www.ctc.ca.gov/educator-standards/speced. pdf, p. 67-68.

22. *Ibid.*, Page 74

23. *Ibid.*, Page 3

24. http://www.ed.state.nh.us/Certification/rules507-01to612-05.htm#Ed 612.07

25. 3 ILLINOIS ADMINISTRATIVE CODE CH. I, S.226.300 SUBTITLE A SUBCHAPTER F SUBPART D: PLACEMENT, Section 226.300 Continuum of Placement Options

26. http://www.state.nj.us/njded/educators/license/1143.htm

27. New Jersey Code, 6A:14-3.1(a) and (b)

28. 34 CFR 300.7(a)(1)

29. 34 CFR 300.456(a) On-site Private School Services

30. 34 CFR 300.551

31. http://www.tsbvi.edu/programs/iowa.htm

32. see http://www.qsac.com/ and http://www.qsac.com/ProgServ/SEIT.htm

33. New York State United Teachers, NYSUT Information Bulletin #990038, http://www.nysut.org/research/bulletins/20001218consultantteacher.html#implementation

34. 34 CFR 300, Appendix A, p. 12470

35. Proposed change: 614(a)(1)(D)(ii)(II) ABSENCE OF CONSENT FOR SERVICES

36. Proposed change: 614(b) EVALUATION PROCEDURES, (5) SPECIAL RULE FOR ELIGIBILITY DETERMINATION

37. Proposed change: 614(b) EVALUATION PROCEDURES, (6) SPECIFIC LEARNING DISABILITIES, (A) IN GENERAL

38. Proposed change: 614(b) EVALUATION PROCEDURES, (6) SPECIFIC LEARNING DISABILITIES, (B) ADDITIONAL AUTHORITY

39. Proposed change: 614(d)(1)(A)(I)(I)(cc)

40. Proposed change: 614(d)(1)(A)(I)(III)

41. Proposed change: 614(d)(1)(B)(ii)

42. 34 CFR 300.342 When IEPs must be in effect.

43. 34 CFR 300.347(a)(4)

44. http://www.kidstogether.org/ct-danl.htm. Tip: Go to the library for a copy of this Court of Appeals case in the Federal Reporter (second series) if the internet copy is difficult to read.

45. 1990 IDEA Regulations, 34 CFR 300, Appendix C, page 73, 1. Purpose of the IEP

46. As is the case in New York where consultant teacher services are listed as one of the elements on the continuum of services (New York State, Part 200, Section 200.6(d) Continuum of services.

47. 34 CFR 300.347(a)(1)

48. *Evans v. Board of Educ. of Rhinebeck*, 930 F.Supp. 83 (S.D.N.Y., 199, p. 936)

49. *Hendrick Hudson Dist. Bd. of Ed. v. Rowley*, 458 U.S. 176 (1982)

50. 34 CFR 300.347(7)(a)(7)

51. 34 CFR 300.343(a)

52. 34 CFR 350(b) Accountability

53. 34 CFR 300.350(b)

54. 34 CFR 300.350(a)(1)&(2)

55. *Daniel R.R. v. State Board of Education*, United States Court of Appeals, 1989, 874 F.2d 1036 (5th Cir.), 1050.

56. http://www.michigan.gov/documents/tc_FA_P&C1_23120_7.html

57. Revised Administrative Rules for Special Education, effective June 6, 2002, Michigan State Board of Education, Michigan Department of Education http://www.michigan.gov/documents/2002-06-06MichiganAdmRulesSpEd_34533_7.pdf

58. 34 CFR 300.235(a) Permissive Use of Fund

59. Consultant Teacher Services, NYSUT Information Bulletin 990038, December 2000, see http://www.nysut.org/research/bulletins/20001218consultant-teacher.html#excerpts

60. see 34 CFR 300.344 IEP team

61. 34 CFR 300, Appendix A, p. 12472

62. SR-105-17

63. Ibid

64. 34 CFR 300.513(a)

65. 34 CFR 300.531

66. Senate Report 94-168, House Report 94-332

67. See Burns, E. (2001). Developing and Implementing IDEA-IEPs, Thomas, Springfield, IL., p. 9.

68. see 34 CFR 300.345(a)&(b)

69. 34 CFR 300.345(d) Conducting an IEP meeting without a parent in attendance.

70. 34 CFR 300.344(a)(2)

71. 34 CFR 300.346(d)

72. 34 CFR 300.346(a)(v)

73. 34 CFR 300.308(a)

74. 34 CFR 300.346(a)(2)(v)

75. 34 CFR 300.346(a)(2)(v)

76. 34 CFR 300.5

77. 34 CFR 300.308(b)

78. 34 CFR 300.6

79. 34 CFR 300.520(b)

80. *Evans v. Board of Educ. of Rhinebeck*, 930 F.Supp. 83 (S.D.N.Y., 199, p. 936)

81. see NYS Part 200.4(d)(2)(v) and part 2006(d)

82. 34 CFR 300.342.(b)(3)(i)

83. 34 CFR 300.342.(b)(3)(I)

84. see http://arkedu.state.ar.us/dirmemos/static/fy9900/408.html
85. Arkansas Department of Education, Rules and Regulations Governing Special Education and Related Services http://arkedu.state.ar.us/pdf/2.00.pdf
86. see the Vermont Department of Education at http://www.state.vt.us/educ/Cses/sped/main.htm
87. see West Kentucky Special Education Cooperative http://www.wkec.org/specialed/Resources/Request_for_Services.doc.
88. The Kentucky Alternate Assessment Project is an excellent site for alternate assessment http://www.ihdi.uky.edu/kap/faq.asp
89. Alaska Comprehensive System of Students Assessments (CSSA) Alternate Assessment, Guide to Collecting Materials for the Students Portfolio, August, 2001, See: http://www.eed.state.ak.us/tls/assessment/Alternateoptional/Standards.doc
90. 34 CFR 300.532(e)
91. 34 CFR 300.532(c)
92. 34 CFR 347(a)(5)
93. 34 CFR 300.347(a)(5)
94. 34 CFR 300.532(C)(2) Documenting Test Accommodations
95. 34 CFR 300.533
96. 34 CFR 300.532(b)
97. 34 CFR 300.550(b)(1)
98. See Washington Assessment Program Accommodation Checklist at http://www.blarg.com/~building/spneeds_ospiaccom2.html
99. The Chicago Public Schools, OFFICE OF SPECIALIZED SERVICES High School Edited by Dr. Shirley Baugher, which provides a variety of interesting curriculum accommodations. http://www.cps.k12.il.us/AboutCPS/Departments/OSS/Publications/publications.html
100. 34 CFR 300.125(a)(1)
101. 34 CFR 300.532(g)
102. 34 CFR 300.533
103. 20 U.S.C. 1413(a)(4)(A)
104. *Roncker v. Walter,* 700 F.2d 1058 (1983), p. 1063
105. 34 CFR 300.347(A)(2)(i & ii)
106. 34 CFR 300.235(a)(1)
107. see New Jersey Department of Education http://www.state.nj.us/njded/educators/license/1123.htm
108. 347 U.S. 483, *Brown et al. V. Board of Education of Topeka* et al. Appeal from the United States District Court for the District of Kansas.* No. 1. Argued December 9, 1952. Reargued December 8, 1953. Decided May 17, 1954.
109. from the 20th Annual Report to Congress, Table AA14 (1987-88 data), 23nd Annual Report to Congress, Table II-8 and Table AA2 (Page A-2), and the Twenty-fourth Annual Report to Congress, Number of Children Ages 6-21 Served Under IDEA, Part B by Disability, During the 2000-01 School Year, AA3

110. SLD-specific learning disabilities, Speech-speech and language impairments, MR-mental retardation, ED-emotional disturbance, OHI-other health impairments, Multiple-multiple disabilities, Hearing-hearing impairments, Orthopedic-orthopedic impairments, Visual-visual impairments, TBI-traumatic brain injury, Dev. Delay- developmental delay

111. Data from the Twenty-fourth Annual Report to Congress, Table AB2, Percentage of Children Ages 6-21 Served in Different Educational Environments Under IDEA, Part B, During the 1999-2000 School Year, pages A-110 to A-137.

112. 34 CFR 104.3(j)(1)

113. School and District Accountability, Legal Assuranceshttp://www.cde.ca.gov/ccpdiv/conapp/assurance.htm

114. California Educator, Volume 5, Issue 9, June 2001, California Teachers Association: http://www.cta.org/CaliforniaEducator/v5i9/feature_support.htm

115. 34 CFR 300.307(a)(2)(I)

116. see 34 CFR 300.307(b)

117. 34 CFR 300.7(c)

118. Arkansas has a very good IEP for indicating adaptation and modifications (which is included in the ADE regulatory document "Special Education and Related Services: Procedural Requirements and Program Standards(ADE 2000)," Appendix A, Required Forms, item #3.) Thanks to Marcia Harding, Associate Director Special Education, Arkansas Department of Education for permission to use this form.

119. 34 CFR 300.24(a)

120. 34 CFR 300.306(e)

121. 34 CFR 300, Appendix A, Question #2

122. 34 CFR300.504(b)

123. 34 CFR 300.136

124. 34 CFR 300, Appendix A

125. 34 300.622(b)(2)

126. 34 CFR 300.347(3)

127. 34 CFR 342(b)(3)

128. 34 CFR 300.347(a)(3)

129. Ibid.

130. 34 CFR 300.346(a)(2)(i)

131. 34 CFR 300.24 Related Services

132. Standards of Quality and Effectiveness for Education Specialist Credential Programs (Including University Internship Options) and Clinical Rehabilitative Services Credential Programs Handbook for Postsecondary Institutions and Accreditation Reviewers, California Commission on Teacher Credentialing, State of California, December 1996: http://www.ctc.ca.gov/educator-standards/speced.pdf, p. 150.

133. 34 CFR 300, Appendix A, Question #22

134. 34 CFR 300.307(a)(2)(ii)

135. AOTA, Standard VII: Transition Services, http://www.aota.org/general/otsp.asp
136. 34 CFR 300.344(a)(6)
137. see Special Education Class Size/Age Range Requirements, Illinois Administrative Code 226.720 & 226.730 (Case Load/Class Size).
138. Co-Teaching: Are Two Heads Better Than One in an Inclusion Classroom? by Millicent Lawton Harvard Education Letter's Research Online. http://www.edletter.org/past/issues/1999-ma/coteaching.shtml
139. State of South Dakota, Department of Education and Cultural Affairs, Office of Special Education. (1998). Individual Education Plan (IEP).
140. 34 CFR 300.344(a)(2)
141. Federal Register, Vol. 42, No. 163, August 23
142. 34 CFR 300.9(c)(2)
143. Twenty-fourth Annual Report to Congress, Percentage of Children Ages 6-21 Served in Different Educational Environments, Under IDEA, Part B, During the 1999-2000 School Year, All Disabilities, Table AB2
144. see 34 CFR 300.342(b)(2)
145. see http://www.tsbvi.edu/programs/caseload.htm, R 340.1749 Teacher consultant: caseload; and also see http://www.tsbvi.edu/agenda/caseload.htm
146. Pennsylvania State Standards [Section 342.42(j); see Pennsylvania Class Size and Caseload www.pde.psu.edu/bbpages_reference/40001/400015635.html
147. http://www.tsbvi.edu/programs/iowa.htm
148. http://www.tsbvi.edu/programs/aspea.htm
149. 34 CFR 300.347(a)(6)
150. 34 CFR 300.347(a)(6)
151. SR 105-17, IDEA
152. Part 200.4(d)(2)(v)
153. Part 200.6(d)(2)
154. see Appendix A, Question #14 from the 1997 regulations for a brief discussion of interim placements.
155. http://www.sro.nysed.gov/00-032.htm
156. 20 USC 1400(c)(5)
157. Appendix A, 1997 regulations
158. 34 CFR 300.551(a)(1)
159. See Part 200.1 and Part 200.6, Regulations of the Commissioner of Education, Pursuant to Sections 207, 3214, 4403, 4404 and 4410 of the Education Law, Part 200–Students with Disabilities (includes all amendments through January 6, 2000)
160. New York State, Part 200, Section 200.6(d) Continuum of services.
161. 34 CFR 300.136(a)(1)(ii) and 34 CFR 300.136(a)(4)
162. 34 CFR 300.28 Supplementary aids and services
163. Or, as stated in Greer v. Rome City School District, 950 F.2d 688 (11th Ctr. 1991), the whole range of supplemental aids and services.
164. 34 CFR 300.28

165. 34 CFR 300.306 Nonacademic services. (a) Each public agency shall take steps to provide nonacademic and extracurricular services and activities in the manner necessary to afford children with disabilities an equal opportunity for participation in those services and activities. (b) Nonacademic and extracurricular services and activities may include counseling services, athletics, transportation, health services, recreational activities, special interest groups or clubs sponsored by the public agency, referrals to agencies that provide assistance to individuals with disabilities, and employment of students, including both employment by the public agency and assistance in making outside employment available.

166. Ibid.

167. IDEA-1990, 34 CFR 300, Appendix C, Question #48

168. Burns, E. (2003). Supplementary Aids and Services, Charles C Thomas, Springfield, IL.

169. Greer v. Rome City School District, 950 F.2d 688 (11th Ctr. 1991)

170. Burns, E. (2003). Supplementary Aids and Services, Charles C Thomas, Springfield, IL.

171. 34 CFR 300.24(a)

172. 34 CFR 300.346(a)(v)

173. 34 CFR 300.550(b)(2)

174. Daniel, 874 F.2d 1036 (5th Cir.), p. 1050.

175. 34 CFR 300.26(b)(3)(ii)

176. 34 CFR 300.456(a) On-site. Services provided to private school children with disabilities may be provided on-site at a child's private school, including a religious school, to the extent consistent with law.

177. Part 200.6(a-l)

178. Part 200.6(l)

179. 34 CFR 300.7(c)

180. 29 USC 794

181. 34 CFR 104.3(j)

182. Appendix A to 34 CFR 104

183. 34 CFR 300.7(c)(10)

184. 34 CFR 300.534(b)

185. State of Wisconsin, Department of Public Instruction, Department of Public Instruction Model Special Education, Policy Document, John T. Benson, State Superintendent, 3/1995

186. 34 CFR 300.7(a)(9)

187. 34 CFR 307(a)(9)

188. 34 CFR 300.26(b)(3)(ii)

189. http://law-gopher.uark.edu/arklaw/libraryr/reserve/negocomp/oberti.html

190. see 34 CFR 300.552

191. *Roncker v. Walter*, 700 F.2d 1058 (1983), p. 1063

192. 34 CFR 300.551(b)(2)

193. Twenty-fourth Annual Report to Congress, Table AD2, Number of Students With Disabilities Exiting Special Education by Age Group, During the 1999-2000 School Year, pages A-307 to A-309.

194. Data collection documentation for IDEA (data collection forms). See http://www.ideadata.org/docs/ExitingPtB.pdf, TABLE 4, REPORT OF CHILDREN WITH DISABILITIES EXITING SPECIAL EDUCATION, 2002-2003 SCHOOL YEAR, p. 2, Authorization: 20 U.S.C. 1418(a)(1)(A)(v) and 1418(a)(2)\

195. 34 CFR 300.343(c)(1)

196. 34 CFR 300.533(a)(2)(i)

197. 34 CFR 300.533(a)(2)(ii)

198. see p. 16 in Burns, E. (2001). Developing and Implementing IDEA-IEPs: An Individualized Education Program Handbook for Meeting Individuals with Disabilities Education Act (IDEA) Requirements. Charles C. Thomas, Springfield, IL.

199. *Daniel R.R. v. State Bd. of Educ.*, 874 F.2d 1036 (5th Cir. 1989)

200. The "mainstreaming" provision can be found in Public Law 105-17 at 612(a)(5); in the United States Code at 20 U.S.C. 1412(a)(5); and in the Regulations at 34 CFR 300.550.

201. This does not eliminate or modify the need for a continuum of alternative placements (regular classroom, resource room, self-contained classroom, residential facility, etc.). The funding mechanism by a State cannot obviate providing each child with the least restrictive environment. For example, students cannot be placed in a self-contained classroom simply because only students in such classrooms have disabilities and thus are used in the determination of needed funds. In this situation placement in a special education class is the sole vehicle for determining and providing services, and such a placement would preclude regular classroom participation.

202. 34 CFR 300, IDEA Regulations, Appendix A

203. Twenty-fourth Annual Report to Congress, Table AB2, Percentage of Children Ages 6-21 Served in Different Educational Environments Under IDEA, Part B, During the 1999-2000 School Year, ALL DISABILITIES

204. Twenty-fourth Annual Report to Congress, Table AB7, p. A-219, Age Group 6-21, Number of Children Served in Different Educational Environments Under IDEA, Part B by Age Group, During School Years 1990-91 Through 1999-2000.

205. 34 CFR 300.550(b)(1)

206. 34 CFR 300.552(e)

207. 34 CFR 300, Appendix A, Question #14, IV. Other Questions Regarding the Development and Content of IEPS

208. 34 CFR 300.24(9)(iv)

209. 34 CFR 300.24(13)(iii & iv)

210. 34 CFR 300.24(v)

211. 34 CFR 300.136(f)

212. P.L. 107-110: http://www.ed.gov/policy/elsec/leg/esea02/index.html

213. 789 F.Supp. 1322 (D.N.J. 1992), p. 1332

214. U.S. District Court for the Western District of Pennsylvania, Civil Action No. 00-249 Erie

215. 34 CFR 300.136(f)

216. 34 CFR 300.136(a)(1)(ii)

217. 34 CFR 300.342(b)(2)

218. Paraeducator Handbook; The NEA Paraeducator Handbook was prepared by the Handbook Subcommittee of the Paraeducator Task Force Committee: http://www.nea.org/esphome/nearesources/para-handbook.html

219. WASHINGTON STATE CORE COMPETENCIES FOR PARAEDUCA-TORS, Office of the Superintendent of Public Instruction Special Education, Paraeducator Project, see Washington Administrative Code (WAC) 392-172-200 (3) Staff Qualifications (http://www.wa.nea.org/Prf_Dv/PARA_ED/RCMDTNS.HTM).

220. 34 CFR 300.342(b)(3)

221. 34 CFR 300.342(b)(2)

222. WASHINGTON STATE CORE COMPETENCIES FOR PARAEDUCA-TORS, Office of the Superintendent of Public Instruction Special Education, Paraeducator Project

223. Ibid.

224. 34 CFR 300.534(b)

225. 34 CFR 300.552(e)

226. 34 CFR 300.347(a)(2)

227. 34 CFR 300.521(a)

228. 34 CFR 300.522(b)

229. 34 CFR 300.551(b)(2)

230. http://www.pps.k12.or.us/depts/speced/rsrcteach.shtml

231. see Vermont Department of Education Special Education Regulations and other Pertinent Regulations from the Vermont State Board of Education Manual of Rules and Practices, Effective August 16, 2001, 2366.7.2 School District Reimbursement for Special Education Costs http://www.state.vt.us/educ/new/pdfdoc/pgm_sped/sped_regs_08_16_01.pdf

232. see Smith, T., Polloway, E., Patton, J., & Dowdy, C. (1995). *Teaching children with special needs in inclusive settings.* Boston: Allyn and Bacon, p. 71.

233. Dunn, L.M. Exceptional Children in the Schools. Holt, Rinehart and Winston. New York, 1963.

234. 34 CFR 300.551(b)(2)

235. 603 CMR 28.06(2)(d)

236. 34 CFR 300.300(a)3)(ii)

237. National Council on Disability (2000), *Back to school on civil rights: Advancing the Federal commitment to leave no children behind.* 1331 F Street, NW, Suite 1050, Washington, D.C., p. 100.

238. IDEA-1997, 601(c)(1)

239. 34 CFR 300.550(b)(2)

240. 34 CFR 300.29(a) Transition Services

241. 34 CFR 300.132

242. 34 CFR 300.347(b)

243. 34 CFR 300, Appendix A, p. 12473

244. 34 CFR 300.347(b)(2)

245. Twenty-fourth Annual Report to Congress on the Implementation of the Individuals with Disabilities Education Act U.S. Department of Education, 2000, Part III-19-iii-21 (Chapter 3).

REFERENCES

Burns, E. (1998). *Test accommodations for students with disabilities.* Springfield, IL: Charles C Thomas.

Burns, E. (2001). *Developing and implementing IDEA-IEPs: An Individualized Education Program (IEP) Handbook for meeting Individuals with Disabilities Education Act (IDEA) Requirements.* Springfield, IL: Charles C Thomas.

Burns, E. (2003). *A handbook for supplementary aids and services: A best practice and IDEA guide "to enable children with disabilities to be educated with nondisabled children to the maximum extent appropriate.* Springfield, IL: Charles C Thomas.

Council of Administrators of Special Education. (1992). *Student access: A resource guide for educators. Section 504 of the Rehabilitation Act of 1973.* Albuquerque, NM: Author. ERIC No. 349 769.

Dunn, L.M. (1968). Special education for the mildly retarded—Is much of it justifiable? *Exceptional Children, 35,* 5-22.

Friend, M, & Bursuck, W. (1996). *Including students with special needs: A practical guide for classroom teachers.* Boston: Allyn and Bacon.

Iwata, B.A., Dorsey, M.F., Slifer, K.J., Bauman, K.E., Richman, G.S. (1982). Toward a Functional analysis of self-injury. Reprinted in *Journal of Applied Behavioral Analysis,* 1994, 27, 197-209.

Johnson, G.O., & Kirk, S.A. (1950) Are mentally handicapped children segregated in the regular grades? *Exceptional Children,* 17, 65-68 and 87-88.

Love, Harold D., (1972) *Educating exceptional children in regular classroom.* Springfield, IL: Charles C Thomas.

National Council on Disability (2000), *Back to school on civil rights: Advancing the Federal commitment to leave no children behind.* 1331 F Street, NW, Suite 1050, Washington, D.C.

New York State Education Department, Regulations of the Commissioner of Education, Part 200, 200.4(a)(1)(vi), January, 1998.

Rena B. L. and Doorlag, D.H. (1983). *Teaching special students in the mainstream.* Columbus, Ohio: Charles E. Merrill.

Rothstein, L. F. (1995). *Special education law (2nd ed).* New York: Longman.

Smith, T., Polloway, E., Patton, J., & Dowdy, C. (1995). *Teaching children with special needs in inclusive settings.* Boston: Allyn and Bacon.

Twenty-fourth Annual Report to Congress on the Implementation of the Individuals with Disabilities Education Act, U.S. Department of Education, 2002, Washington, D.C.: http://www.ed.gov/about/reports/annual/osep/2002/index.html. For annual reports Seventeenth through Twenty-fourth see: http://www.ed.gov/about/reports/annual/otherplanrpts.html

INDEX